MURDER,

MADNESS

AND

MAYHEM

MURDER, MADNESS

AND

MAYHEM

TWENTY-FIVE TALES OF TRUE CRIME AND DARK HISTORY

MIKE BROWNE

Collins

Murder, Madness and Mayhem

Published by Collins, an imprint of HarperCollins Publishers Ltd

First edition

HarperCollins books may be purchased for educational, business or
sales promotional use through our Special Markets Department.

HarperCollins Publishers Ltd
Bay Adelaide Centre, East Tower
22 Adelaide Street West, 41st Floor
Toronto, Ontario, Canada
M5H 4E3

www.harpercollins.ca

Library and Archives Canada Cataloguing in Publication

Title: Murder, madness and mayhem : twenty-five tales of true crime and dark history /
Mike Browne.
Names: Browne, Mike, author.
Description: First edition. | Includes bibliographical references.
Identifiers: Canadiana (print) 20210272198 | Canadiana (ebook) 2021027770X |
ISBN 9781443461597 (softcover) | ISBN 9781443461603 (ebook)
Subjects: LCSH: Murder. | LCSH: Cold cases (Criminal investigation) | LCSH: Disasters. |
LCSH: True crime stories.
Classification: LCC HV6515 .B76 2021 | DDC 364.152/3—dc23

Printed and bound in the United States of America
LSC/C 9 8 7 6 5 4 3 2 1

This is for anyone who thinks you cannot do the thing
your heart truly desires. You can.

Hell is empty, and all the devils are here.
—*THE TEMPEST*, WILLIAM SHAKESPEARE

CONTENTS

PART 4: NOTABLE DISASTERS

FOREWORD

What is it about the worst of human nature that so many people find fascinating? It may be the quest to understand the depraved mind of a psychopath, or perhaps it's the glimpse into the darkest parts of humanity that makes true crimes worth studying.

As long as the human race endures, there will be tragic incidents of death and disappearance that will go unexplained. But as the stories in this book show, no matter how long they linger out in the cold, they remain an important part of our history.

Mike Browne has distinguished himself as a great resource for true crime history through his years of research for his *Dark Poutine* podcast, heard around the world by thousands of fans. This is his first shot at writing about some of the most fascinating crimes he has covered over the years that have made a personal impact on his own life.

Action fans will appreciate the exciting coverage of deadly disasters such as the space shuttle *Challenger* explosion and the Indian

Ocean tsunami. Mike also reminds us of cases that have bizarre twists and turns to them, as in the kidnapping of Jayme Closs or "the Boozing Barber."

Even more captivating is the array of stories he calls the perpetual puzzles, where he describes intriguing cases like the Oak Island mystery or the story of the unknown man.

You will find it hard to put this book down and even harder waiting for his next release!

Alan R. Warren
Host of the *House of Mystery* radio show
NBC Radio, Los Angeles, California

INTRODUCTION

I've always loved stories, reading them and telling them, and the darker, the better. Growing up in a small town like Bridgewater, Nova Scotia, the stories I loved were quite often from some other place in some other time. It's not that Bridgewater is boring—plenty is going on there. It is a great little town to grow up in, but I did not realize what I had there until years after I had left.

I believed that the real, exciting stories were happening elsewhere, to folks other than me. I wanted transportation to anywhere other than where I was. Comics and magazines were my vehicles of escape. I fantasized about being an army man and fighting the Nazis like DC Comics' Sgt. Rock and the men of Easy Company. I dreamt of finding ancient tombs filled with gold and treasure buried under the Sphinx, like Howard Carter, the archaeologist I learned about in *National Geographic*.

I spent a lot of time in my head.

The week before my 12th birthday, though, I had a rude awakening, and my simple life was not so simple anymore. Something happened that jerked me out of childish reverie into an adult world of darkness for which I was not ready. It was my first encounter with real evil and my introduction to the criminal mind.

It was July 29, 1981. I got up early to watch the wedding of Lady Diana Spencer and Prince Charles on television. After the wedding I got dressed and went to the park behind our house. I threw on my favourite jacket, a red pullover windbreaker. A few of my closest pals all had the same one. It was the type that folded up into a fanny pack. We were like a little gang of harmless hoodlums running around town in our cheap windbreakers. Thanks to that windbreaker I felt like I belonged, which was important to me because I was shy and awkward, with low self-esteem.

At the park, in front of the DesBrisay Museum, I received a prize, a navy and neon-green Adidas kit bag, and had my photo taken for the local newspaper. I had received the most monetary pledges in town for my participation in the first Terry Fox Run to raise awareness and earn money for cancer research. The photo would be in the next weekly edition of the *Bridgewater Bulletin*.

For the rest of the day, I played floor hockey with my pals at the Michelin Tire plant's social club. A number of my windbreaker-wearing friends were there. We had a great day.

When it was time to go home, a friend's mom offered me a ride, but I didn't accept her offer. I decided to walk the 2.5 kilometres (1.6 miles) home in the dark, alone. Dad had always said if you need a lift, call, but I didn't. I was almost 12 years old, after all— time to start acting like a grown-up.

After I crossed Dufferin Street, where York Street turns into Alexandra Avenue, I noticed a man following me. My "spidey sense" began tingling right away. Something wasn't right.

I picked up my pace, and so did he, until he was almost on top of me. Instinctively, I knew to let him pass, so I bent down to tie my shoe. I could feel his gaze burning into me as he walked by, but now he was in front of me. I let him get a few metres ahead so I could watch him.

The man turned down a dead end, Park Street, just before the hill leading to the town park and duck pond. I knew he didn't belong there because I was familiar with all five families who lived along the short lane.

As I approached Park Street, the stranger turned around and came back toward me. He asked me for the time when he caught up to me at the intersection. I was less than 100 metres (330 feet) from my family's home when the stranger grabbed me. He put my arm behind my back and started dragging me toward the darkened woods. He told me not to scream or he would break my arm.

I asked him what he intended to do with me, and he told me. He said vile things to me that no child should ever have to hear. But then something inside me snapped. I don't recall what I said, but I screamed and broke free of his grip. I ran to the home of a family I knew, which was just steps away. As I banged on their door, screaming for help, I saw my assailant scampering back the way we had come.

The police were called, and my dad also arrived minutes later. After I calmed down enough to tell the story, we climbed into the police cruiser and drove around for 15 minutes looking for the creep who had assaulted me. We didn't find him.

The police and the adults in my life tried to comfort me by telling me "It could have been worse." That's true; it could have been. Still, I grappled with nightmares and felt like a freak for being afraid. I was ashamed that the experience had upset me so much. I had a secret. Mom and Dad told me not to talk about it, and I didn't. No one, not even my closest friends, knew what had happened to me.

The next week, when I saw the local paper, there on the front page was the photo of me taken on the day of my assault. I was wearing the same clothes my monster had seen me in. I was horrified—he could easily recognize me. My full name was there in the caption. In those days it was as simple as looking in the telephone book to find out where someone lived. Because there were only two families with the last name Browne in the directory at that time, I knew my attacker would likely figure it out. I began to be afraid he might come for me, that I was not safe at home.

A couple of months later, just as I was beginning to get over my fear and anxiety, I saw the man again. I was hanging out with my friend Dominic, one of the guys I had been playing floor hockey with on the night of the attack. He and I had gone for lunch at a restaurant where his father worked. As we walked through the restaurant, I noticed a familiar face sitting at one of the tables. Our eyes met. It was the man who'd grabbed me. I recognized him and he recognized me. I walked past him, pretending I hadn't seen him. I felt him staring at me as I walked by. Once Dominic and I reached the kitchen, I felt sick to my stomach. I can't recall whether I ate anything, but I did not mention the sighting to anyone. I was embarrassed by my victimhood.

I saw the man again that same day in his car. He was parked across the street from the school. I felt the implied threat and said nothing to anyone about it. I saw him again a couple more times in his car—he'd drive by slowly, glaring at me. I also saw him a few times walking along the same street where he had assaulted me; at least once he was with a boy about my age. Again, belittling myself as a coward, I said nothing to anyone.

Afterwards, rather than deal with the pain that everyone seemed to think I shouldn't be feeling, I shoved it deeper down inside and told myself to get over it. But I didn't. I couldn't. I couldn't stand the sight of the clothing I'd been wearing on the night of my assault. The red windbreaker I had been so proud of now anchored me to that night. The monster had tainted it for me, and unable to look at it anymore, I hid it, stuffing it far back into a cupboard above the coat closet in our entryway. There it sat behind seasonal outerwear, sleeping bags and raincoats, and I never laid eyes on it again.

Hiding the windbreaker is symbolic of how I dealt with my assault as well. I turned inward on myself and became depressed, and just over a year later I turned to drinking and drugs to bury the pain as deeply as possible. It was not until years later that I learned the man's name, and it was years after that before I was comfortable approaching the police with it. I was in my early 40s by that time. The Bridgewater Police sent me a photo lineup, but I was unable to identify the man definitively. The photo they sent was recent and the man looked very different. Since I could no longer say for sure it was him, the detective on the phone told me they could not charge him with anything. I asked if he had been known to them. The detective told me they were aware of him but would not elaborate. I don't want to know specifics, but I assume I was not his only victim.

Even though it was not the optimal outcome, I am still glad I came forward. I have been able to move on since.

Around the time of my first assault, I found Max Haines in my grandmother's newspaper collection. Haines was a Nova Scotia–born journalist and author famous for his weekly crime column. I began reading dark, hair-raising stories about people like the man who had attacked me. I learned what "It could have been worse" could mean as I consumed story after story about horrendous crimes. After Haines, I began reading true crime classics like Vincent Bugliosi's *Helter Skelter* and Truman Capote's *In Cold Blood*. The true crime bug had me in its grip and has not let me go.

Reading true crime helped me begin to understand the mind behind the monster who came for me all those years ago. But, sadly, that first experience was not my last and may have helped colour the reactions that led me into a second, more violent encounter in my early 20s.

Thanks to my then alcoholism and drug abuse, I had fallen in with some people who were living similar lifestyles. A man, whom I had called friend, assaulted me, leaving me with physical and emotional scars I still carry.

I was invited to my friend's house one day in 1990. There I met his girlfriend at the time, and I liked her right away. She and I became fast friends, and soon after she and my friend broke up. I enjoyed her company, she enjoyed mine, and soon we were together. My friend, who had encouraged the relationship at first, eventually became jealous, demanding I end the relationship so he could swoop in for another try. I refused. It was too late; I was already committed to the young woman.

My friend was no longer a friend but a rival. Word got back to me through mutual acquaintances that he was out to get me. I was physically afraid of him, mostly because of his size; he was almost a foot taller and had at least 40 kilograms (88 pounds) on me. I had already seen signs of his volatility, and he'd overtly threatened me more than once. We bumped into him at a parking lot one day, and he confronted me, telling me I had a decision to make about my relationship, or else. Since it was daytime and the location was very public, I felt confident enough to stand firm. He took no action at the time and left in a huff, but I knew he meant business. After that, I became fearful of going out. I even had a vivid nightmare where he'd beaten me badly. That dream, I know now, was a premonition.

One spring evening after a threatening phone call from my rival, I was in the kitchen of my parents' home grabbing a late-night bowl of Rice Krispies. Mom and Dad were in bed. As I pulled the milk from the refrigerator, I was startled by a voice coming from the open window right next to me. I turned and saw him, in shadow. I don't recall exactly what he said, but he indicated we needed to talk, man to man. I agreed and he said he would meet me in the park that bordered the back of our home at that same museum, in the same spot where I had my photo taken for the Terry Fox Run nine years before.

I put on my shoes, met him outside and followed him silently in the darkness up through our hedge and to the designated spot. As soon as we arrived, he was in my face, intimidating me with his size and pushing me against the brick wall. He threatened me, telling me if I did not leave my girlfriend, he would hurt me. Even knowing I had no chance against him, I made some feeble attempts at pushing back, but he easily bested me physically.

Seeing there was no more reasoning with him, I told him I was firm in my decision to stay with my girlfriend and turned to leave. It was then that he said, "This is over, right now!" He grabbed me, flung me like a rag doll against the brick wall and began punching me in the face. As my head took repeated blows from his fists from the frontal assault, the back of my skull bounced off the brick wall behind me, concussing me. As the world began to turn black, one of the punches landed square on my nose, shattering it and dislodging my septum (the cartilage down the middle of the nose) and pushing it to the right. The screaming white pain in my nose jolted me back to reality. I managed to break free and tried to flee.

My attacker pursued me. He was yelling something; I can't be sure what he said. I was screaming too, for help. He jumped onto my back and the momentum pushed me to the sidewalk I was using for my escape. He started pummelling the back of my head, driving me face first into the concrete of the walkway. There was more pain as two of my right front teeth chipped. I was helpless, and the world started going black again.

It was then that I heard a car horn and saw lights flashing. The parking lot of the museum was a lovers' lane of sorts, and the driver of the vehicle there must have seen the attack and wanted to help. As the horn blared, my attacker was startled just enough for me to be able to get to my feet and run home, with my attacker screaming threats behind me.

When I reached home, I locked the door and went to my parents' bedroom to tell them I had been attacked. I was bleeding from my broken nose. I had cuts on my face and bumps and bruises all over my head, including two nasty black eyes.

Dad called the police. They came and took a statement, and it was decided I would pursue assault charges against my attacker. But he was already gone. The police could not find him to charge him for several months, during which time my family began receiving hang-up phone calls at all hours. One call even involved a threat against my mother. I was afraid to go outside, and my drinking and drug use escalated. I relied heavily on narcotic painkillers to take the edge off. I couldn't stand the pressure anymore and ended up in the psychiatric hospital for a few weeks that fall.

The police eventually found him, and the following year, I went to court to face my attacker, who, of course had pleaded to a lesser offence. By that time the relationship with my girlfriend had soured and I had come to believe I had deserved everything I got. I testified against the man and he spoke in his own defence, saying it was me who had threatened him, a liar to the last. He was found guilty and sentenced to two years of probation. I have seen his name in the paper since, for other offences.

After a few more years of drug and alcohol abuse, I finally reached out for help with my depression and addictions. The early years of my recovery included numerous false starts and failed attempts at the world of storytelling, something I have always been drawn to.

Along the way, my true crime interest developed into an obsession that was further fuelled when I began listening to podcasts. I was obsessed with Adnan's story in *Serial* and loved shows like *The Trail Went Cold*, *The Minds of Madness* and *Last Podcast on the Left*. As podcasting became more accessible, I started to think it might be something I wanted to try. I asked friends with podcasting knowledge about how to get started, and they were extremely helpful.

I bought a microphone and some other gear with a quarterly bonus from work and began planning an all-Canadian true crime and history podcast. I wanted a memorable name for the show, so I meditated on it for some weeks, writing obsessively during my downtime. There was already a podcast called *Canadian True Crime*, so I needed another name. I decided I wanted a title that sounded truly Canadian, with a little humour thrown in to lighten the mood of all the serious content. The name *Dark Poutine* just popped into my mind, and I snagged the URL immediately.

Thanks to connections and shout-outs on other shows, *Dark Poutine* took off. But it exploded after *My Favorite Murder* hosts Karen Kilgariff and Georgia Hardstark gave us a shout-out during the recording of their 2018 Vancouver show. I'm grateful to the ladies from *MFM* every day for mentioning us. Just 30 seconds brought us thousands of Murderinos, and our episode downloads tripled overnight.

I keep writing, networking and recording every week. Every Monday, our listeners have a new show to listen to on their commute or whenever they find a moment to tune in. I have fallen in love with podcasting, and thanks to a series of fortunate events, I get to do it full time.

I have been able to use my experiences as the survivor of two assaults and recovery from mental illness and addiction to give *Dark Poutine* a unique perspective on true crime and dark events through compassion and understanding. This empathetic approach shows in the numbers, with millions of episode downloads over the past four years. What I am most proud of, though, is that we have built a dedicated community of listeners, with over 9,000 of the most loyal fans in our extremely active Facebook group, Dark

Poutine Yumber Yard, and its subgroups. The Yumber Yard got its name after a flub I made in one episode. Funny how even awful mistakes and horrific experiences can lead you exactly where you belong.

In this book are 25 bite-sized stories of true crime, mysteries, oddities and dark history. Two of the stories are rewrites of a couple of my favourite episodes, and the others are fresh content, most of which would not have made it into the *Dark Poutine* rotation because of their more international flavour. All of them are tales that have drawn me in over the years, and I wrote them all in the same victim-centred tone you hear on the show week to week. I hope you enjoy reading this as much as I have enjoyed writing it.

PART ONE
Murder with a Twist

The following seven true crime stories come with some
atypical elements, including weird motives, unusual
perpetrators and bizarre murder weapons.

Chapter 1

GIRL GONE

One of the most shocking and closely followed cases in recent true crime history comes with a relatively happy ending compared with the tragic and violent way it began.

At 12:53 a.m. on the morning of October 15, 2018, a frantic, garbled 911 call came in from the residence at 1268 13½ Avenue, U.S. Hwy 8, west of the City of Barron, Wisconsin. There is screaming throughout the 45 seconds of the call, from what seems to be two different female voices. Little is decipherable from the harrowing audio, other than the Barron County dispatcher trying to get information from the caller. The screaming voices become muffled, and the call goes to silence after what sounds like the racking of a shotgun. There is another click that sounds like a misfire.

Police arrived at the small bungalow no more than four minutes after the initial call came in. The residence was quiet as police approached cautiously. Shortly after the three responding officers arrived, Deputy James Pressley commented on the 911 call he had just reviewed to fellow deputies Erik Sedani and Jon Fick.

"The tapes did not sound good," he said.

The Barron County deputies checked the perimeter for other exits from the residence. Finding none, they approached the front door. The condensation on the outer storm door prevented a clear view inside, but the inner wooden front door was open. Officers called out as they entered, with their guns drawn.

The motionless body of a shirtless man lay just inside in the hallway near the door. The scene was horrific. There was no doubt that he was deceased. His head and upper torso showed the type of trauma the officers' training told them was a close-range shotgun blast. Brain matter, blood, bone and other pieces of flesh covered the wall near the dead man's body. The body was later identified as that of homeowner James M. Closs, 56. A spent shotgun shell was lying near Mr. Closs's corpse.

"Suicide," Deputy Sedani can be overheard saying on audio recordings taken from the bodycam mics worn by the deputies present and later released to the public.

Deputy Pressley wasn't so sure. "You don't know that. There were several voices. I don't see a gun, guys. Let's not write it off as a suicide."

The badly splintered wooden door and its frame indicated that someone had forced their way in, possibly with a kick. There were other signs of a violent struggle. There was debris strewn about in the front door area, and a chair by the kitchen table was overturned and broken.

The deputies discovered another shotgun shell and a phone in the hallway in front of the open bathroom door. The door was damaged and appeared to have been kicked open.

Inside the bathroom, Deputy Fick was horrified to discover another gruesome scene. Slumped against the wall in the bathtub was a deceased red-haired woman. Denise Closs, James Closs's 46-year-old wife, was dressed in a grey hoodie, black leggings and socks. She too had suffered a close-range shotgun blast to the head.

A spent shotgun shell was found on the lawn beside the front stairs. A closer inspection of the front door showed powder burns and a hole indicating someone had shot through the door, which suggested the use of slugs rather than shot. Autopsies on Mr. and Mrs. Closs confirmed this.

Slugs are massive, large-calibre projectiles that inflict catastrophic damage on their target. The perpetrator intended to kill and leave no witnesses. Thankfully, death would have been instantaneous, and Mr. and Mrs. Closs did not suffer.

While clearing the house, the deputies noted a bedroom decorated as though it belonged to a young female, possibly a teen or tween. The room, the police learned, belonged to James and Denise Closs's 13-year-old daughter, Jayme. Investigators checked under beds, in closets, in the attic and any other place she might be hiding, but she was not there. The house was empty save for the two corpses of Jayme's mom and dad.

Police collected a cellphone belonging to Jayme from the counter in the darkened kitchen. For the teen to leave home without her phone was another red flag. It is unusual for anyone, especially a teen, to leave home without their phone.

The officers surmised that Jayme was the real target of the attack and was abducted by whoever had killed her parents. The shooter, the murder weapon and Jayme had disappeared into the cold Wisconsin night.

Speaking with other investigators, Deputy Fick remembered seeing a maroon-coloured car with grey or silver trim, possibly a Ford Taurus, headed in the other direction as he and the other deputies responded. It pulled over and yielded as he flew by. Fick said he did not see a licence plate on the front of the car as he passed, only a black frame where it should have been. It was a lead, albeit a thin one.

Detectives gathered items from the home that they believed would provide samples of Jayme's DNA in the hope of later identifying her if required. As is the practice in suspected child abduction cases, local authorities called in the FBI to assist. An Amber Alert went out with Jayme Closs's particulars. She was 152 centimetres (5 feet) tall, weighing 45 kilograms (100 pounds), with green eyes and long strawberry-blond hair.

As the case grabbed national headlines, the rumours flew across all the social media platforms. Armchair detectives cruelly speculated Jayme was somehow involved in her parents' murder. Authorities denied that assumption. They stated that Jayme was not a suspect at all. She was a victim, and, if she was alive, they believed she was in grave danger.

Growing groups of volunteers searched for Jayme Closs over the next few days. A week after she had disappeared, 2,000 people, two-thirds of the population in tiny Barron County, showed up to search for the missing middle school student who loved dance and ran cross country. Locals held a rally for Jayme Closs titled "A Gathering of Hope" one evening at the Barron High School football stadium.

On October 24, 2018, the FBI put up a $25,000 reward for information leading to Jayme's safe return. Three days later, Jayme's parents, Denise and James, were laid to rest. Mourners packed the funeral venue—scores of family, friends and community members wanted to remember the much-loved Closs couple. They also prayed for Jayme's safe return and the capture of whoever had done these awful things to this innocent family. The FBI and police were there too, watching for anyone who stood out, but no one did.

That same day, in a weird turn of events, a man was arrested after breaking in and tripping motion detectors in the Closs residence, which police had since locked down as a crime scene. A K9 unit apprehended the man. He was Kyle Jaenke-Annis, 32, of nearby Cameron, Wisconsin, who said he had recently started a job as a packaging operator at a nearby Saputo plant. When the officers searched him, they found that Kyle had personal items belonging to Jayme Closs—some of her underwear, a pink tank top and one of Jayme's dresses.

Jaenke-Annis rambled throughout his interview with police, bouncing from one idea to another, his thought processes disjointed and scattered. It was difficult to determine his motivations for the break-in. Kyle indicated he was trying to help investigators by being in the house. He also spoke of violent fantasies involving revenge amid rants about child molesters. Kyle said he knew he would get caught. He wanted to see who was looking for Jayme and speak to the FBI to offer his assistance. He claimed he could go places where the police could not.

The break-in was not the first time Kyle had been to the Closs residence since hearing about the crime via social media. He admitted he had been there on Monday morning as well. Kyle had walked over to watch the investigators moving in and out of the house, gathering evidence.

Kyle Jaenke-Annis was charged with felony burglary and held so the cops could try to determine if he knew anything about the crimes. Kyle did not appear to have any information about the crime itself, although he claimed he wanted to find help find Jayme. Investigators determined Jaenke-Annis was not the perpetrator of the murders or Jayme's kidnapping. He had wasted precious resources and investigators' time.

Over the next month, the searches for Jayme wound down. There was no sign of her. Police followed up on numerous leads and questioned many known sex offenders from the area without any breaks or solid tips.

On November 15, 2018, the Barron County Sheriff's Department posted an update on its Facebook page. The post indicated that the case remained the number one priority. The sheriff's department said they were reviewing video from the area and looking into other digital evidence, and they would continue following up on leads. The department had daily contact with FBI and DCI agents also working on the case. Because hunting season was just about to open, the department asked hunters and property owners to report anything suspicious. The post ended with Sheriff Fitzgerald thanking everyone for their continued support in the efforts to bring Jayme home.

The reward for Jayme's return now stood at $50,000.

The FBI Milwaukee Twitter account posted an update on November 28, 2018:

> *The Jayme Closs "Tree of Hope" on display in the lobby of the Barron County Justice Center reminds the public we still need your tips to help #FindJayme . . . Our thoughts are with Jayme's family and friends this holiday season.*

The Twitter post also included a phone number, a photo of Jayme Closs smiling and another picture of the FBI Justice Center's Christmas tree.

On the afternoon of January 10, 2019, at 4:10 p.m., in Gordon, Wisconsin, Jeanne Nutter, a former social worker, took her dog for a walk. A distraught teenage girl approached Jeanne. The terrified girl was inappropriately dressed for the weather, wearing only leggings, a light T-shirt and dirty men's shoes that appeared to be on the wrong feet.

The girl begged for help and asked where she was before identifying herself as Jayme Closs. She had been missing for 88 days, gone without a trace, but now here she was, dishevelled, dazed and gaunt, but very much alive.

Jayme was terrified, pointing back to the house she had come from, only two doors down from Jeanne's cabin, and talking a mile a minute. Jayme told Jeanne she had been kidnapped and held there by a 21-year-old stranger named Jake Thomas Patterson.

Jayme recounted her harrowing story. She told Jeanne that a man who was previously unknown to her came into her home and shot her dad, shot her mom while she was calling 911, and then abducted her.

Jeanne reassured Jayme and made for the nearest house.

Peter Kasinskas was cleaning fish when he was startled by pounding on the kitchen door. In rushed his neighbour, Jeanne, with her dog and a young girl.

Jeanne told Peter that the girl at her side was Jayme Closs and implored him to call 911. Kristin Kasinskas, Peter's wife, recognized Jayme right away and called 911. As she spoke with police, Kristin did her best to put Jayme at ease, offering her something to cover herself with and a glass of water. Based on the information given by Jayme through Kristin, police vehicles made their way to the residence at 14102 South Eau Claire Acres Circle. Other deputies went to look for Jake Patterson and his vehicle.

Jayme identified herself again to the first officers to arrive. Since the killer was still on the loose, they whisked the shaken but grateful teen into a police cruiser's front seat and drove her out of the area to safety. The officer driving Jayme noticed a red car matching Jake Patterson's vehicle's description headed in the other direction on Eau Claire Acres Circle. The officer reported the sighting to other officers in the area.

Douglas County sheriff's deputy Matt DeRosia received the call about the red car coming his way, and when it passed, the officer noticed there was a single male occupant. DeRosia ran the licence plate, and it came back as belonging to the house where Jayme claimed she had been held.

The deputy pulled out and followed the car as it went past the driveway of its registered address. Other police cruisers quickly joined. Rather than follow too much farther and risk a dangerous chase, DeRosia turned on his flashing lights and pulled the car over.

The officers drew their sidearms and cautiously approached the car. They asked the man inside if his name was Jake Patterson; he said it was. The deputies ordered the man to step out of the car with his hands raised.

As Jake got out of the car, hands in the air, he said he knew why he had been stopped.

Jake Thomas Patterson, a 21-year-old labourer, calmly allowed himself to be cuffed and put into a squad car. When he was in the back of the vehicle, Jake asked what the charges were. The officer holding Jake told him he would get the details when they were at police headquarters.

The wheels were set in motion to acquire the proper warrants to search Jake's car and his residence for evidence related to the kidnapping of Jayme and the murder of her parents.

Upon hearing of Jake's capture over the cruiser's radio, Jayme smiled. Her immediate trauma was coming to an end, but she would still have to undergo invasive medical exams and intense questioning about her ordeal.

Under interrogation, Jake Patterson spoke at length to police interviewers about what he had done. He said his obsession with abducting a girl started sometime in 2015, and he had been fantasizing about it since then. One day on his way to work, Jake happened to see Jayme Closs getting onto the school bus and became interested in her. He later watched her walk home and began to formulate his plan.

In the weeks leading up to the murder and kidnapping, Jake had made two visits to the Closs home with the intent to abduct Jayme but had chickened out. Although he didn't follow through, both attempts were valuable dry runs. Jake became more familiar with the property each time, and he knew he would work up the courage eventually.

After stealing a licence plate from another vehicle and affixing it to his car, in the wee hours of October 15, 2018, Jake was ready to make his move. He took great pains to ensure he would not leave any evidence at the scene. Jake shaved his head and his beard; he vigorously cleaned his Mossberg 500 shotgun with a cloth to remove his fingerprints and loaded it with six slugs that he had also wiped down individually.

After a shower, Jake put on jeans, a black pullover with gloves and a black balaclava to hide his identity. He put heavy, brown steel-toed boots on his feet before leaving home to go to the Closs residence.

Jake pulled into the Closses' driveway, and as he approached the home, he saw James Closs through the window of the darkened residence. Jake pointed the shotgun at James and yelled for him to get on the ground, but Jake wasn't sure the man heard him because he didn't react.

Jake went up to the door and began pounding, demanding entry. When Jake saw James Closs looking out through a small window in the front door, he put the gun against the glass and shot the man through the window.

Jake tried to kick the door open but was unsuccessful, so he shot through the lock. He shoved James Closs's body out of the way, stepping over it as he entered the home. Using a flashlight to find his way around, he saw that every door in the small bungalow was closed.

Jake could see light shining under one of the doors in the hallway. He made his way there and heard sounds and a pair of panicked female voices coming from inside. The door was locked. He yelled for the people inside to open up, but his commands were met only with screams.

Frustrated, Jake decided he couldn't wait anymore. He obliterated the flimsy door with a few kicks, then finally used his shoulder to pop it open. Inside, he found his target, Jayme, and her mom, Denise, huddled together inside the family's bathroom. Denise told Jake she had called 911 and showed him the phone. Jake ripped the phone out of her hand and threw it into the hallway.

Jake produced a roll of duct tape and told Denise to put it over Jayme's mouth, but Denise refused, so he had to do it himself. After Jayme was secured, Jake coldly put the gun to Denise's head, pulled the trigger and ended her life. Jake claimed he looked away as he executed the innocent woman.

Jake dragged Jayme outside and forced her into the trunk of his car. Not wanting to draw attention to himself, he then calmly drove the speed limit for nearly 130 kilometres (80 miles) back to his residence outside Gordon, Wisconsin.

Along with other evidence from the crime, Jake later burned Jayme's clothes in his fireplace. Afterwards, he went to Walmart and bought Jayme more clothing. He put the shotgun into the trunk of another car in his driveway, where police later found it.

Jake said he forced Jayme to sleep in his tiny twin bed with him at night. He admitted to having had sexual fantasies about the teenager but said he felt too guilty to have sex with her. Jake and Jayme would talk and play board games late into the night. When he was not around, or others were in the house, which was a rare occurrence, Jake would force Jayme under his bed and warn her to be quiet. Jake would then put bins and laundry baskets full of free weights and dumbbells around the bed to prevent her from leaving. It was not a secure prison, but Jake knew she was afraid of him and would not try to escape.

And Jayme *was* afraid, but escape she did. Now Jayme was able to tell her side of the story too.

Jake would leave Jayme there, alone in the dark under his bed, sometimes for as much as 12 hours while he went out for one reason or another, mostly to work. During these extended periods of solitary confinement, Jake would provide Jayme with adult diapers to urinate and defecate in, and often little to no food or water.

One time, Jake noticed Jayme had moved the bins a bit. He became livid and struck her on the back with a tool he used to clean the blinds.

Terrified, Jayme would lie there going over and over in her mind the brutal murder of her parents. She knew death was a real possibility. What would happen if Jake became bored of her? Jayme knew she had to get away before that happened.

After being alone for six hours the day of her escape, Jayme decided she had to take a chance and flee. She pushed and kicked the hampers full of weights out of the way and crawled out from under the bed. Having no shoes of her own, Jayme put on a pair of Jake's and ran out into the cold.

Wanting to avoid trial, 21-year-old Jake Patterson pleaded guilty to two intentional homicide counts and one count of kidnapping. Jake was emotional, and his voice shook as he spoke to the judge, admitting what he had done.

At Jake's sentencing, family attorney Chris Gramstrup read a statement from Jayme, who was in the courtroom. Jayme's statement said, in part:

> *Last October, Jake Patterson took a lot of things that I loved away from me. It makes me the most sad that he took away my Mom and my Dad. I loved my Mom and Dad very much and they loved me very much. They did all they could to make me happy and protect me. He took them away from me forever. Jake Patterson can never take away my courage. He thought he could control me, but he couldn't. I feel like what he did is what a coward would do. I was brave. He was not.*
>
> *He can never take away my spirit. He thought that he could make me like him, but he was wrong. He can't ever*

change me, or take away who I am. He can't stop me from being happy and moving forward with my life. I will go on to do great things in my life, and he will not.

Jake Patterson will never have any power over me. I feel like I have some power over him, because I get to tell the judge what I think should happen to him. He stole my parents from me. He stole almost everything I love from me. For 88 days he tried to steal me, and he didn't care who he hurt or who he killed to do that.

He should stay locked up forever.

The judge threw the book at Patterson, sentencing him to two consecutive life sentences without the possibility of parole or release for the murders. The judge gave Jake the maximum sentence of 25 years for Jayme's kidnapping, also to be served consecutively.

Jayme Closs is living with family and is doing as well as can be expected, considering the living nightmare she endured.

The prisoners' code does not look kindly on men who hurt children, and Jake Patterson has been no exception. Jake got into a fight with another inmate shortly after the trial. The other prisoner was upset to have a skinner, jail slang for a pedophile, in his prison section. Prison officials put Patterson into protective custody after that.

Kyle Jaenke-Annis, the man found in the Closs home after the murders, had not been involved in the crime at all. He did not know Jake or Jayme. He pleaded down to a single count of misdemeanour theft on May 3, 2019. The man who claimed he only wanted to help received a sentence of two years' probation for breaking into the Closs home. Jaenke-Annis was just a troubled person who inserted himself into the case.

Chapter 2

SPELL MURDER FOR ME

On the evening of October 6, 1988, a 30-year-old man walked into the police station in Grand Rapids, Michigan. Kenneth Wood, an employee at a local GM plant, claimed he had a story to tell and that he could not live with his burden any longer. He needed to spill his guts.

As Ken spoke, Detective Tom Freeman thought at first he was listening to a tall tale made up by an angry man simply to cause trouble for his ex-wife. Yet the details of Ken's story were odd but compelling.

Ken said that one weekend in August of 1987, his ex-wife, Cathy Wood, told him a secret. Cathy said she and her co-worker and lover, Gwen Graham, had murdered residents of the Alpine Manor nursing home between January and April of that year. Gwen and Cathy both worked at the home as nurse's aides and were also live-in lovers.

Cathy said Gwen had come up with a sick plan to prove their love for each other. The idea was to commit several murders,

15

making a twisted game of it by attempting to spell the word *M-U-R-D-E-R* using their victims' initials. Ken mistakenly remembered the first victim's name, referring to her as "Margaret," the *M* in the series. The woman's correct name was Marguerite Chambers, a 60-year-old Alzheimer's patient.

Cathy told him that, as she stood watch, Gwen smothered Marguerite with washcloths—one under the chin and over her mouth to hold it closed and the other rolled up and placed firmly under the frail woman's nose, cutting off her air supply.

After Marguerite's murder, the killers could not find a victim for the *U* for their macabre spelling bee but kept killing regardless.

Cathy and Gwen had targeted women close to death, as they would be easier to dispatch and less likely to arouse any kind of suspicion. The pair also made sure they chose women with severe dementia as their victims, so no one would believe them even if they managed to survive the attempts on their lives.

Cathy justified the murders to Ken as mercy killings, claiming they were actually relieving the suffering of these women by murdering them. Cathy also admitted she was divulging her secrets to Ken because she was trying to stay away from Gwen, whom she had recently broken up with. Cathy believed that by betraying her ex-lover, she would never go back.

Detective Freeman asked Ken why he had taken so long to talk to the police. Ken told him that after Cathy's confession, he considered that she might be lying to him. Cathy was a notorious bullshit artist. She had also threatened to kill herself if he talked to the cops. Ken didn't want to see their daughter grow up motherless, regardless of their poor relationship.

The thought that Cathy and Gwen had gotten away with murder ate away at Ken though. But then he realized that if Gwen and Cathy got back together, he might be their next victim. He told the cops he was terrified of them both. But not too scared, since just recently he had taken Cathy on a trip to Las Vegas.

Ken provided some general background details on Cathy and what he knew of Gwen and their relationship to the police. The conversation left Detective Freeman with the feeling that several big questions still needed answering. Was Kenneth Wood telling the truth, or was he just a jilted ex-husband? More pressing, the detective needed to determine if there had been murders at Alpine Manor that had gone undetected.

Catherine May Carpenter, the oldest of three, was born in Michigan on March 7, 1962, to an alcoholic truck driver and his wife, who worked as a bookkeeper. Cathy's father went away to serve in the Vietnam conflict and returned more violent and angry than before. Cathy grew taller and heavier than many of the other children her age. She was ridiculed for her size, not only by her peers but publicly by her father as well.

Cathy's relationship with her mother wasn't much better. Her mom was busy with her bookkeeping work, so as the oldest, Cathy had to do all the chores, including caring for her younger brother and sister. To escape, Cathy would close her bedroom door and lose herself in books, often overeating for comfort. She developed a real hatred for the world and did not confide anything in her very few friends. She felt she was alone and that her friends would eventually betray her anyway.

Cathy desperately wanted the love she read about in books, but secretly, she didn't believe it would ever happen for her. She was overweight and more than 183 centimetres (6 feet) tall—she felt she was an unlovable freak.

Cathy and Ken Wood first got together when she was 16 years old. The older boy seemed interested in her, so she clung to him. There was still a part of her that did not believe Ken's apparent love for her could be real. She would often have her friends feign interest in Ken to test him. But he always stayed true to Cathy.

Once she knew she had her hooks in him, Cathy demanded all of Ken's attention. She wanted to possess him, forcing him to give up activities he enjoyed and friends he had been close with in favour of spending all his time with her. Ken was a pushover and always did as Cathy commanded.

Cathy eventually realized that Ken was her way out of the violent and loveless home where she had grown up. After a particularly rough fight with her folks, Cathy saw her chance and moved in with her all too willing boyfriend. Cathy became pregnant almost right away, and the pair were married when she was just 17.

Cathy was not a good fit for motherhood. She'd admitted in the past that she hated children, after having to care for her younger siblings for years. Now that she was a mother to her own child, she was bored and lazy. She began eating way too much, and she grew to weigh more than 135 kilograms (300 pounds).

Eventually, Ken became fed up with her and was more than happy when Cathy suggested she get out of the house and get a job. In 1986 Cathy landed a job as a nurse's aide at the 400-bed Alpine Manor nursing home and went to work with elderly patients who suffered from varying forms of dementia.

Gwendolyn Gail Graham was born on August 6, 1963, in Santa Monica, California, and was also the oldest of three. Gwen didn't come from a happy home either. The family moved a lot because Mack, her father, had trouble holding down a steady gig. As a result, they were poor, and the kids knew not to get attached to a school or friends as they would probably be moving again before long. Her family settled in Tyler, Texas, when Gwen was nine years old.

Gwen later recalled the abuse she suffered at the hands of her frustrated parents, and in Lowell Cauffiel's book on the murders,

Forever and Five Days, Gwen's mother admitted to hitting Gwen with an electrical cord when she was only 18 months old, saying that "with all the kids underfoot, she sometimes "lost [her] cool." Gwen's father, Mack, was a hard man too, and refused to pick up a crying child because, he said, "It spoils them."

When she got older, Gwen would burn her arms with cigarettes and would often cut herself. The self-harming behaviours had started as a way for Gwen to cope with the sexual abuse she was suffering at her father's hands. She later disclosed that her father had begun sexually assaulting her when she was very young, and the abuse had continued into her teens.

Gwen was prone to nightmares and developed several odd phobias. She was afraid of the sound of a flushing toilet, she claimed in *Forever and Five Days*, because as a child she had once watched as her father forced her mother's head into a toilet and held her there as it flushed. She was terrified that her mother would be sucked down into the drain.

Gwen hated men and began having relationships with other women in her teens, which her father disapproved of. When she was 17, Gwen moved in with a woman almost 10 years older to escape her home life, and began drinking excessively. She then followed her lover north to Michigan and landed in Grand Rapids, where she ended up working at Alpine Manor as a nurse's aide.

Gwen, who was 160 centimetres (5 feet, 3 inches) tall, met Cathy at Alpine Manor and was smitten with the tall, powerful woman with the bleached platinum-blond hair. Cathy had lost over 45 kilograms (100 pounds) by this time, thanks to the physical work at the home.

Cathy and Gwen began partying together with other co-workers, often drinking and drugging to excess. Ken and Cathy were having lots of trouble in their marriage, and these parties and the attention Cathy got from Gwen was a welcome distraction.

As was her pattern when the going got rough, Cathy bailed on her marriage. In the summer of 1986, she moved into Gwen's place after a big fight with Ken. It took only a few days as roommates before the two women became physically involved. Cathy had had a couple of lesbian experiences before marrying Ken, so she was more than open to Gwen's advances. While Cathy was a force to be reckoned with everywhere else, Gwen was the boss in the bedroom.

Gwen and Cathy spent as much time together as they could at work. But Gwen's supervisor noticed that her performance took a nosedive after Gwen and Cathy became a couple. Gwen was distracted and began forgetting simple tasks she usually had no trouble completing.

Supervisors separated the pair and had them complete their duties in different parts of the facility, on opposite shifts, to fix the situation. But the couple always seemed to find their way back together, including swapping duties or shifts with other staff to remain close to each other. They would tend to patients together, often closing the door to the room while they worked, which was against policy.

Detective Freeman began his investigation the day after Ken Wood disclosed his secret. Initially, nothing really seemed off. Sure, patients at the nursing home had died while Gwen and Cathy were on shift, but no more than usual. No one else on the Alpine Manor staff seemed to think anything was amiss.

But when Detective Freeman brought Cathy Wood in for an interview, the whole situation blew wide open. She was surprisingly forthcoming, confirming Ken Wood's claims of murder in bits and pieces. Cathy distanced herself from the murders at first, claiming to be afraid of Gwen, who she said had killed the patients herself. According to Cathy, Gwen had committed as few as five and as many as eight murders at Alpine Manor between January and April of 1987. Cathy also said Gwen would steal small personal items from each of her victims to relive the crimes.

Cathy admitted they had attempted to spell M-U-R-D-E-R using the victims' names, and also revealed she had played lookout during at least five of the murders while Gwen carried them out. She said Gwen would kill the frail patients by holding washcloths over their mouths until they smothered to death. Cathy stopped short of admitting to any physical participation in the killings.

Cathy also told the shocked investigators about a macabre ritual she and Gwen would perform after each of the murders. One of the women would brazenly report that they had found the patient deceased in her room while doing their rounds. Cathy and Gwen would feign sadness for the death, then volunteer to prep the patient they had just killed for her removal by local funeral homes. They relished the time they spent together washing their victims and wrapping them up for pickup. Cathy admitted the ritual gave them a thrill and made them feel invincible.

After Detective Freeman's interview with Cathy, he created a list of eight potential victims:

- Marguerite Chambers, age 60, died January 18, 1987, at 8:30 p.m.
- Myrtle Luce, age 95, died February 10, 1987, at 2:30 p.m.
- Mae Mason, age 79, died February 16, 1987, at 4:00 a.m.
- Ruth VanDyke, age 98, died February 26, 1987, at 2:40 a.m.
- Belle Burkhard, age 74, died February 26, 1987, at 4:25 a.m.
- Wanda Urbanski, age 90, died March 2, 1987, at 10:50 p.m.
- Edith Cook, age 98, died April 7, 1987, at 2 a.m.
- Lucille Stoddard, age 70, died May 1, 1987, at 7:48 p.m.

All but two of the victims, Marguerite Chambers and Edith Cook, had been cremated, but investigators acquired court orders to exhume Chambers's and Cook's remains. Unfortunately, Marguerite's corpse was in terrible shape because water had leaked into her coffin. Edith Cook's remains, the medical examiners noted, were more intact.

In his book *Skeletons in the Closet: Stories from the County Morgue*, Tobin Buhk revealed that the autopsies on the women noted no signs of struggle or defensive bruising on either body. Investigators also found no fibres on the bodies that would indicate the use of washcloths to commit murder. The official cause of death on the death certificates of both women was a heart attack. Under closer examination, neither body showed any markers for heart disease nor evidence of any other natural cause that might have killed them.

Dr. Stephen Cohle, the Kent County medical examiner, noted it was not what was present but what was missing that told the tale of the women's murders. If the women had not died of natural causes, then their deaths were from some external cause, he reasoned, leading him to determine that both the deaths were homicide by way of suffocation.

Prosecutors felt that Cathy's admissions were more than enough to convict her of the killings, and police arrested her immediately. Right away, Cathy agreed to a plea bargain that would have her testify against Gwen Graham in exchange for a single conviction of second-degree murder, for which she would be sentenced to 20 to 40 years behind bars. Authorities then arrested Gwen on five charges of first-degree murder, each charge coming with a life sentence if convicted.

Sometime before the investigation began, Cathy and Gwen had broken up and Gwen had started dating another nurse's aide at Alpine Manor. Cathy was furious, which was why she decided to tell investigators about the murders.

After the ugly breakup, Gwen Graham wanted to escape from the ongoing drama between herself and Cathy, so she relocated back to Tyler, Texas, to be closer to her family. She was arrested there in December of 1988. Gwen denied everything, saying that no murders had ever taken place. She adamantly claimed that all eight patients had died of natural causes. Gwen told investigators that Cathy was angry with her for leaving and had made the whole thing up. Making up the story of multiple murders was Cathy's revenge for Gwen's abandonment.

At the trial, Cathy Wood testified against Gwen, telling her hair-raising tale to 12 jurors. Cathy claimed she was lovestruck and intimidated by Graham—despite the fact she wrote bizarre poetry to Gwen in code about the murders. She painted Gwen as an evil and bloodthirsty monster who relished being dominant in their relationship and enjoyed the power she felt from killing her frail victims. Although Cathy mentioned the souvenirs Gwen had supposedly kept to relive the crimes, police never recovered any personal items belonging to the victims in Gwen's possession.

Cathy testified about their failed game to spell M-U-R-D-E-R with each victim's initials. In Cauffiel's book *Forever and Five Days*, she also admitted that after the first killing, the women had begun saying they would love each other "for forever and a day," a phrase she had used in a poem written to Gwendolyn Graham after the fifth murder that was later submitted by prosecutors as evidence at their trial. They changed the number of days, increasing it by one after each killing, as a code to account for each of the murders. The poem ended with, "You'll be mine forever and five days."

Prosecution witnesses corroborated Cathy's testimony about Gwen's drug and alcohol abuse and her penchant for violence. When drinking, she would often get into fistfights with other women. Several witnesses testified that Gwen and Cathy often fought as well, but one witness revealed that on one occasion Cathy had bested Gwen and thrown her across the room. Gwen and Cathy had also been seen physically attacking Ken Wood when he came by to pick up some personal items from the apartment. Cathy was not the only person who knew about the murders either; other friends testified Gwen had gone into detail about the murders to them as well.

Gwen took the stand during the defence portion of her trial and tearfully denied everything. The jury did not buy her tears, however. It took the jury just five hours to come back with guilty verdicts on all five first-degree murder counts and a single count of conspiracy to commit murder. Gwen Graham received five life sentences.

A two-part television documentary called "Cathy Wood and Gwen Graham: The Lethal Lovers," part of a TV series called *Serial Killers* released in 1995, featured jailhouse interviews with the two women, and both spoke about their time together. Gwen claimed she'd left Cathy because she was "tired of her playing games." She said that Cathy set her up for murder because she was angry and jealous about Gwen's new relationship after they broke up. Gwen maintained her innocence during the interview, claiming she wasn't even in the room when the women died. She reiterated her position that Cathy had concocted the whole story in her "sick mind" after their breakup. "I hate her for what she's put me through," Gwen said tearfully.

Cathy's interview told a different story. Cathy was much more composed than Gwen and claimed that Gwen had told her she killed in an effort to relieve tension. Cathy, at least, admitted responsibility in the interview and said that even though she did not commit the murders herself, she knew it was partially her fault that the victims had died.

A prosecutor confirmed that without Cathy's testimony, they would've had no case at all against Gwen. In the eyes of investigators, Gwen was the instigator and was more dangerous than Cathy, so the plea bargain, a deal with the devil, was offered to Cathy for her testimony, to ensure Gwen Graham was put away for a long time.

In a strange twist to the story, on June 25, 2019, Cathy's daughter, Jackie, called in to the *Howard Stern Show* and began freely talking about her mother's crimes. Jackie mentioned that she was eight when her mother had gone to prison, and she'd visited her mother in jail until Jackie moved out of state when she was 21. She repeated Cathy's story that Cathy had been the lookout while Gwen committed the murders, but she insinuated that they were not mercy killings, that Gwen and Cathy had killed for fun. Jackie also mentioned that her mother was coming up for parole, and things were looking good for her release.

Four months later, in October 2019, after 30 years in prison, Cathy Wood was granted parole by a Kent County judge, her earliest release date set to November 5, 2019. The conditions attached were that Cathy could never work with vulnerable adults or children and that she should never again set foot in the Alpine Manor nursing home.

Members of the victims' families sued to reverse the decision and keep Wood incarcerated at the Tallahassee Federal Correctional Institution in Florida, despite the fact that her maximum discharge date was June 6, 2021, and she'd be getting out in less than two years regardless. Catherine May Wood was released on January 16, 2020, and moved to South Carolina to live with her sister.

Thanks to Cathy's plea, and the additional testimony against her, barring a miracle, Gwen Graham will stay in jail for the rest of her life. She currently resides in the Huron Valley women's prison and still maintains her innocence. In the 1995 interview, Gwen still blamed the murders on her ex-lover, stating, "It's all a game of control. As long as [Cathy] doesn't tell the truth, as long as she holds on to the truth, I sit here, and she has control over my whole life."

The families of the victims sued Alpine Manor for hiring the two women who murdered their loved ones. The company has since folded, and another corporation now runs the home.

Chapter 3

THE BOOZING BARBER

Between 1965 and 1987, Gilbert Paul Jordan (born Gilbert Paul Elsie), an alcoholic barber and career criminal from Vancouver, British Columbia, allegedly killed as many as 10 women and attempted to kill at least four more. His weapon of choice was ethanol, also known as ethyl alcohol—the same kind you find in your evening cocktail. Jordan would kill his victims with a deadly overdose, and the slayings were called "the Alcohol Murders" by some in the press.

Gilbert Paul was born on December 12, 1931, to Winifred and Edward Jack Elsie in Vancouver, and the family resided in what is now the affluent Kitsilano neighbourhood. Gilbert was the second of the three Elsie boys. His older brother's name was Bud; his younger brother's name was Robert.

Gilbert's dad went by his second name, Jack, a practice Gilbert Paul would adopt later on because he loathed the name Gilbert and preferred to be called Paul. After working numerous labour jobs, Jack eventually settled into life as an employee at the Royal

Bank of Canada. His interest in finance was also shared by his son Gilbert.

Jack's wife, Winifred Elsie, was a domineering woman and a devout Methodist. Jack and Winifred eventually divorced, and both remarried and started new families. The boys lived with Jack, to remain in familiar schools, but also because Jack made more money than Winifred, who worked as a salesclerk at a local store.

Years later, in an article published in the *Vancouver Sun* on November 4, 2000, Bud Elsie expressed that he had a hard time understanding how his brother ended up the way he did. Bud could not cite any specific trauma or other event from their childhood that could have explained Gilbert Paul's murderous behaviour. As a child, Gilbert Paul did have difficulty making friends, and his classmates thought he was anti-social. Because he was short and stalky, some of his schoolmates began referring to him as "Chubs" or "Chubby," nicknames he hated.

Gilbert Paul eventually left school altogether at the age of 16 and began drinking heavily around Vancouver's west end beaches, often remaining drunk for days. His mother, Winifred, was disgusted by her son's drinking and refused to take phone calls from him when he would call her drunk.

Gilbert Paul's life soon began to deteriorate. He loved cars and began doing body work on vehicles. He travelled to Los Angeles to seek work in 1949 but was unsuccessful and came home. Gilbert Paul began taking odd jobs, but they barely helped him scrape by. As his alcohol addiction began to grow, he settled on a life as a criminal. Stealing was his thing, and although he started with smaller items, he eventually began stealing cars. On July 17, 1950, when he was 18, Gilbert Paul's adult criminal record began. His first conviction in adult court was for an auto theft in Vancouver, which earned him a 12-month jail sentence. Between 1952 and

1960, he was charged six more times for theft-related offences and was convicted of four. For two of those convictions, Gilbert Paul was sentenced to 12 months in prison each time.

In 1961, Gilbert Paul's criminal history took an ominous twist. He was found by RCMP in a gravel pit in his car alone with a five-year-old girl. Gilbert Paul had abducted her from a reserve in Mission, B.C., but further details of the incident are unknown. Because of the girl's young age, her ability to be a reliable witness was questioned and the Crown entered a stay of proceedings. The case did not come up again. It is unclear whether Gilbert Paul sexually interfered with the girl.

In early December of 1961, Gilbert Paul received another conviction for theft. Then, later that month, drunk, he held up traffic on the busy Lions Gate Bridge by threatening to throw himself into the water 60 metres (200 feet) below. The Crown later withdrew charges relating to that stunt, but he spent two months after the incident in what was known then as the Riverview Mental Hospital in Coquitlam.

Shortly after getting out of the mental hospital, in March of 1962, Gilbert Paul picked up two women from the seedy area of Hastings Street near Main Street. The trio drank in the car near Coal Harbour. When one of the women got out of the car, feeling ill from too much vodka, Gilbert Paul sped off with her purse and the other woman passed out beside him. Elsie took the woman to a secluded area in North Vancouver, where he raped her. Afterwards, the women went to the police and he was arrested and charged with sexual assault and theft.

At a court appearance to face the charges a week later, Gilbert Paul yelled, "Sieg heil!" at Magistrate Arthur Pool, then clicked his heels together and made the straight-armed Nazi salute. His courtroom antics earned him another six months in jail, this time for contempt. During the period of incarceration before his rape trial, a psychiatrist assessed Elsie and determined him to be mentally ill, although the official diagnosis is unknown.

Gilbert Paul was acquitted of the sexual assault charges when the court determined that his alleged rape victim was too drunk to recall with any surety what had taken place in his car. He was convicted on the two counts of theft over $50 for driving off with the second woman's purse and sentenced to two years for each offence. He later appealed his convictions, won and was released.

During his latest stint in jail, Elsie had taken a course on how to be a barber. His new profession and his love of alcohol earned him the nickname "the Boozing Barber."

On the morning of January 18, 1965, a housekeeper found the nude body of an English-born switchboard operator named Ivy Rose (Doreen) Oswald in a room at the Lyle Hotel in Vancouver. Gilbert Paul Elsie and the young lady had checked in and staggered to their room arm in arm the night before. A pathologist determined Ivy's blood alcohol content (BAC) to be 0.51. Strangely, she was not known to be a heavy drinker. Yet, somehow, she had surpassed the 0.31 to 0.45 BAC where death can occur from alcohol poisoning. With a BAC between 0.16 and 0.30, the average person would lose consciousness. Ivy's autopsy also revealed superficial and recent bruises on her chin, lips and scalp, but at the time, these were deemed inconsequential and unrelated to her death.

Police picked up Elsie for questioning and held him at the city jail while police investigated. He had a few of Oswald's belongings on him when they caught him, proving he had been with her. Elsie admitted that he and Oswald had been drinking and had sex all night. But he claimed he'd found her dead in the morning. Ivy Rose's death was ruled accidental, and police released Elsie without charge.

Elsie applied to have his surname changed to Jordan only four days after Oswald's death. His brother Bud later told the *Vancouver*

Sun, in an October 22, 1988, article, that his brother had changed his name "because of the embarrassment [his crimes were] causing the family. My stepmother was particularly sensitive to it."

The new surname didn't slow Gilbert Paul Jordan down; in fact, his crimes accelerated. Between 1966 and the end of 1971, he was charged with 18 different offences that included theft, assault, indecent acts, heroin possession and drunk driving. Two of the drunk driving charges he was arrested for occurred on the same day in Delta, B.C. For many of his other crimes, the Crown often had to drop charges against him because of a lack of evidence. Elsie, now Jordan, was a slippery fellow and got away with a lot.

In 1971, Gilbert Paul Jordan moved north to Prince George, a rough-around-the-edges logging town in British Columbia's Central Interior. Even though he married in 1972, his dangerous, anti-social antics continued.

From late 1973 throughout 1975, Gilbert Paul Jordan was convicted of a trio of sex offences and others related to violence and alcohol. One conviction for indecent exposure came from an incident in April 1973, when the now 42-year-old exposed himself to a group of children in Mackenzie, B.C.

After another short stint in prison, Jordan returned to Prince George, and in October of 1975, he offered a woman a drive and then attempted to sexually assault her. A passerby who heard Jordan's 23-year-old victim screaming thwarted the assault.

Jordan finished off the year with another sexual assault in December. He met a woman outside a Prince George liquor store, offered her a ride and took the woman to his home, where they drank heavily together. The woman passed out and later came to as Jordan was trying to sexually assault her in his bathroom. She escaped, but not before Jordan beat and choked her.

Jordan was convicted of the October and December assaults and sentenced to two years less a day for each crime. The sentence for the first assault was appealed and reduced to six months.

The Crown then decided to try him as a dangerous offender because of his chronic and increasingly violent behaviour. In Canada, if a trial finds a person to be a dangerous offender, they can be subjected to an indeterminate term of incarceration, even if the crime they are serving time for is not punishable by life in prison. It is almost impossible for dangerous offenders to receive parole because the designation indicates their behaviour is habitual and they pose a risk to society if released.

A string of expert witnesses testified that Jordan was a high risk to re-offend. Yet the court denied the Crown's dangerous offender application, and Gilbert Paul Jordan was a free man once again.

Once out of jail, Jordan moved to Alberta, and there he continued committing crimes, including being nude in a public place and a string of other indecent acts. He also raped an intellectually challenged woman he had taken from a mental institution against her will. The Crown dropped charges of rape, theft, assault causing bodily harm and kidnapping against Jordan in favour of a guilty plea to assault that earned him 26 more months in prison. After this jail term, he returned to Vancouver and began his life as a murderer in earnest.

Gilbert Paul Jordan was not a down-and-out bum. He was actually quite well off. Taking his father's advice, Jordan had been investing money over the years and acquired even more money from an inheritance. Somehow, this alcoholic career criminal had been able to amass enough of a fortune to keep himself drunk and well-defended throughout his numerous legal entanglements.

In 1980 Jordan opened a barbershop in downtown Vancouver, where he started his newest crime spree. He would buy loads of alcohol and then entice vulnerable alcoholic women from Vancouver's Downtown Eastside back to his barbershop to party with him. He told his friends that the women loved him, but his friends all knew better: the women loved him for his money and his alcohol supply.

Jordan bragged about having drunken sex with as many as 200 women a year throughout the 80s. Even though some of the women he was partying with turned up dead, the authorities failed to notice a pattern until it was far too late.

On November 30, 1980, Mary Laurentia Johnson, 42, died in Jordan's company at the Aylmer Hotel. Her blood alcohol content (BAC) was 0.3 percent.

Barbara Anne Paul, 27, had been on a four-day alcoholic binge with Jordan at the Glenaird Hotel when she died on September 11, 1981. She had a BAC of 0.41.

On July 30, 1982, Mary Doris Johns died while drinking with Jordan at his Kingsway barbershop. Her blood alcohol content was a whopping 0.76.

At the time, investigators determined accidental alcohol overdose was the cause of death in all three cases. The police didn't seem to notice the fact that women were turning up dead after being in Jordan's company. Every death, the police decided, had been death by misadventure caused by a high-risk lifestyle. That Jordan might be a murderer was not even a consideration.

Jordan briefly stopped killing in 1983 when he fell in love with and married a woman named Maria Elvira. But his drunkenness, infidelity and physical abuse led Maria to flee and file for divorce after only four months.

Undeterred by his brief failed marriage, Jordan quickly picked up where he had left off, and women continued to turn up dead after spending time with him.

Patricia Thomas, 40, died at the barbershop on December 14, 1984, during one of Jordan's parties. Her BAC was 0.51. Patricia's body showed injuries that had occurred close to the time of her death. Investigators determined her injuries to be the result of falling while intoxicated, and her cause of death was, once again, deemed an accidental alcohol overdose.

On June 29, 1985, Patricia Josephine Andrew, 45 and a mother of four, died at Jordan's barbershop. The responding paramedics found the woman naked and unresponsive on the floor of the shop. She had an astonishing BAC of 0.79, almost 10 times the level at which someone is too drunk to drive. Jordan claimed he and the woman had been bingeing on Chinese cooking wine for days before she died. The coroner found signs of chronic alcohol abuse during her autopsy and ruled Patricia's death accidental and unnatural, but not homicide.

Around this time, in trouble again for unrelated crimes, Gilbert Paul Jordan told the court he was trying to turn his life around. Jordan blamed booze for his poor life decisions and decided to attend 12-step meetings. But he never managed to stop drinking for any significant period of time.

On September 25, 1986, Velma Dora Gibbons, 38, was found dead and semi-nude in a room at the notorious Balmoral Hotel in Vancouver's skid row. She had died with a BAC of 0.63. Chinese cooking wine was the only alcohol found in the room. Her death was ruled accidental due to acute alcohol poisoning. She had been seen with Gilbert Paul Jordan in the hours leading up to her death.

Veronica Norma Henry, 33, was found deceased on November 19, 1986, in a room rented by Jordan at the Clifton Hotel. She had a BAC of only 0.04. Pathologists ruled her death to be accidental, even though she had fresh cuts and bruises on her face. Henry too had been seen with Jordan on the day of her death.

On October 12, 1987, 27-year-old Vanessa Lee Buckner was found naked and dead with a near-impossible BAC of 0.91 at the Niagara Hotel. Buckner's mother, a nurse, and her father, the owner of a construction firm, didn't believe their daughter had accidentally overdosed on alcohol, even though she was known to lead a high-risk lifestyle. For years Vanessa had struggled with addiction to drugs and alcohol. However, on the day of her death, she seemed happy and spoke to her parents of the future. She had given birth to a child only two weeks before.

Gilbert Paul Jordan had called to anonymously report Vanessa's death from his room at the nearby Marble Arch Hotel. Police traced the call, picked up Jordan and questioned him. Even though his story didn't make a lot of sense, police released him. However, after Jordan was let go, Vancouver Police Department homicide investigators finally began to look back at all the alcohol deaths that seemed to be connected to him.

The last woman to die was 53-year-old Edna Marie Shade. On November 8, 1987, Edna's naked body was found in a room at the Glenaird Hotel with a blood alcohol level of 0.77. Witnesses had seen her with Gilbert Paul Jordan earlier that day.

Cops put Jordan under surveillance immediately and watched him as he trolled for new victims along the city's skid row. Police had to intervene, and thwarted what they believed to be another four attempts to poison Indigenous women with alcohol so Jordan could have his way with them after they passed out. Police even overheard him coaxing women to drink more than they wanted to, promising them cash.

According to Regina (the Crown) v. Jordan, Case 010079, police listening outside of hotel room doors heard the accused say to women such things as "Have a drink, down the hatch, baby, 20 bucks if you drink it right down; see if you're a real woman; finish that drink, finish that drink, down the hatch, hurry, right down; you need another drink, I'll give you 50 bucks if you can take it."

After the fourth close call, Jordan was arrested and charged with first-degree murder for the death of Vanessa Lee Buckner. It was his first and only homicide charge.

In 1988, the court convicted Gilbert Paul Jordan of manslaughter rather than first-degree murder because, although the Crown was able to prove he was negligent in Vanessa Lee's death, they did not show sufficient proof he had intended to kill her. The judge sentenced the 57-year-old career criminal and suspected serial killer to 15 years in prison.

Jordan was released in 1994 after serving only six years. He was incarcerated again after failing to meet his parole conditions, which included avoiding any licensed establishments near Vancouver's downtown and the company of any women where liquor was served.

Another woman with Jordan came dangerously close to dying of alcohol poisoning in the York Hotel in Swift Current, Saskatchewan, in August of 2004. Barb Burkley, an alcoholic and resident of the low-rent hotel, required hospitalization and almost died after a night of binge drinking with Jordan. Afterwards, Jordan took off, heading west. Two days later he was picked up by the police and briefly held on suspicion of attempted murder. A slippery career criminal, Jordan was not talking, and Barb had been too drunk to give a coherent statement. Cops reluctantly let Jordan go, citing a lack of evidence to proceed with charges.

Jordan returned to British Columbia and was in and out of prison for the rest of his life for various offences, mostly parole violations. His final victim was himself: he died alone in a Victoria, B.C., hotel room of cirrhosis of the liver on July 7, 2006. He had finally drunk himself to death.

In an article written by Jim Beatty for the *Vancouver Sun* printed on November 4, 2000, Gilbert Paul Jordan talked about his life and minimized his involvement in the women's deaths by saying, "They were all on their last legs." Still unwilling to take responsibility for his crimes, he added, "I'm not a criminal. But I've got a terrible criminal record because of booze."

Jordan's choice of victim was much more common than his murder weapon. Drug-addicted and alcoholic women who support themselves as sex workers are often targeted by serial murderers globally. Jordan chose his victims from Vancouver's notorious Downtown Eastside, and they were almost exclusively of Indigenous heritage.

The same downtown area where Jordan chose his victims later gained notoriety thanks to another serial killer. Port Coquitlam pig farmer Robert "Willie" Pickton also chose from the same pool of victims and killed as many as 49 women between 1983 and 2002.

Sadly, because of a lack of understanding and empathy about addiction, these women, who are often society's most vulnerable, tend to be easy pickings for predators like Jordan. These factors allowed him to go on killing, relatively undetected, for years, something that probably would not have happened if his victims were pretty college coeds.

Chapter 4

THE ELEMENTARY SCHOOL
MURDERER

In December of 1968, a sensational double-murder trial began in the Moot Hall Assize Court in Newcastle upon Tyne, England. Two boys, Martin George Brown, four, and Brian Edward Howe, three years old, had been brutally murdered in May and July of that year.

It was not the victims as much as the perpetrators that caught the attention of news reporters and the public. Two young girls, inseparable friends and neighbours, had committed the heinous crimes. Though unrelated, the pair happened to share the same last name. Norma Joyce Bell was 13 years old, but the dominant of the two, Mary Flora Bell, was only 11 years old when she strangled both little boys as the older girl looked on.

After the arrests, the same question was on everyone's mind. What on earth would drive these two young girls to carry out such horrific acts?

Mary Bell, called "May" by her family and close friends, was the eldest of four children, with two younger sisters and a younger brother. She'd been born in Newcastle, England, on May 26, 1957, out of wedlock, to Elizabeth "Betty" McCrickett, 17, who had been banished to a convent when her parents discovered she was pregnant. Betty was so disturbed after Mary's birth that she did not want to see the child and begged for her daughter to be taken away from her.

A few months after Mary's birth, Betty met 21-year-old Billy Bell, an alcoholic bad boy and small-time criminal. The two were soon married, and Mary called Billy "Dad," although it was never clear who her biological father was.

Mary knew her dad was a troublemaker and looked up to him for it. She thought of him as a modern-day Jessie James, like the outlaws portrayed in the television westerns she would watch with him when he was not out drinking and thieving. Betty and Billy's most significant crime against Mary and her future siblings was neglect. When their parents were off trying to put together what little money they could, Mary and her siblings were often left on their own.

Betty was the parent who took the blame for creating the little monster that Mary had become. Mary later claimed that to make ends meet, Betty had become a sex worker, travelling as far as Glasgow to service her clientele. Mary also claimed Betty would bring her work home with her, practising sadomasochism with the men in their tiny house, even with her children present. Mary later recalled sitting on the couch at four years old and watching as her mother had intercourse on the bed with a stranger. Worse still, Mary claims that Betty forced her to participate in sexual acts with some of the men, describing her experiences in harrowing detail in Gitta Sereny's book *Cries Unheard*.

Mary's teachers noticed odd behaviour right from her first days in school. Mary would hide under her desk in the classroom and refuse to come out. Her moods were erratic too: some days she would be outgoing and energetic; other days she was sullen and withdrawn.

Mary would kick, pinch and punch classmates but then get upset when no one wanted to play with her. There was no one to help Mary, to redirect her from the violent and tragic path she was on.

Mary's family moved to a house on Whitehouse Road in the Scotswood district of Newcastle upon Tyne in the summer of 1967, when she was just 10 years old. In the late 1960s the slums in Scotswood were in transition. The neighbourhood had a post-apocalyptic feel as older row homes, filled to overflowing with low-income families, were torn down to make way for modern multi-unit flats. When they weren't in school, Mary and the other neighbourhood kids played amid the debris of demolished houses and inside the many hazardous abandoned buildings that were waiting for the wrecking crews.

Mary's friend Norma Bell was one of 11 children, and she lived in a tiny house two doors down from Mary. Although poor as well, Norma's family was hard-working and had a better reputation than Mary's parents. Norma's younger sister Susan was first to play with Mary, but Mary soon became bored with the girl, who always followed the rules, and found herself spending time with the more rebellious and unpredictable Norma. Norma was two years older than Mary but was not as smart, and she was easily manipulated by the younger girl. Mary was intelligent and precocious, willing to take on pretty much any dare posed to her by her peers. She was fearless and relished in having Norma as a sidekick.

But Mary Bell's tendency toward violence was a growing concern for those around her. A former teacher told author Gitta Sereny that on one occasion, she caught Mary Bell with her hands around a smaller child's throat, applying pressure. When the teacher admonished Mary for hurting the little boy, Mary coldly asked whether it would kill him.

On May 11, 1968, a call came from a pub in Scotswood requesting an ambulance and police attendance. Mary Bell and her friend

Norma reported that a three-year-old boy had been injured while playing in the empty houses nearby. Mary and Norma both claimed they had not seen what happened to the little boy, but they had heard shouts coming from a group of sheds behind the house they were playing in. They said they ran to see what was causing the commotion and discovered the toddler. He was bleeding from a wound to the head and covered in his own vomit. They carried the boy to the Delaval Arms pub, where the barkeep called for help.

The next day, May 12, 1968, another call came to police, this time from a local mother. She said that three girls, two aged 6 and the other 7, claimed they had been assaulted by two older girls, Mary Bell, 10, and Norma Bell, 13.

Constable I. Charlton interviewed one of the victims, seven-year-old Pauline Watson. Pauline told the officer that Mary Bell had told her to get out of the sandpit where they were playing. When Pauline refused to leave, Mary Bell clamped her hands around Pauline's neck and squeezed hard. When Pauline's friend Susan tried to intervene, Mary did the same thing to her. After Susan broke free from Mary's grip, the younger girls ran home and told their mothers what had happened.

Norma was interviewed and laid the blame squarely on Mary Bell, claiming she had witnessed the whole thing. Mary countered, saying she had not been present the entire time and claiming she had seen Pauline running and clutching her throat. When Mary asked what happened, Norma told her that the other youngster had fallen and hurt her neck.

Pauline seemed afraid to talk about the incident in the days afterwards. The police dropped the affair after warning Mary and Norma not to be involved in any further violent incidents.

At 3:30 p.m. on May 25, 1968, a small group of boys playing in an abandoned, partially boarded-up home at 85 St. Margaret's Road stumbled upon the body of a little boy lying near a window.

Blood and foam were coming from his mouth, and his body was cold to the touch. The terrified older boys ran to call for help. Police and an ambulance crew arrived five minutes later and tried to resuscitate the child, but it was too late.

The dead boy was Martin George Brown, aged four years and two months. His aunt, Rita Finlay, had been watching him that Saturday afternoon. Martin had gone down to a shop for candy, she told investigators, where the shop owner sold him a lollipop at 3:15 p.m. Just 15 minutes later and only 300 metres (980 feet) away, he was found dead. Whatever happened to the young boy had happened quickly.

Mary and Norma, who had been a babysitter for the Finlays, knocked on Rita's door that afternoon to tell her one of the children was hurt, but Rita did not believe them. Even so, she went to investigate and arrived just in time to see little Martin's body as paramedics carried it to the waiting ambulance.

At first, medical investigators assumed that Martin had ingested poison, perhaps some substance in the house. But an autopsy determined there was nothing unusual in his digestive tract or in his blood. There were also no marks on his neck or any other signs of strangulation.

It would be two weeks before Martin Brown's family was able to finally lay him to rest. The cause of his death was still unknown, but many believed it was just an unfortunate accident.

Mary Bell's behaviour became more bizarre in the weeks after the boy's death. She prattled on about death and drew disturbing and violent pictures in her schoolbooks. She was also involved in several other concerning incidents.

On Mary's 11th birthday, the day after Martin's death, she visited Norma Bell and her siblings to play. The children were outside that afternoon when Norma's parents heard one of them cry out. Mr. Bell ran out to find Mary Bell throttling his 11-year-old daughter, Susan. He separated the two and sent Mary away. Mary screamed that she would tell her father that Mr. Bell had struck her. According to Susan, the altercation began over a birthday card. Even though Susan had sent Mary a card, and told her so, Mary called her a liar, chased her down and began choking her. Mr. Bell told Susan she was not to play with Mary again.

Two days after Martin's death, on May 27, employees at a local nursery school arrived at work to find the building had been broken into and vandalized over the weekend. Amid the papers and other school supplies strewn about were several hastily scrawled notes with hateful messages toward police and Martin Brown. One cryptically read, "I murder so that I may come back," and another stated, "WE did murder Martin brown Fuckof [sic] you Bastard."

In the days before Martin's funeral, Mary Bell knocked on the door at the Brown residence. Mary asked Rita if she could see Martin. When Rita told Mary he was dead, Mary said she knew Martin was dead, but that she wanted to see him inside his coffin. Rita was mortified by the callousness of Mary's request and slammed the door in the young girl's face.

Six days after Martin's death, Mary and Norma tripped an alarm breaking into the nursery school again. Although police suspected them, the girls denied responsibility for the previous break-in. The Crown charged the little girls with breaking and entering and released them to their parents pending trial in juvenile court on the charges.

The summer got worse for the tight-knit neighbourhood when another little boy turned up dead. On July 31, 1968, a cherubic blond-haired boy named Brian Howe, only three years old, went missing at around 3:30 p.m. He was last seen in the afternoon playing with his brother, Norman, his dog, named Lassie, and two girls with bicycles, Mary Bell and Norma Bell. Lassie and Norman returned home, but Brian stayed behind with the two girls.

Mary Bell joined in the search for little Brian. As groups scoured the neighbourhood, Mary pointed to some concrete blocks in an area full of junk and discarded building materials near the train tracks. She suggested that perhaps Brian was there, among the blocks. The older searcher dismissed Mary's idea and went off to look elsewhere. Mary went home to supper at 7:30 p.m.

That evening, there was still no sign of Brian, so his parents called the police to aid in the search. Police found the boy, dead, just after 11:00 p.m., lying between the concrete blocks that Mary Bell had gestured toward earlier. Like Martin Brown, he had foam and blood coming out of his mouth. But unlike Martin, Brian had distinct bruises and scratches on his neck. Police recovered a pair of broken and bent scissors near his body.

Because of the nature of Brian's injuries, police believed right away that another child had killed him. It was not immediately clear who or, better yet, why. Then another bizarre clue surfaced during the post-mortem, when the pathologist found what appeared to be a letter M carved into Brian's skin. Someone had also cut off hanks of his hair, scratched his legs and mutilated his genitals with the scissors.

Police went right to work questioning people, specifically children, in the neighbourhood. On the day after discovering Brian's body, police blanketed Scotswood in force, talking with and taking statements from more than a thousand children ranging in age from 3 years old to 15.

Mary Bell and Norma Bell stood out right away thanks to the inconsistencies in their answers to police questions, and were visited by police multiple times. Mary claimed she had seen a local eight-year-old boy, whom she named, playing with scissors like the ones found near Brian's body. She said she had witnessed the same boy using the scissors while attempting to cut the tail off a local cat.

Police had not published photos or mentioned scissors in the newspaper accounts of the crime. The police checked on the young boy Mary had mentioned and verified that his alibi put him somewhere else at the time of Brian Howe's death. Mary Bell's lies made her a prime suspect in the killing, mostly because her tales contained details that no one outside of authorities knew.

After changing her story at least twice, on the evening of August 4, 1968, Norma Bell could not contain her knowledge of the slaying anymore. Norma nervously told investigators that Mary had admitted to killing Brian Howe, had taken her to see the body and had also described how she had done it.

Norma's first statement to Detective Chief Inspector Dobson implied that she and Mary Bell had found Brian and that he was already dead when they got there. She claimed she had tripped over something and looked down to see it was Brian Howe's head. Norma described how the dead boy was situated, what his face looked like and what he was wearing. She said there was a mark on the boy's nose and that his lips were purple, all consistent with what the police observed on finding the tot's body.

The details Norma gave next shocked the experienced chief inspector. After Norma touched the boy's face, Mary grabbed her around the neck. Norma claimed that is when Mary told her she had taken Brian there to kill him, that she had squeezed the life out of him and enjoyed doing it. Mary threatened Norma, warning her not to tell anyone.

Only hours later, at 12:15 a.m., investigators were knocking on Mary Bell's door. Police interviewed the 11-year-old until 3:30 a.m. Despite the pressure, Mary continued to deny involvement in Brian Howe's murder.

Norma had imparted a lot of information in her newest statement, so investigators brought her in again the next afternoon. Norma Bell said her previous report had been factual, but there was even more. She owned up to having been present while Mary murdered Brian Howe. Mary had chased two boys playing with Brian away so she and Norma could be alone with him.

Norma said Mary had grabbed Brian Howe's neck and throttled the little boy, taking him down to the grass, still choking him as hard as possible. Norma claimed it seemed like Mary was acting "funny," like something had come over her. The harder little Brian fought to tear Mary's hands away, the more focused Mary got. Mary's hands had become tired from strangling the boy, and she asked Norma to take over. Norma claimed that is when she had run away.

Police questioned Mary again. When they reiterated what Norma had told them earlier, Mary threw the blame right back on Norma. Mary claimed Norma was making it up to keep herself out of trouble.

Both girls were arrested and charged with the murder of Brian Edward Howe and remanded into custody to await trial. By this time, investigators were treating Martin Brown's death as murder as well. The fact that these two girls had been present on that property, and Mary Bell's odd behaviour afterwards, including the nursery school break-in and notes matching both girls' handwriting, indicated possible guilt. Grey wool fibres found with Martin Brown's body matched Mary's dress exactly. Police investigators believed that the lack of marks on Martin's neck was explained by Mary's lack of hand strength, but she had indeed strangled him. Even though both girls continued to deny involvement in Martin Brown's death, the Crown also charged them with that murder.

According to Gitta Sereny's book *The Case of Mary Bell*, during the trial in December of 1968, Mary was asked, "Why did you pretend that you and Norma had murdered Martin Brown if it wasn't true?"

Her response was chilling. "For a giggle."

Psychiatrist Dr. Robert Orton had interviewed Mary Bell to determine her fitness for trial and possible mental illness. He testified that he had diagnosed preteen Mary Bell as psychopathic and incapable of feeling any guilt or remorse for her crimes.

At Newcastle Assizes on December 17, 1968, Norma Bell was found not guilty on the two murder charges. Because of her age and what the court deemed diminished responsibility, Mary Flora Bell was found not guilty of murder but guilty of manslaughter in the deaths of Martin Brown and Brian Howe. Mary was to be held in prison "at her Majesty's pleasure," meaning she would stay in prison indefinitely.

In 1977, a year after Mary Bell moved from a juvenile detention centre to an adult prison, she escaped briefly, making the news once again. Mary finally got her release from prison in 1980 when she was 23 years old. Granted immunity because of her young age at the time of her crimes, Mary has moved and changed her identity numerous times. She gave birth to a little girl on May 25, 1984, and she became a grandmother in 2009. Her current whereabouts are unknown.

Chapter 5

BAD APPLES

Motherly is not the first adjective that comes to mind when looking at the mug shot of Gertrude Nadine Baniszewski, which was taken as officials processed her for parole from the Indiana prison system. Gertrude had a severe, depressed look, with shockingly overplucked eyebrows highlighting her sad eyes. Her gaunt face, smart yet understated grey dress over a clean white shirt and massive 60s-style hairdo make her look like Faye Dunaway's portrayal of a disturbed, abusive mother, Joan Crawford, in *Mommie Dearest*.

Gertrude looked as though she smelled like hairspray, intense perfume and an ashtray. She was a prodigious smoker and was never without a cigarette between her skeletal fingers. Every room in her home had an ashtray overflowing with butts stained by Gertrude's bright lipstick.

In 1966, Baniszewski had been convicted of the first-degree murder of 16-year-old Sylvia Likens, a boarder who had lived in her home with her physically disabled younger sister, Jenny Likens.

With the help of two of her children, Paula, 18, and John, 13, and two neighbourhood boys, Coy Hubbard and Richard Hobbs, both 15, Gertrude, 37, mentally, emotionally and physically tortured Sylvia and Jenny. She later turned her attention solely to Sylvia, ultimately starving the teenager to death in the family's basement.

Sylvia Marie Likens was born in Lebanon, Indiana, on January 3, 1949, between two sets of fraternal twins, to carnival workers Lester and Betty Likens. Diana and Danny were two years older, and Jenny and Benny were a year younger than Sylvia. She was the monkey in the middle and stood out for it.

Sylvia's parents were not well situated but did what they could to provide for their five children. They travelled, often leaving Sylvia and Jenny behind with relatives to give some stability in their lives and ensure consistency in education for the two girls.

Sylvia was outgoing, pretty and confident. She kept her mouth closed when she grinned impishly, trying to hide the space in her smile where a tooth should have been. The tooth had been knocked out long ago during a collision with one of her brothers while roughhousing. Her friends called her "Cookie."

Sylvia grew into a responsible youngster, helping to earn the family money by doing chores for neighbours and babysitting. She loved music too. The Beatles were her favourite group, and when she could, she'd purchase a Beatles record and listen to it over and over, with her little sister at her side.

Shy little Jenny Likens survived a bout with polio but wore a leg brace and walked with a pronounced limp after her illness. Sylvia was close to Jenny. She felt responsible for the younger girl since her parents were on the road much of the time.

Sylvia's eventual murderer was born as Gertrude Van Fossan just before the big stock market crash in 1929. She was the third of six children in the family. Gert's father favoured her, and her mother responded jealously, irrationally hating her young daughter for it. When Mr. Van Fossan was out of the house, Gert would be neglected by her mother entirely or bullied by her siblings at her mother's urging.

When Gert was 10 years old, her 50-year-old father dropped dead while helping her with homework. She was devastated. The only person who seemed willing to provide her with any love at all was gone.

Gert took the blame for putting the family behind the eight ball financially during the Great Depression. Her mother acted like it was her fault that her father, the family's provider, had died, and reminded her every chance she could. After years and years of mental, emotional and physical abuse, Gertrude grew into an angry young woman.

She dropped out of school at 16 and married her 18-year-old boyfriend, John Stephan Baniszewski, and had four children. Their marriage was not much of a respite from her previous homelife. John was physically and verbally abusive with Gertrude, but she hung in with him for 10 years, using makeup to cover the bruises, before they divorced.

Gertrude had a short-lived relationship with another man before she went crawling back to the familiar but brutal relationship with John Baniszewski. They remarried. They had two more children and Gertrude had a few miscarriages as well. Eventually, Gertrude and John split, once and for all, in 1963.

Gertrude quickly found another man, Dennis Wright, who was more than a decade her junior. The two married soon after meeting, and Gertrude became pregnant with her seventh child.

Dennis Wright was only in his early 20s and he quickly tired of being dominated by Gertrude, who acted more like his mother than his wife. She behaved even worse when she was pregnant. Dennis took off the night after his son's birth, leaving Gert in the hospital, high and dry, with a gaggle of kids, including a newborn they'd named Dennis Jr.

Gert melted down into a significant depression and spent much of her time hiding in her room, leaving her eldest daughter, then 17-year-old Paula Baniszewski, to step into the role as caregiver for the household. Paula was trying to get her own life together, and her mother's hatefulness was holding her back, but out of a sense of duty, she stuck around.

In 1965 Lester and Betty Likens came calling on their old friend Gert, with Sylvia and Jenny in tow. They were having trouble finding a place to board Jenny and Sylvia while they went off to work with the carnival. None of their relatives could take the girls this time. Gertrude was more than happy to take them in for $20 per week, and Lester paid the first week in advance. She told Betty the extra money would help with the bills that were piling up.

They made the deal in the living room of Gertrude's home at 3850 East New York Street in Indianapolis. Had the Likens seen the rest of Gertrude's house, they might have taken their girls elsewhere. Gertrude, depressed and stoned out of her mind on phenobarbital and other medications, was a terrible housekeeper. There was barely any food in the cupboards, and certainly not enough for two more growing girls.

It didn't take long before Gertrude began abusing Jenny and Sylvia. Gertrude berated and slapped both girls when money from Lester failed to arrive on time. Gertrude called the girls bitches and whores as she screamed that she had taken care of them for nothing that week. Although a money order from Lester arrived the next day, an apology from Gertrude did not.

Jenny quickly learned to keep her mouth shut and stay out of Gertrude's way. So Gertrude focused her wrath on Sylvia. Gertrude reprimanded Sylvia, calling her a thief and a liar, telling her she was a bad influence on Gert's kids.

Sylvia had not been stealing. She had been turning in bottles she, Jenny and Gertrude's younger kids had scavenged around the neighbourhood for change that they converted to candy. The kids liked Sylvia for it, but immature Gertrude took umbrage at anything that took attention, or money, away from her. Gertrude often gave Sylvia vicious beatings with a heavy wooden paddle for her perceived slights.

Even though Sylvia did what she could to minimize the chances of another beating, it seemed she could do nothing right. Gert would call Sylvia a pig just for eating a meal. But if Sylvia refused to eat, Gertrude would slap her and force the food down her throat. If Sylvia threw up, Gert forced her to eat that too. Sylvia could not do anything to please Gert.

Sylvia was so beaten down by Gert she could not bring herself to tell her parents about the abuse during a brief visit late in the summer. Having Gertrude glaring at her throughout the entire visit did not help Sylvia's courage either.

On the bus ride back home, Gertrude let Sylvia know she had done well at the meeting with her parents. For the next little while, things seemed to improve, giving Sylvia a false sense of security.

One ray of light in Sylvia's life was that she was pretty and popular with the neighbourhood boys. Soon a number of them began hanging around the house more than usual. Gertrude seethed as Sylvia received attention from the young men. It was the kind of admiration the plain-looking Gert had never experienced.

In front of her children and the local kids, Gertrude would claim that Sylvia thought she was better than the rest of them. The jealous woman would encourage the children and neighbours to join in and berate her, and they often did, giggling as Gertrude raged against 16-year-old Sylvia.

One afternoon, Sylvia opened up to Paula and Stephanie, the oldest Baniszewski girls, along with Gertrude and some neighbourhood kids. Sylvia admitted to having had a boyfriend she had kissed and allowed to touch her breasts over her sweater. As all the others sat in stunned silence, Gertrude flew into a rage. She called Sylvia a slut and a whore, then slapped her and knocked her right out of her chair. Screaming as the others watched, then laughing, Gertrude punched Sylvia and kicked her hard between her legs.

When Sylvia cried and tried to close her legs against the assault, Gertrude called on the boys to hold Sylvia's legs open so she could kick more freely. They obliged, and the attack continued. From that day on, Sylvia's groin became one of Gertrude's favourite targets.

After the assault, Sylvia was no longer allowed to sit anywhere in the house. Even the pile of dirty laundry that she used as a bed was dispersed by Gert's kicking feet before Sylvia was allowed to lie down at night.

As the fall began and the girls returned to school, the beatings at Gertrude's house continued. Sylvia and Jenny continued to go to school this whole time but missed many days with mysterious illnesses, later showing up at school with yellowing bruises on their bodies.

At her mother's urging, Paula, now 18, joined in on the beatings. Paula punched Sylvia so hard in the jaw on one occasion that she thought she'd broken her wrist. Gertrude lied to 15-year-old Coy Hubbard, Stephanie Baniszewski's boyfriend, saying that Sylvia had been calling Stephanie a slut. Gertrude manipulated the teen-ager into dragging Sylvia into the basement. There he used Sylvia as a practice dummy for judo throws until he was too tired to do it anymore.

When Coy finished, Gertrude told him he was a good boy and offered Sylvia up for similar treatment any time he liked. Everyone else went back upstairs, turned out the light and shut the door behind them. Sylvia was left bruised and battered on the dirt floor of the cellar in the dark. There would be no dinner for Sylvia that night, and this would be the first of many nights alone in the dank, dark basement without any food.

The abuse continued, and each day, as soon as Sylvia dutifully came home from school in the afternoon, the torture would begin. Gertrude cursed at Sylvia, burned the girl's fingers and put cigarettes out on her skin.

Gertrude had convinced everyone that Sylvia was a liar and a thief and invited the other kids to burn Sylvia too, and they happily joined in. Gertrude also knew how to manipulate young men— she acquired the loyalty and attention of a few of them by satisfying them sexually.

In one particularly humiliating incident, while beating Sylvia with a belt, Gertrude forced Sylvia to strip off all her clothes in front of the other children. Gertrude handed Sylvia an empty pop bottle and told her to give the boys a show. When Sylvia balked at inserting the bottle into her vagina, Gertrude forced the bottle into the girl, who screamed in pain. As she walked back up the stairs, Gertrude called Sylvia ridiculous, leaving her writhing and bleeding on the cellar floor.

Jenny Likens would sneak into the basement at every opportunity to visit Sylvia and tend to her the best she could, but she was terrified of Gertrude too. Having seen how brutal and violent her "caretaker" could be, Jenny kept her mouth shut. Jenny herself had even slapped Sylvia after being threatened by Gertrude, which made her feel complicit in the whole affair.

The pop bottle incident was the beginning of the end for Sylvia Likens. She no longer left the house and was kept in the basement for further humiliation and torture. Gertrude began charging the neighbourhood children a quarter to view or participate in Sylvia's abuse.

One day, to clean Sylvia up, Gertrude drew her a bath of scalding hot water. With the help of her male teenage accomplices, Gertrude forced Sylvia into the tub. Sylvia's skin reddened as Gertrude roughly rubbed salt into her wounds. This cruel and painful method of disinfection would take place multiple times over the next weeks.

Sylvia was now living exclusively in the basement, sleeping naked and cold on the dirt floor. She was not permitted to use the toilet, and Gert beat Sylvia when she urinated on the floor. Gert's cruelty was escalating, and more than once, she forced Sylvia to eat her own excrement. Sylvia's only nutrition was a bowl of broth, which she drank from the bowl. Utensils were another luxury that Gertrude said she did not deserve.

In mid-October, with the assistance of one of her daughters and 15-year-old neighbour Ricky Hobbs, Gertrude branded Sylvia with a sharp sewing needle, writing, "I'm a prostitute and proud of it!" across her abdomen.

After witnessing what was going on at Gertrude's house, a neighbourhood boy told his parents what he had seen. John Dean wrote in his book *House of Evil* that the boy told them there was a girl in the basement with "sores all over her." The parents, in turn, reported the claim to the school, and a public health nurse was sent to 3850 East New York Street to investigate.

Gertrude answered the door, cool as a cucumber, with her youngest on her hip. Playing innocent, she invited the nurse in after learning of the neighbours' concerns. Jenny listened, terrified, in another room, as Gert claimed Sylvia, who'd become a prostitute, had run off and was no longer welcome in the house. Gertrude claimed she had no idea where Sylvia was.

The nurse left, along with Sylvia's last hope for salvation. Sylvia was starving to death in the basement.

Just days before she died, Dean wrote, Sylvia told her sister, "Jenny, I know you don't want me to die. But I'm going to die. I can tell."

Sylvia was not the only one who was aware she was dying. Gertrude was becoming concerned that she might be found out, so she cooked up a plan. One evening, after a scalding hot bath and more salt for Sylvia's wounds, Gertrude forced Sylvia to write a letter explaining to her parents what had happened to her. Gertrude dictated, as Sylvia wrote.

> *Dear Mr and Mrs Likens,*
>
> *I went with a gang of boys in the middle of the night. And they said that they would pay me if I would give them something, so I got in the car and they all got what they wanted . . . and when they got finished they beat me up and left sores on my face and all over my body.*
>
> *And they also put on my stomach, I am a prostitute and proud of it.*
>
> *I have done just about everything that I could do just to make Gertie mad and cause [sic] Gertie more money than she's got. I've tore up a new mattress and peed on it. I have also cost Gertie doctor bills that she really can't pay and made Gertie a nervous wreck and all her kids.*

Gertrude told her son John, 13, of her plan to dump Sylvia's body in a nearby forest after she died, which she knew would be soon. Sylvia overheard the conversation and tried to escape but was too weak to make a clean getaway. Before she could reach the door, she was tackled, beaten and tied up.

Sylvia was fading fast and was unable to eat the couple of crackers that Gertrude so generously allowed. Gert punched Sylvia in the stomach and spitefully fed the crackers to the family dog in front of the starving teen.

The next day, October 25, 1965, would be Sylvia's last full day alive. John and Gertrude took turns beating Sylvia with a wooden paddle. During the beating, Gertrude somehow managed to hit herself in the eye, blackening it. Fifteen-year-old Coy Hubbard joined in and beat Sylvia unconscious with a broomstick.

Sylvia made one last-ditch effort to attract help to save her life. After she came to in the middle of the night, Sylvia used a shovel to bang on the walls and ceiling, hoping a neighbour would overhear and come to the rescue. A few of the people living nearby later reported hearing a racket, but none bothered to call the police or investigate further.

The next morning, during Sylvia's scalding hot bath, Stephanie Baniszewski and neighbour Richard Hobbs noticed she was still and no longer breathing. Sylvia Marie Likens, only 16 years old, was dead. Stephanie Baniszewski ran out and called police from a pay phone.

When the police arrived, Gertrude pretended to be upset. They found Sylvia Likens's pyjama-clad body on a dirty mattress in one of Gertrude's bedrooms. Gert claimed Sylvia had just shown up the day before, after disappearing for some time. Gert said that when Sylvia came home, the girl was in terrible shape. She claimed Sylvia looked as though she had been beaten. Sylvia was emaciated and dirty, and she had a letter in her hand, which Gert then provided to the officers. Gert claimed she had put the poor child to bed to rest and had found her dead that morning.

Seeing her chance, as described in *House of Evil*, Jenny Likens whispered to one of the responding officers, "Get me out of here, and I'll tell you everything."

Sylvia's body told a tale of extended torture. She died from a hemorrhage of her brain, which was swollen inside her skull. She had suffered shock and extreme malnutrition. Sylvia had cuts and bruises all over her body, and her genitals were swollen. The poor girl's skin was also peeling off from the scalding baths, and she had over 100 burn marks. Jenny's tale and the examination of Sylvia's body were enough to have Gertrude Baniszewski, who was still feigning ignorance, arrested and charged with first-degree murder.

Gertrude's 18-year-old daughter, Paula Baniszewski, a new mother, was charged with second-degree murder. Gertrude's son, John Baniszewski, 13, and two boys from the neighbourhood, Richard Hobbs and Coy Hubbard, both 15, were charged with manslaughter. Four other local youths were charged with injury to person, but those charges were later dropped for lack of evidence.

The three boys were convicted of manslaughter and sentenced to 2 to 21 years in prison. They served only 2 years each.

Paula was convicted of second-degree murder and sentenced to life. She won a retrial on appeal and pled guilty to manslaughter, spending only two more years in prison. Paula changed her name upon release, but her past caught up with her in 2012, when her true identity was discovered. She lost her job as a teacher's aide when her participation in the grisly murder and torture of Sylvia Likens came to light.

Gertrude claimed she could not recall her actions because of her many medications. Regardless, the evidence of her cruelty earned Gertrude a conviction for first-degree murder in Sylvia's death, and she received a life sentence. Gert also won a new trial but was convicted of first-degree murder for a second time, and the judge re-sentenced her to life in prison.

Even after protests by Sylvia's family and all those who remembered her crime, Gertrude was released in 1985. She changed her name, moved to Iowa and died of lung cancer in 1990.

Jennifer Faye Likens, the star witness at all the trials, married and had two children, a boy and a girl. She passed away in 2004 at the age of 54.

Chapter 6

SING A SONG OF MURDER

Edward Joseph Leonski did not appear to be the kind of person you would peg as a brutal, fetishistic serial killer. Described as friendly, cheerful and talkative, Eddie had a broad, warm smile and bright eyes. Although tall and powerfully built, he was baby-faced and looked younger than his 24 years. On the surface, Eddie seemed uncomplicated, even harmless. Underneath, however, Eddie seethed with a hatred of women that was fuelled by a loathing for his controlling mother. He also had an odd, sexually motivated desire to possess the voices of three young women he viciously strangled to death.

Eddie was born on December 12, 1917, in Kenvil, New Jersey, the middle of five children, with two older brothers and a younger brother and sister. When Eddie was very young, the family moved to New York City and lived on the fifth floor of a tenement building at 424 East 77th Street.

Although shy, Eddie loved lifting weights and playing baseball, as well as boxing and wrestling. Sports and fitness were an excellent escape from Eddie's unhappy home life and an ideal outlet for the bonfire of rage growing inside him.

Eddie's father, a Russian-born labourer, drank himself into a stupor as often as he could, dulling the pain of the tongue lashings he endured daily from his bipolar Polish-born wife. Eddie's mother regularly howled at the family patriarch, screaming that he was lazy and useless. In turn, Eddie's father would take out his frustrations on his children by verbally berating them and physically abusing them. Eventually, Leonski Sr. left his wife and family, leaving them to fend for themselves. Eddie resented his father and claimed to barely remember him as time passed.

Even though Eddie was his mother's favourite and outwardly appeared to be a mama's boy, he secretly hated her. In his teens, he grew into a large young man, but somehow his mother was always able to make him feel small. He also resented how much she depended on him to take care of her as he got older. She spent time in and out of psychiatric wards, and she'd developed a drinking problem. Eddie's siblings were not much help either when it came to caring for their mother. Eddie felt as though he was the parent in the house. Eddie did all right in school but left in junior high and enrolled in an all-boys secretarial college, where he earned a solid B average. But clerical work was not for him. He hated sitting at a desk all day and longed for more physical work, so he landed a job as a store clerk at Gristede Brothers, Superior Food Market.

As the world went to war for the second time in less than 25 years, Eddie was happily slinging groceries when he got drafted into the United States Army. He didn't want to go, because his mother still struggled with her mental health and still needed help, but he knew he couldn't avoid the draft.

Eddie's younger brother, the fourth of the boys, whom Eddie was fond of, had also been drafted. But he landed in a psychiatric hospital after a breakdown soon after his conscription. The youngest Leonski, Eddie's sister, had distanced herself from the family and was making a life of her own.

Private Leonski of the 52nd Signal Battalion was one of the thousands of U.S. troops who landed in Australia in 1942, to act as a deterrent to the potential Japanese invaders. But the island continent was also a launching point for Allied troops intent on pushing the Japanese all the way back to their own island, exacting revenge for the attack on Pearl Harbour in Hawaii less than a year before.

The Army is typically a brotherhood of shared experience, but Eddie did not have many close friends, nor did he seem to want them. He seemed to enjoy beating the living daylights out of opponents in the boxing ring during recreation, though. He was unpredictable when drinking, and the other soldiers in Eddie's unit thought he was a braggart and a weirdo. Eddie even bragged to one soldier about a sexual affair he'd had with his brother's wife and claimed she was still sending him letters.

Eddie also had an addictive personality. According to a transcript from his trial, he told a psychiatrist, "When I eat candy, I eat a pound. When I eat ice cream, I eat a quart." He smoked a pack of cigarettes a day, and following in the footsteps of his alcoholic parents, Eddie developed a love of booze. He spent a lot of time drinking himself stupid in the pubs and bars around Melbourne, just as he had back in the States during basic training.

An odd thing that one of his superiors noticed was that you could always tell when Eddie was drunk because his voice would go up an octave. Soon, his excessive drinking began getting him into trouble.

The Australians resented the Yank soldiers because they were late to the war and loved to bed Aussie girls. Since Eddie Leonski liked to fight when plastered, this worked out great for him. Just a sideways glance at an Aussie tough guy in a bar, or an unwanted advance on a local's girlfriend, was enough to start a brawl. Eddie would take on all comers, and there were plenty, Aussie and Yankee alike. Eddie didn't discriminate.

Eddie did not come out on top every time, however, despite his enormous size and boxing prowess. Sometimes alcohol got the better of him. Other times he was outnumbered. One night, in particular, Eddie was jumped by six civilians who beat and choked him.

Eddie's fellow soldiers would deride him about the previous night's escapades during his brief periods of sobriety. Suffering from frequent alcoholic blackouts, Eddie believed they were lying to him about what had gone on. He honestly could not recall what happened the next day.

When Eddie was on one of his alcohol-fuelled benders, he went AWOL for days at a time. In late March, Eddie's misconduct had earned him 30 days in the stockade. But even when imprisoned, Eddie managed to get his hands on more hooch. Though handcuffed, he even escaped at one point but was recaptured soon after because of his drunkenness.

Eddie was released from the stockade on April 20, 1942. But he had learned nothing from his time behind bars. Instead, he took off on another binge that lasted a full three weeks.

Out of the fear of Japanese bombing raids at night, all major Australian cities observed brownout rules during the war. Although not as strict as the blackouts seen in England and Europe, the brownout rules were in place to darken targets to thwart bombardiers, who still used sight as their primary targeting tool. It was hard to bomb something you could not see. The windows of every home and business were covered completely. Drivers could still drive, but the speed limit was a turtle-like 30 kilometres per hour (20 miles per hour) after sundown since all headlights were covered with black tape, leaving only a tiny slit to light the way. Streetlights stayed dark, giving cities an eerie, almost empty feel. It was also the perfect cover for criminals who prowled at night.

In early May of 1942, women started turning up dead in Melbourne. The first woman to die was 40-year-old Ivy McLeod. She was last seen leaving a male friend's home around 2:00 a.m. on Sunday, May 3, 1942, after a lovely evening of food, pleasant conversation and two shared beers. Ivy had only a four-minute walk to the train station, so she was sure she would be okay to make the walk alone.

The Bleak House Hotel on Victoria Avenue, near Beaconsfield Parade, was just a short walk from the train station at Albert Park and the home where Ivy McLeod had visited. At 7:00 a.m., an employee, Harold Gibson, went outside to do some maintenance work and spotted a man he would later describe as a tall, fit-looking American soldier walking quickly from the doorway of a nearby beauty salon, which was still closed up from the day before. Gibson saw what appeared to be a pile of clothes where the man had emerged. He went to investigate and found a partially nude woman lying there. Gibson tried to rouse her, but the woman did not move when he shook her, and her skin was cold to his touch. Gibson called the Albert Park police station to report the body, and in minutes the area was swarming with Melbourne police officers.

Ivy McLeod was dead. Her clothes had been shredded so severely she was almost naked. What remained of her clothing lay beneath her body. Her belongings had not been what her killer was after. Her purse was found beside her, undisturbed. All her personal belongings were inside the bag, as was the $33 she had in her wallet. Investigators surmised that the attack had been sexually motivated. However, there were no signs of sexual assault. Ivy was battered and bruised, and it was clear she had struggled with her attacker. She had a fractured skull, and both her eyes had been blackened. The cause of Ivy's death was determined to be suffocation due to compression of her windpipe. Someone had strangled her.

The man Gibson had seen leaving the doorway where he discovered Ivy could have been any of the 15,000 American soldiers in Melbourne. Since they all wore the same clothes and had the same haircut, there was not much in the way of a description to go on.

That same morning another GI ran into Eddie Leonski drinking away his hangover in a bar a short distance from the murder scene, where the police were still investigating Ivy McLeod's death.

Six days later, at around 4:00 a.m. on Saturday, May 9, 1942, a night watchman named Henry McGowan was doing his rounds when he found a woman's handbag lying in the street in front of 89 Flinders Lane, its contents scattered about on the road. Henry picked everything up and took it all with him, hoping to return it to its grateful owner.

An hour later, at 5:00 a.m., Henry saw what appeared to be a person lying on the front steps of a residential apartment building called Morningside House at 13 Spring Street, just a short distance from where he had discovered the purse. It was the body of another deceased woman. The woman's clothes were in disarray, and she lay splayed out on the steps. Her top had been pulled down and was bunched at her hips. Her skirt was hiked up around her waist, exposing her genitals. Investigators found that the woman, like the previous victim, had been beaten, strangled and left exposed for all to see. The landlord at Morningside House confirmed that the woman was renting a room on the top floor of the residence. It appeared as if her attacker had grabbed her as she made her way to the door.

The woman's family identified her as 32-year-old Pauline Buchan Thompson, from Bendigo, 130 kilometres (80 miles) away. She had come to Melbourne and rented a room to pursue a singing career during the war, entertaining the troops. In addition to her beautiful singing voice, Pauline was well known for her charity work and fundraising efforts.

She had spent the previous afternoon with her husband, Leslie Keith Thompson, a police constable in Bendigo, and their son. Husband and wife saw each other as often as they could and were very much in love. Her husband and little boy had seen her off at the train station at 5:40 p.m. the previous evening.

Witnesses at the Music Lover's Club recalled seeing Pauline the night before, drinking and having a friendly conversation with a stocky American GI after a dance. None of them could give more than a general description of the man.

Connecting the two murders was not a reach for the police. Detectives were beginning to wonder if they had a psychopath on their hands. News of the murders left women in Melbourne terrified. If a policeman's wife could become the victim of this murderer, everyone was in danger. The newspapers soon nicknamed the perpetrator "the Brownout Strangler."

Only 18 hours after the discovery of Pauline Thompson's body, a colleague of Eddie Leonski's found him blubbering in the mess hall at camp. Eddie told fellow soldier Private Anthony Gallo he had killed someone, but Gallo dismissed Eddie's confession as drunken rambling; however, he would live to regret disbelieving Leonski.

The police were unable to come up with any useful leads over the next couple of weeks. City and military police patrolled Melbourne's streets to prevent another attack or, better yet, capture the strangler as he stalked his next victim.

Three days later, two other women narrowly escaped the strangler's clutches on the evening of May 12, 1942. Both were accosted at the doors of their homes in separate incidents within an hour of one another. Both got a close-up look at the American soldier who had tried to strangle them. The man had run off into the rainy, darkened night after they had broken free, screaming.

It was later discovered that the same American soldier boldly bummed a cigarette from a patrolling policeman only minutes after the attack on the first woman. Luckily, the cop remembered the soldier's face well.

Then, two days later, on May 14, 1942, another woman was followed home by an American soldier. This time, fearing for her life, the woman hurriedly opened the door and called out to her uncle. The older man came running and confronted the soldier, getting a good look at him, before the trespasser laughed and scampered off into the night.

A third woman died five days later when the killer struck again in the early morning hours of May 19, 1942.

It had been raining intermittently, and at 7:00 a.m., near Camp Pell, a base filled to bursting with American soldiers, a butcher named Albert Whiteway spotted a woman's body lying face down in the mud. As with the other victims, the killer had ripped the woman's clothes to ribbons. Her hat and umbrella lay nearby on the damp grass.

The other unsolved murders had been so well publicized in the newspapers and on the radio that the butcher and another passerby who came upon the scene immediately assumed they had discovered another murder victim, and the men ran to call the police.

Gladys Hosking, 40, was splayed out, just like the other victims had been. Her killer had beaten her and violently torn her clothes off before strangling her. Her money was still in her purse.

Soldiers questioned by detectives said they had seen Gladys the night before, walking and sharing her umbrella with an American soldier. One soldier, as he was chatting with a couple of detectives, spotted the GI he was describing and pointed at him excitedly.

"That's him!" he yelled.

It was 24-year-old Eddie Leonski.

Unable to believe their luck, detectives sauntered up to Leonski and arrested him on the spot without a fuss. People who had gotten a good look at him, including the three surviving victims, repeatedly picked him out of later lineups.

Eddie soon confessed to the three murders, but the legal wrangling over who got to try the American soldier was more problematic. Australian authorities wanted to prosecute him because the victims had all been Australian women, murdered on Australian soil. The American Armed Forces, however, wanted to try him, to send a message about what would happen to American service members who committed crimes while in host countries.

In the end, the Americans won out and Eddie faced a military court martial. Eddie's confessions contain little information about the motive for the slayings. But there are some interesting things of note in the transcripts from the trial.

When writing about his second victim, Pauline Thompson, Leonski said, "She had a nice voice and she sang as we walked along. We turned a corner, there was nobody around. I didn't see anybody, I just heard her voice. Then we came to the stone steps, they were long steps. I grabbed her around the neck. She stopped singing. I said, 'Keep singing, keep singing.' She fell down. I got mad then and tore at her—tore at her, I tore her apart."

In his confession about the murder of Gladys Hosking, Leonski wrote, "I asked her to walk on with me and show me the way to the camp. She said 'Alright.' We came along and soon came to a very dark part of the street. She stopped and said, 'There's the camp over there.' She had a lovely voice. I wanted that voice. She was leaving to go to her house and I did not want her to go. I grabbed her by the throat. I choked her. I choked her. She was so soft. I thought 'What have I done.'"

After dragging Gladys to a more private spot, Eddie was put off by the sounds she was making. He wrote, "She made funny noises, a sort of a gurgling sound. I thought I must stop that sound, so I tried to pull her dress over her face."

Eddie Leonski was convicted of the three murders on July 17, 1942, and sentenced to die by hanging. On November 9 at Pentridge Prison in Coburg, Australia, Eddie was executed after General Douglas MacArthur personally signed his death warrant.

Chapter 7

ANTIFREEZE AND
A COLD HEART

A t 2:00 p.m. on Monday, August 22, 2005, a call came in to
the 911 dispatch centre servicing Clay, a township in Onondaga County just outside Syracuse, New York. Stacey Ruth
Castor, the woman who had placed the call, sounded frantic as
she begged for help. Stacey said her husband, David, had locked
himself in their bedroom the day before, after an argument, and
was not answering the door or his phone, nor had he shown up for
work that morning.

Stacey, who was at work when she placed the call, claimed that
48-year-old David was depressed and behaving strangely. He had
been drinking far too much, more than he usually did.

Stacey told dispatchers that she and David had argued on Friday night before he vacillated between asking Stacey and her children to leave and begging her to stay, and then made veiled threats
about what might happen were she to leave him.

Sergeant Robert Willoughby, of the Onondaga County Sheriff's
Office, told Stacey to meet him at her home with the key as soon as

possible. Stacey agreed, stating that she hoped David had not done anything impulsive.

When Willoughby arrived at the Castors' house, he saw Stacey sitting on a lawn chair in front of the residence, casually smoking a cigarette. Stacey opened the door for Sergeant Willoughby and told him where the bedroom was. Stacey said she had waited outside because she was too afraid of what awaited her inside.

Willoughby knocked on the bedroom door and announced himself while trying the knob, but the door was locked. He pounded harder and called out to David through the door. No one answered. Willoughby went outside and looked through the bedroom window but couldn't see through the closed blinds.

He came back inside and forced the door open with a kick. The door gave way easily. David Castor was inside, lying naked on the bed. He had no pulse or any other vital signs. He was cold to the touch and stiff from rigor mortis.

The room was a disaster area. It stank, and there were clothes and bedsheets in piles on the floor. David had vomited in numerous spots on the bedroom floor and in the adjoining bathroom. There was vomit all over David's face and torso too, and it had also pooled underneath his head.

There were two glasses and a bottle of Hiram Walker apricot-flavoured brandy on the nightstand, but there was also a blue plastic bottle of PEAK antifreeze next to the bed. One of the glasses contained a liquid that looked and smelled like antifreeze. Willoughby wondered if David had poisoned himself.

The officer called Stacey to the bedroom. When Stacey saw David, she asked if he was all right. When Willoughby told her David was dead, Stacey began yelling and crying. She screamed at Sergeant Willoughby to bring her husband back, refusing to believe he was dead.

Stacey's histrionics continued throughout the day, even after an ambulance had taken David's body away. She bawled and cried with friends who came by to console her as detectives and technicians gathered evidence in the bedroom.

At first glance, it appeared that David had died by suicide. Yet something didn't seem quite right to investigators. From the beginning, Stacey's behaviour seemed off. She seemed almost too upset.

A search of the home turned up some further clues that something might be amiss. As evidenced by the scene, David's death had taken some time. Underneath the bed, investigators found a loaded shotgun. Poisoning is not a cleaner, more straightforward or painless way to die. If David had killed himself, as the scene suggested, investigators wondered why he hadn't used the shotgun. Why torture himself with poisoning?

When Stacey was questioned about her activities over the weekend, she claimed she had gone shopping at Walmart but could not produce a receipt to corroborate her story. Detectives dug through the trash in the kitchen to look for the receipt but could not find one. They did, however, find a nearly new turkey baster in the garbage. The turkey baster had drops of green liquid inside and smelled of antifreeze. It was bagged as evidence, as were the glasses, bottle and antifreeze container in the bedroom.

In an eight-page statement to police recorded the next day, Stacey, now eerily calm, admitted there were problems in the marriage and that she was having an affair with another man.

Stacey's first husband, Michael Wallace, the father of her two girls, had died from an apparent heart attack at only 38 years old in 2000. Stacey and David Castor met a year after Michael died and were married on August 16, 2003. They had just celebrated their second wedding anniversary.

There were other issues in the marriage too. Stacey's daughters had not gotten along with David. The girls did not want their father replaced and fought a lot with their stepfather, who they felt was overbearing.

Stacey said David had been depressed for some time, but when his father passed away a month earlier, his alcohol intake increased dramatically, and his mood quickly got much worse. He was grumpy and sullen all the time.

Stacey claimed that after a seven-hour-long verbal argument on Friday, David had gone on an epic drinking binge, to the point of becoming quite sick over the weekend. Stacey said she had tended to him, helping him to the bathroom to vomit, and had even offered to call an ambulance at one point, but David refused.

When the interviewing officer asked Stacey why David would drink antifreeze to kill himself, her answer was odd. She said David might have gotten the idea from an episode of *48 Hours* they had seen the year before. In that show, a woman had murdered both of her husbands by lacing their green Jell-O with antifreeze. The episode had rerun in the last month, and Stacey and David had watched it again.

Stacey was careful to build a detailed alibi and painted herself as a caring partner. One red flag to detectives was that Stacey's answers were too detailed, a classic sign that an interviewee is hiding something and might have rehearsed their responses. She seemed able to recall minute details about the previous four days that the average person would not remember under questioning.

Police also interviewed numerous family members and close friends of David Castor. Without exception, they insisted there was no way that David would have killed himself. They all said he was just not that kind of guy.

Onondaga County's deputy chief medical examiner, Dr. Robert Stoppacher, performed the autopsy on David Castor's body. His findings were not a surprise, but they were unusual and a cause for concern. There were crystals in David's kidneys consistent with the ingestion of a large, highly toxic amount of ethylene glycol, the main ingredient in antifreeze. David had died when his kidneys had failed.

In all his years as a practising medical examiner, Dr. Stoppacher had not previously seen a single case of suicide by antifreeze. It was known to happen but was rare, especially in males. Death by ethylene glycol poisoning is a terrible and painful way to die.

According to the U.S. Agency for Toxic Substances and Disease Registry (ATSDR), stage 1 (central nervous system depression) of antifreeze poisoning occurs between 30 minutes and 12 hours after oral ingestion. The effects on the central nervous system are horrendous. They include intoxication, euphoria, lack of coordination, slurred speech, drowsiness, irritation, restlessness and disorientation. There is also severe nausea and vomiting.

Between 12 and 24 hours after ingestion, stage 2 (cardiopulmonary toxicity) sets in. The heart races, the blood pressure rises, and the patient will show symptoms of shock. When a person is in shock, the body's organs don't get enough blood or oxygen. If untreated, this alone can lead to permanent organ damage or even death. The patient's breathing rate increases as the lungs become inflamed—respiratory distress sets in, followed by the onset of metabolic issues.

If shock or any other symptoms have not yet killed the patient, then stage 3 (renal toxicity) begins between 24 and 72 hours after ingestion. The kidneys start to fail, causing excruciating pain as patients lose their ability to urinate and excrete the poison their systems cannot metabolize. With no medical intervention, as seen in David Castor's autopsy results, death follows.

Stacey said she had been with David alone in the house on Saturday between 4:00 p.m. and 11:00 p.m. She had to have known what he was doing if he was poisoning himself with the antifreeze. His violent vomiting sprees would have been loud, and in the state he was in, someone would have had to help him to and from the washroom. Stacey claimed she had last spoken with David 24 hours before Sergeant Willoughby broke down the bedroom door, finding her husband deceased.

As the investigation continued, more pieces of evidence raised questions for detectives, pointing to something other than suicide as the cause of David's death. The two glasses in the bedroom tested positive for traces of alcohol. Only one tested positive for ethylene glycol. There was only one clear set of prints on either glass, and they were Stacey's. Her fingerprints were the only ones found on the glass with the antifreeze in it. It was odd that David's fingerprints were not present on the glass he had supposedly used to poison himself.

Testing also concluded that the turkey baster found in the trash contained ethylene glycol, and David's DNA was on its tip.

The clichéd old motive of murder for money was there too. Stacey stood to profit from David's passing to the tune of at least $200,000. Stacey was the one who had discovered and presented David's will after his death. In it, David left Stacey the bulk of his estate, leaving his son from a previous marriage only a few things, including a car he had restored. The rest of the family found this odd. It was not like David, known for his generosity, to leave everyone else out of his will, and so little to his son.

Stacey had David's body prepared for viewing at the same funeral home she had used for her first husband, Michael Wallace, who had passed away only five years before. At Stacey's request, David was also buried in the family plot, right beside her first husband. Stacey's name was on both men's headstones.

Despite Stacey's odd behaviour, her extended family stood behind her. Among other relatives with the same ideas, Stacey's mother surmised that if someone had murdered David, it was not Stacey who had done it, but Stacey's daughter Ashley, who was just about to turn 16. Ashley and David were known to have loud, hateful arguments. Many of the fights were over his attempts to discipline the teen when she acted up, which was often, and when David felt Stacey was, in his opinion, too lenient. Investigators did speak with Ashley, but it was Stacey who seemed to be hiding something.

A year passed, and questions about David's death continued to nag at investigators and some of his friends and family members. Many suspected that Stacey had poisoned David, but there was no real proof, just a gnawing suspicion.

Detectives got permission to wiretap Stacey's home. They were hoping she would trip up and admit to something over the phone. Stacey, though, was careful about what she said, and the electronic surveillance was fruitless. Perhaps she was on to them, they thought.

Police were watching her too. They had set up cameras pointed at the Castor residence as Stacey began remodelling the house. There were also cameras set up at Stacey's two husbands' gravesites, but Stacey never visited the cemetery after the funeral, not once—strange behaviour for a grieving widow who claimed she missed them both so much.

Police also began looking deeper into Michael Wallace's death. It's rare for a 38-year-old man to die of a heart attack. Perhaps some of the answers to David Castor's passing lay in the circumstances surrounding Wallace's premature death. The family had accepted cardiac arrest as the reason for Michael's demise because he had partied hard and was abusing drugs and alcohol. He'd gotten numerous DUIs over the years and was rarely sober. Michael's sister told investigators that Stacey had blocked an autopsy; she was adamant that she did not want one.

Stacey did not cry at Wallace's funeral or at the graveside during his interment. Some praised Stacey's stoicism, but others were suspicious, calling her cold. Soon after his death, Stacey collected on Michael's life insurance policy. All $50,000 went to her.

As police investigated further, another suspicious death came to light. In 2002, Stacey's father had taken ill with lung disease. He seemed to be recovering when he suddenly died. Stacey, who was tending to him, was one of the last people to see him. Michael

Wallace's brother-in-law, John Corbett, remembered her going into his room with a can of pop right before the older man passed away. Stacey oversaw the dispersal of his remaining assets, most of which went to her. There were rumours that she had killed him and had him cremated almost immediately to cover her tracks.

With too many odd coincidences to ignore, police decided to exhume the body of Michael Wallace and requested the court's permission, which a judge soon granted. Investigators hoped that Michael's body would still be in a condition to provide answers to his cause of death. After the exhumation, a proper autopsy was performed on the body, including a screening for poisons, specifically ethylene glycol. The results of the examination indicated that Michael Wallace had not died of a heart attack. He too had been killed by antifreeze poisoning. These findings made Stacey Castor suspect number one in the deaths of both of her husbands.

Investigator Detective Dominick Spinelli brought Stacey in on September 7, 2007, and spoke with her. She solidly denied any knowledge of Michael's poisoning.

An ABC News article accompanying a 20/20 story covering the case recounted some details of Stacey's questioning that day. The article quoted Detective Spinelli speaking about his interview with Stacey Castor. He had asked Stacey about the drinking glasses investigators discovered in the bedroom where David had died. Detective Spinelli said Stacey had earlier claimed she had poured David some cranberry juice, and she again confirmed that. While showing Stacey a photo of the glasses in place at the scene, Spinelli asked Stacey if she recalled which glass she had poured the juice into. Stacey looked at the photos and then made a slip of the tongue, saying she had poured "antifree" into one of the glasses. She quickly corrected herself, claiming she had meant cranberry juice.

Spinelli did not pick up on Stacey's slip of the tongue at the time, but it would prove crucial later in confirming Stacey as the perpetrator of David's murder.

A couple of days later, police met with Ashley on her first day in college to watch her reaction when they informed her that her father, Michael Wallace, had died of ethylene glycol poisoning, just like David Castor. Ashley was shocked and upset—she seemed surprised by the information. She called her mother right away. Stacey told her to come home and have a few drinks because she'd had a "hard day." Although Ashley was only 19 and still underage, she and her mother got drunk together that night with alcohol Stacey provided. Ashley woke up the next morning with a terrible hangover.

Then on September 13, 2007, Stacey summoned Ashley home for a second time. The last few days had been challenging. Stacey suggested the two of them should get drunk again to blow off some steam. Just as she had the week before, Stacey gave Ashley Sprite with vodka. Ashley thought the drink tasted terrible, but Stacey told her to keep stirring it. Ashley got drunker than the previous weekend and passed out at around 1:00 a.m.

Ashley's younger sister tried to rouse the older girl the next morning, but she didn't respond. The younger girl screamed for Stacey, who came into the room and immediately dialled 911. Stacey screamed hysterically at the dispatcher that her daughter had taken pills or something and would not wake up and that she was making strange sounds in her throat.

The younger sister left the room for a moment, and when she returned, she found what appeared to be a typewritten suicide note beside Ashley's bed. The letter also included a rambling 750-word confession to the murders of Ashley's father, Michael Wallace, and her stepfather, David Castor. The signature was also typewritten. The letter indicated that Ashley had decided to take her own life out of guilt for the murders by getting drunk on vodka and taking an overdose of pills.

Ashley was minutes from death when she arrived at a local hospital by ambulance. She lay comatose for a few hours but slowly began to come around after doctors undertook measures to save her life.

When Ashley woke up, there was a detective there to question her. He asked her about the note in which she admitted to the murders of her father and her stepdad. Ashley recalled later that she had no idea what the cop was talking about. None of it made sense to her. Ashley had been 11 years old when her father died.

When Detective Spinelli saw the "confession" note, something stood out to him right away. Twice, the author of the letter dropped the *z* and *e* at the end of *antifreeze*, typing "antifree," the same thing Stacey Castor had said in her interview only one week before. Police now felt they had enough evidence to charge Stacey with the murders.

While Ashley Wallace was still in the hospital, Stacey Castor was charged with one count of second-degree murder in the death of David Castor and one count of attempted murder for her poisoning and attempted frame-up of her daughter.

Before her trial, investigators discovered that Stacey and a friend had forged David's will. They also found drafts of Ashley's confession note on Stacey's personal computer. The date stamps on the files were from the night of the attempt on Ashley's life. Police also heard, on one of the wiretap recordings, the sound of Stacey typing as she chatted with a friend on the phone at the exact time the files had been saved to the computer's hard drive.

Stacey's defence team went after Ashley, accusing her of the murders, but in the end, justice was served. On February 5, 2009, Stacey Ruth Castor was found guilty of second-degree murder in the death of David Castor, her second husband, and of the attempted second-degree murder of her elder daughter, Ashley, by feeding her vodka laced with enough pills to knock out a horse.

In her victim impact statement, as published on 9WSYR.com, Ashley told the judge: "I never knew what hate was until now. Even though I do hate her, I still love her at the same time. That bothers me, it is so confusing. How can you hate someone and love them at the same time? I just wish that she would say sorry for everything she did, including all the lies."

The court sentenced Stacey Castor to 51 years in prison. She died of a heart attack, while still behind bars, on June 11, 2016.

PART TWO
Perpetual Puzzles

These mysterious stories remain unresolved and
lead to more questions than answers.

Chapter 8

THE OAK ISLAND MYSTERY

I n Mahone Bay on the south shore of Nova Scotia, just a 40-minute drive down the old #3 highway from Halifax, the province's capital, lies Oak Island and "the Money Pit," home to one of history's most fascinating and enduring mysteries. In the late 1700s a curious group of teens discovered a strange indentation in the ground on the island and began to dig, finding hints of what appeared to be buried treasure. Over the last 225 years numerous groups of treasure hunters have attempted to uncover the secrets of the Money Pit, and many sightseers have toured the island, looking into the watery pits and boreholes, wondering what the heck, if anything, lies buried down there.

The drive to uncover the island's secrets is about more than the treasure itself. Inside every serious seeker's psyche there's an ego-fuelled little voice nagging at them. That voice tells each treasure hunter that it could be them who succeeds where everyone else has failed; that their name could go down in history as the person responsible for letting the world know what precisely lies beneath the earth on the island. Some have even gone so far as losing their lives in the often dangerous undertaking of searching for its buried treasure. The earliest theories about the origins of the treasure are that a pirate, possibly the famous William Kidd, hid millions of kilograms of pirate gold on the island while running from authorities, who were hot on his trail before his capture and execution in 1701. There are several areas in the New World where Captain Kidd's treasure is rumoured to be buried. Oak Island is just one of them. There are other verified accounts that Kidd buried treasure along the east coast of North America, including the cache at Gardiners Island, off New York State, which was uncovered, sent to England and used as evidence in his piracy trial.

There are many theories about what might be buried on Oak Island. Some people believe there are treasure vaults containing manuscripts that prove philosopher Francis Bacon penned the famous plays attributed to William Shakespeare, a theory that tends to upset theatre nerds, literary scholars and serious historians. These same theorists maintain there's an elaborate underground system with complex booby traps that point to Bacon's involvement. They believe that Bacon's well-known experimentation with mercury as a method of document preservation paired with the presence of mercury and bits of manuscript discovered in an Elizabethan-era dump on the island's north end also hint at his relationship with the island.

Some people believe the legendary Knights Templar chose the remote site to hide Biblical artifacts, including the Lost Ark of the Covenant and the Holy Grail. Many treasure hunters on the island have been freemasons, a secret society that has been around as long as the Knights Templar. Perhaps they know things the rest of us do not.

The missing crown jewels of France have made an appearance in some of the lore surrounding the island. While unproven, there are claims that as French revolutionaries were about to overtake Marie Antoinette's palace, she gave some of her jewels to a trusted maid. The maid escaped with them before fleeing to Nova Scotia, which was territory held by the French as a part of New France. To assist their beloved queen, the story goes, French loyalists and engineers created secret vaults and tunnels to hide the treasure. Marie Antoinette went to the guillotine in 1793 and was never able to retrieve her possessions, and the secret location of the jewels died along with her.

There have been even wilder theories about Oak Island's secrets as well. Some have surmised that ancient aliens might have buried secrets on the island, like plans for advanced technologies they believed we were not ready for. Only when we achieve a certain level of knowledge on our own will humans be prepared to level up with alien knowledge. Perhaps these alien secrets will even provide us the ability for intergalactic space flight.

Of course, skeptics believe there is nothing at all buried on Oak Island. They contend that the story of secret treasure is entirely a fabrication, since there is no record of the island being mentioned until sometime between the 1840s and 1860s. They contend that vaults found while drilling are natural caverns and not humanmade at all. Later discoveries of gold links, coins and the parchment mentioned earlier, along with ciphers and other artifacts, are explained away as items left by treasure hunters to attract more cash to their flagging efforts or as the detritus of previous treasure companies' efforts to unearth the loot.

So far, it seems the skeptics might be correct. There has been no solid proof that there is any treasure at all on the island. Despite that, cohorts of treasure hunters have spent millions of dollars trying to solve a mystery where one may not exist. Every single effort has met with disaster in one way or another. Companies run out of either money or the will to continue. Yet the treasure hunters keep coming.

Locals, mostly farmers and fishermen, wanted no part of Oak Island. For years before the talk of treasure began there had been rumours of strange lights on the island at night. There were tales of the disappearances of several people who had investigated its darkened woods. According to legend, the story of hidden treasure started in 1795 and was passed along verbally for at least the first 50 years. Although some researchers have uncovered contrary information, the story presented here is an amalgamation of the area's most prevalent accounts.

One afternoon, teenager Daniel McInnis (or McGinnis), who had grown up on a local farm, rowed out to the 57-hectare (140 acre) island to go exploring. While walking in the woods, Daniel came across an old pulley and rope system hanging from an oak tree's partially sawn limb. It hung over a depression in the earth that was between 2.5 and 4.5 metres (8 to 14 feet) across.

The mind of the young man went immediately to pirate booty. Many verified stories from 17th- and 18th-century Nova Scotia hold that pirates frequented the area. On the run from authorities chasing them, these buccaneers made landfall in the Maritimes and hid treasure on remote islands there. Daniel must have thought he had hit the jackpot, but further exploration of the find would have to wait since the sun was going down and he did not have the proper tools to excavate his find.

Daniel rowed back to shore, his head full of fantasy, and related his discovery to Anthony Vaughan and John Smith, a couple of his young friends. The trio made a plan to meet early the next morning at Daniel's rowboat with pickaxes and shovels. The next day, they rowed out to the island at daybreak, and Daniel led the way to the spot. They set about digging, no doubt swatting away swarms of blackflies as they sweated in the Nova Scotian summer heat.

The ground was loose, and the digging was easy. Two feet down, the boys were excited to discover a layer of flagstones, which are not native to the island. Scientists later determined that the flagstones had to have come from Gold River, just over 6 kilometres (3.7 miles) away.

The boys flung the flagstones and dirt aside in a fury, sure they were about to find treasure. Instead, they found only more loose soil. They devised a pulley system and attached it to the sawn-off limb of the overhanging tree, just as they believed the shaft's originators had done. After a few days of digging, they reached the 3-metre (10 foot) mark and struck something odd. It was a layer of rotting oak logs, side by side, definitely placed there by human hands. They were elated again, hoping the treasure was just below. After pulling out the logs and tossing them aside, they discovered even more loose earth.

Another 3 metres later, they encountered a second layer of logs, the same as the first, and 3 metres after that was another layer of logs. Frustrated and literally in over their heads, now 9 metres (30 feet) down in an unstable shaft, the young treasure hunters knew they would need help if they wanted to continue.

The boys left the open pit alone for a few years but bought land on Oak Island to ensure the security of their presumed treasure. They married and began to raise their families there. In 1802 a man named Simeon Lynds from Onslow, Nova Scotia, visited, and they told him of their efforts to reach the bottom of the pit. After being shown the hole in the ground, Lynds promised the young men that he could help, but only if he could share the profits from whatever they found there. He went back to Onslow, his mind filled with visions of untold riches just waiting to be claimed.

Oak Island's first professional treasure-hunting group, the Onslow Company, was formed by Lynds and several wealthy businessmen. They pledged their equipment and labour resources to excavate the site for a share of the loot. In 1804, the original shaft was shored up using timbers by the more professional digging crew, and the first organized dig in Oak Island's Money Pit began.

At 11 metres (35 feet), diggers discovered a layer of charcoal. There was a layer of putty at 14 metres (45 feet) and a coconut fibre layer at 17 metres (55 feet). Coconuts are not native to Nova Scotia, which bolstered the idea that pirates might be involved, since the nuts are more common in the Caribbean, a known pirate and privateer hotspot.

Inexplicably, every 3 metres (10 feet), all the way to the 27-metre (90 foot) mark, there were layers of deteriorating oak logs that seemed to mock the diggers, who would remove them and dig on. At 27 metres, atop that layer of logs, lay a strange flat stone. The men from the Onslow Company removed the stone from the pit. Some say the oddly shaped stone had weird markings inscribed on one side, but no one made a tracing of them or recorded the shapes before the stone went missing.

The Onslow Company's last act before finishing work for the night was to use a metal rod to determine the next platform's depth. They learned the next tier of logs was only 2.5 metres (8 feet away), rather than the customary 3 metres (10 feet). Many believed the treasure was just beyond that area, but the young men who had initially started the excavation were more skeptical.

One of the workers took the strange stone home to examine it overnight. He thought he might be able to determine its significance. Although the man could not figure anything out about the stone or its markings, a possible answer arrived the next day. When the crew returned to work in the morning, the formerly dry pit had filled with water to the 10-metre (33 foot) mark. Attempts to pump the water out failed. It appears the stone may have been a sort of boobytrap that triggered the flooding of the shaft.

The crews laboriously sunk another shaft 3.5 metres (11.5 feet) east of the original hole, burrowing 34 metres (110 feet) into the earth. They attempted to tunnel across to the original pit, underneath what they hoped would be a watertight roof to the vault holding the final treasure. When the second shaft filled with water, nearly drowning the diggers who had been tunnelling to the original, the Onslow Company, running low on cash, called it quits and abandoned the entire operation.

The stone changed hands a few times over the years. It was said to have been used in one treasure seeker's home as a fireplace stone. It was finally lost after having been displayed in the window of a downtown Halifax bookseller for decades. According to Randall Sullivan's book *The Curse of Oak Island,* one 20th-century code breaker claimed the stone's scratchings were a message he deciphered to say: "Forty feet down, two million pounds lie buried." However, the origin of the cypher decoded by the expert cannot be definitively traced back to the actual stone and may be apocryphal.

For the next 45 years, John Smith, one of the original boys who dug up the Money Pit, used Oak Island as farmland. In 1849, after a group of wealthy businessmen learned about the legend of buried treasure on the island, the Truro Company was formed and began drilling from a platform they had constructed above the Money Pit's waterline. They discovered wooden planks at 30 metres (98 feet), exactly where the Onslow Company had determined they would be. Their drilling auger went smoothly through the upper platform, which consisted of 13 centimetres (5 inches) of spruce wood. It then met a 30-centimetre (12 inch) gap, followed by 10 centimetres (4 inches) of oak wood, 56 centimetres (22 inches) of loose metal and then another 20 centimetres (8 inches) of oak.

There was something there, but what?

In 1850, the Truro Company dug another shaft adjacent to the Money Pit. They went down to 33 metres (109 feet) and, using shovels, dug toward the original shaft. The side tunnel flooded as they neared what they believed to be a vault, and their efforts failed in precisely the same way as the Onslow Company's had. Workers then discovered five stone-lined drains, nicknamed the finger drains, in Smith's Cove. They believed these led to the Money Pit and were the source of the flooding. Later claims state this was proved correct with a dye test. Workers poured the dye into the flooded Money Pit and, sure enough, it bubbled out of the drains in Smith's Cove.

The group dug another shaft, attempting to meet the drainage tunnel and plug it up, to allow the Money Pit to be pumped dry, but the excavators missed their mark. They sunk a third, 11-metre (35 foot) shaft nearby, but it also flooded.

In the Truro Company's final attempt, they dug a tunnel just south of the Money Pit to 36 metres (118 feet). For this plan, they intended to approach the Money Pit from yet another side tunnel. As the diggers neared their goal, they stopped when they heard a tremendous crash from the Money Pit, and the water in the pit turned muddy.

Modern searchers believe that whatever lay beneath the Money Pit's 30-metre (98 foot) mark was lost to a cave-in—caused by the side excavation—and then fell into another cavern beneath, buried under hundreds of tons of earth and debris.

With their funds and hopes for success running low after the supposed collapse, the Truro Company abandoned their work on Oak Island.

Numerous treasure-hunting groups have come and gone from Oak Island in the years since. In 1861, digging there was resumed by a company called the Oak Island Association. Many others have made attempts to excavate what was believed to be the Money Pit, but flooding continued to be an issue. The location of the flood tunnel has also remained elusive. All efforts have failed to produce anything conclusive, making a total mess of the island. Even the Money Pit's original location has been lost in the process.

The rich and famous have also been interested in the story of Oak Island. As a young man, future U.S. president Franklin Delano Roosevelt was an investor in the Old Gold Salvage group involved in digging there. Roosevelt planned to visit in 1909 but never made it to the island in person. Other famous investors involved with various companies dedicated to solving the mystery include actors John Wayne and Errol Flynn and famed adventurer Richard E. Byrd Jr., a rear admiral in the U.S. Navy.

Numerous myths have sprung up over time, confusing the story of buried treasure even further. One bit of folklore says the treasure will be found only when the last live oak tree on the island dies. There remain hundreds of oaks on the island, so that theory has yet to be put to the test.

Another myth that came from the American publication *True*, a men's magazine from the 1960s, makes an ominous claim that seven treasure hunters have to die before the treasure can be found. There have been six accidental deaths directly related to the digging as of this writing. The first came in 1861, when a worker lost his life in a pump engine explosion. The Money Pit claimed its next victim in 1897, when worker Maynard Kaiser fell to his death in the shaft. Four more men died on August 17, 1965, after being overcome by hydrogen sulphide gas in an 8-metre (27 foot) shaft they believed led to the Smith's Cove drainage tunnels. The dead were Robert Restall, 59 years old, of Hamilton, Ontario, and his son, Robert Jr., only 24; Cyril Hiltz, a 22-year-old native of nearby Martin's Point; and Karl Graeser, a 40-year-old mineralogist from Massapequa, New York.

In a televised news story from 1971, and still remembered by many Nova Scotians today, Triton Alliance sunk a borehole near what was presumed to be the Money Pit and found a cavernous space. Then they lowered cameras down into the murky space via a shaft, called Borehole 10X, near the supposed location of the Money Pit. According to an article published on January 14, 1972, in the *Chronical Herald*, the men gathered around the video monitor back on the surface saw what they believed to be a human hand at 65 metres (212 feet). Others claimed the video showed a treasure chest covered in silt.

Many experts have studied frames from the video and cannot discern any shapes resembling a hand or a chest. Perhaps the treasure hunters' obsession with finding something significant led their minds to fill in the gaps.

The hope of solving the mystery of Oak Island continues to outlive generations of treasure seekers. Every few decades, they go to the island in droves. Most recently, two brothers from Michigan, Rick and Marty Lagina, went to the island in hopes of solving the enigma. They have explored many of the old sites and sunk truckloads of cash into their effort, which has been televised on the popular History Channel show *The Curse of Oak Island*.

The Laginas sent a diver into Borehole 10X, but the water was too cloudy for him to see. There was no sign of the supposed chest or of the human hand. The brothers have discovered numerous artifacts, such as coins, believed to come from the Elizabethan era, and some even much older. The group used sonar to find the underground cavern, which is still believed to contain a chest of some kind, but have not yet reached it.

Thousands of viewers familiar with the famous mystery tune in to the show every episode to watch as Rick and Marty come up empty-handed. Many memes make fun of the television program for its continual cliffhangers with no payoffs. The brothers have thrown millions into their search, but it is beginning to look as though they may not find anything at all.

In his book *The Secret Treasure of Oak Island*, D'Arcy O'Connor called the quest "the world's longest and most expensive treasure hunt." Who knows if anyone will ever solve the mystery. Until that day arrives, the aptly named Money Pit will sit silent, patiently waiting for its next treasure-obsessed victim to arrive and pour millions more dollars down into it.

Chapter 9

WHO WAS THE
PERSIAN PRINCESS?

ncient Egyptians invented mummification around 2800 BC
to preserve the body after physical death. In warmer cli-
mates, such as Egypt, bodies tend to decay quickly, and
Egyptians believed that preservation of the body was important so
the essence, or *ka*, of the recently deceased could re-enter the body
for use in the afterlife.

Mummification was an expensive process that was financially out
of reach for the average Egyptian. The practice was used only for
royals, nobility or the very wealthy. More impoverished Egyptians
did not receive such care after death. Instead, family members
wrapped the bodies of their loved ones in a simple cloth taken from
their homes and buried them quickly with a few trinkets in the desert.

Humans were not the only ones honoured by mummification
in ancient Egypt. Archaeologists have also found scores of mummified animals, including crocodiles, baboons, ibises, fish and
cats. Animals were held in high regard by ancient Egyptians, who
believed that animals were related to various gods.

Each year collectors spend millions of dollars on Egyptian artifacts, sometimes on a single object. Since removing ancient artifacts from Egypt is outlawed, most of these items have been obtained or traded illegally. Using any search engine, one can find many looted antiquities for sale on the Internet, including mummies. The provenance of these mummies, however, is often dubious. One of the most questionable mummies discovered in recent decades was the one referred to as the Persian Princess.

On October 19, 2000, Sindh police officers raided a house in Karachi, Pakistan, as part of a police investigation. There they discovered a video that showed what appeared to be an ancient mummy wearing a golden face mask, lying inside an ornately carved wooden coffin within a stone sarcophagus. It was estimated the body would have been no more than 140 centimetres (4 feet, 7 inches) tall in life.

The resident who had the video, a man named Ali Akbar, an obvious alias, told interrogators that he received the video to pass along to another man, known as Asfandyar, who wanted to smuggle it out of the country to show to potential buyers of black-market antiquities.

Akbar also told investigators that the mummy was currently at a house belonging to tribal leader Wali Mohammad Reeki in Quetta, located in the Pakistani province of Balochistan, a region bordering Afghanistan and Iran. In a joint effort with Balochistani authorities, Sindh police raided Reeki's home and recovered the mummy.

Reeki claimed that an Iranian man named Sharif Shah Bakhi had discovered the casket and its contents in a remote area of Pakistan after a recent earthquake. Agreeing to divide any profit, the two put the mummy up for sale on the black market. There had already been some interest, with an unnamed foreign investor offering them 10 percent of the asking price of 600 million rupees, or close to US$11 million.

Perhaps unaware of the potential value of what they had in their hands, the police unceremoniously shoved the sarcophagus into the back of a van and brought it back to Karachi over nearly 700 kilometres (430 miles) of bumpy road.

Authorities took photographs of the mummy and sent them to a retired professor of antiquities, Dr. Ahmad Hasan Dani, who was an expert archaeologist, historian and linguist from Islamabad. They wanted him to determine if there was any significance to the find. Professor Dani was so excited by what he saw in the pictures that he hopped on the next plane to Karachi to go and view the artifact for himself.

After Professor Dani saw the mummy up close, he told authorities he was sure it not only was important but might even be royalty. Police notified the Pakistani news organizations and invited them to a press conference at the National Museum of Pakistan in Karachi for a glimpse of the mummy. In a video of the event posted by the Associated Press, the public got its first look at the artifact. With Professor Dani at the head of the casket, international reporters and photographers jostled for the best view of what appeared to be the find of a lifetime. A tiny woman lay there resplendent in her coffin, encased in resin, her arms across her chest on top of a bed of wax and honey.

When asked if the mummy was of Egyptian origin, Professor Dani stated he was confused by the presence of cuneiform writing rather than hieroglyphics, which would be typical for an Egyptian artifact. The instrument used to write the inscriptions on the casket, a nib with a pointed tail and thick head, was not known to be used in Egypt at all. More research was needed to determine the mummy's provenance.

Dr. Asma Ibrahim, the curator of Karachi's National Museum, led the research team. She claimed that several factors led her to conclude the mummy was a Persian royal. The image of Ahura

Mazda, the supreme Zoroastrian deity, was carved into the coffin, as were other symbols matching those at Persepolis, a well-known ancient Persian site. The mummy wore a golden crown embossed with seven cypress trees. The cypress was the symbol of Hamadan, Persia's ancient capital. After acquiring a rudimentary understanding of cuneiform from a book, Ibrahim translated the script on the mummy's gold breastplate. According to a BBC documentary on the discovery, the inscription read: "I am the daughter of the great King Xerxes. Mazereka, protect me. I am Rhodugune, I am."

If the mummy was, indeed, a member of the Persian royal family, it would be the first such artifact ever found. Mummification was unheard of in Persia before this find, and if the mummy was real, it would be one of the most important archeological discoveries in centuries.

When the potential value of the mummy leaked in the press, a tug-of-war broke out between various groups, each claiming ownership. The mummy was financially valuable because whoever possessed the remains would receive research funds from international groups wanting to study it.

Some believed the mummy belonged in Egypt. Egyptians claimed the cuneiform inscriptions must have been added after someone had smuggled it out of that country. The Iranian Cultural Heritage Organization said the mummy's origins appeared to be Persian and demanded the Pakistanis turn it over to them. The Taliban government of Afghanistan claimed smugglers had found the mummy within their borders, so they too ordered the artifact's return. Pakistani national officials claimed the mummy belonged in Quetta, since it had been discovered in their country. Ultimately, Pakistan won the ownership dispute and the mummy remained in their national museum, where experts set to work studying it. On the surface, the mummification appeared to follow typical Egyptian preservation rituals. Still, a more in-depth study showed some disturbing inconsistencies, leading experts to believe the mummy to be an elaborate fake.

The first sign the mummy might be fraudulent was that the heart was missing. Egyptian religious practices always included the heart. The second red flag was the cuneiform writing found on the breastplate. The word *Rhodugune*, a Greek translation, came from a much later period. If this were the mummy of Xerxes's daughter, her name would have been written as *Wardegauna*. This discrepancy was significant. It was like finding an iPhone buried with Alexander the Great.

Dr. Ibrahim also found outlines of pencil tracings on some of the markings. The earliest known use of graphite pencils was in the late 1700s, another anachronism that was too flagrant to overlook.

To learn the mummy's age at the time of death, it was taken to the hospital and X-rayed. The body's pelvic bones revealed it to be a woman between 21 and 25 years old. The gold mask and chest plate thwarted a good look inside the skull and torso, so authorities decided to give the mummy a full CT scan.

In mid-December of 2001, the CT scan revealed that the mummy's brain was gone, but it had been removed via a brutal procedure that smashed through her palate and into the cranial vault rather than the ancients' less destructive technique of removing it.

The presence of tendons and ligaments in the mummy's inner ear gave the fraud away completely, revealing that the woman had not perished 2,600 years ago but much more recently, within the last five years. The scan showed that her back had been traumatically broken in what appeared to be a violent blow from a blunt object. Then she had been quickly mummified, most likely within 24 hours of her death. In an instant, the case turned from an archaeological discovery into a police investigation. Investigators now believed that, at the very least, this was a grave robbery, or worse, a murder.

Dr. Ibrahim told a BBC documentary crew she was disappointed when the evidence indicated the mummy was a fake. She admitted her hope of its veracity as an important find had clouded her judgment.

The police knew the elaborate fraud had to have involved more than one person. Archaeologists engaged in uncovering the forgery believed the person who created the mummy might even be a scholar. A lot of planning and knowledge went into creating such an elaborate hoax. Experts who dealt in Persian antiquities believed an Iranian group known for forging ancient Persian art and selling it on the black market was responsible for creating the mummy.

Police ordered an autopsy to discover more about the dead woman. Since touching human remains is frowned upon in the Islamic faith, pathologist Dr. Christopher Milroy was bought in from the United Kingdom to perform the autopsy.

Dr. Ibrahim was in attendance as forensic scientists expertly removed the resin-laden bandages, taking care not to damage the body beneath. As the hard casing peeled away from the corpse, Dr. Ibrahim mistakenly thought the woman had blond hair. Turns out, she wasn't blond. Instead, the woman's hair had been bleached by the chemicals used in her mummification. Doctors determined the fraudsters had used sodium chloride, simple table salt, and baking soda to dry the body out. Carbon dating performed on samples from the woman indicated she had died in 1996. Her neck had been broken, severing her spinal column at the cervical vertebrae. If the back injury had not killed the woman, this injury would have.

After investigators looked at all the evidence, it was impossible to determine whether the young woman had died in a horrific accident or had been murdered. Police launched a homicide investigation, and the men involved in trying to traffic the mummy were arrested and interrogated. None of them owned up to how they had come by the body, and because of a lack of evidence, police could not lay any charges in the woman's death.

A forensic facial reconstruction specialist made a model of what the woman might have looked like in life to help identify her. In 2001, the BBC broadcast photos and videos of the facial reconstruction. Pictures of the woman's face were circulated widely throughout the region where the mummy was found, but no one ever came forward to claim the remains. A Pakistani non-profit took charge of the woman's body in 2005 and laid her to rest in Karachi in 2008.

Who was she? Where had she come from? Who had done this to her? Had she been a target, murdered for her body, or had the fraud's perpetrators acquired her fresh corpse by some other nefarious means?

Since this fraud was detected, other similar mummies, all forgeries, have shown up on the still active black market that now skulks on the dark web. Are people being murdered and turned into mummies for the black market? Or are people's bodies being stolen after death to perpetuate these antiquities frauds? The trafficking of ancient artifacts, both real and fake, is so murky that it's possible we'll never know.

Chapter 10

THE LOVE ME TENDER MURDERS

The 1950s saw the rise of rock and roll. Names like Chuck Berry, Little Richard, Fats Domino and Bill Haley and his Comets ruled the airwaves. But the decade belonged to a puppy-eyed, pompadour-wearing crooner from humble beginnings in Tupelo, Mississippi. The man crowned "the King of Rock and Roll," a moniker later shortened to only "the King," Elvis Aaron Presley has been called a musical prodigy and one of the most significant cultural icons of the 20th century.

His first single, "That's Alright," released in 1954, was also Presley's first gold record. After that, he was on a rocket ship to stardom. Everything he touched turned to gold, his records charting 16 times over the next two years, with four number one hits in early 1956 alone.

The legions of Elvis fans were known for their fanaticism. His sexual appeal, bolstered by cocky confidence and gyrating hips, captured the imaginations of a generation of teenage girls. His concerts were a spectacle, his music drowned out by the shrill screams of swooning fans.

In mid-November of 1956, Elvis made his film debut in the western *Love Me Tender*, playing Clint Reno, a crooning Confederate cowboy caught in a love triangle. The "Love Me Tender" title single, sung by Presley, quickly shot to number one as theatres were packed night after night, mostly with teenage girls, many of whom saw the film multiple times, to their conservative parents' chagrin.

The Grimes sisters, Patricia, 12, and Barbara, 15, of southwest Chicago, Illinois, were obsessed with the 21-year-old singer. They had already trekked into the city to see the heartthrob in *Love Me Tender* 10 times. They could not get enough of him.

When they found out the film would be playing at the more local Brighton Theatre, at 4223 South Archer Avenue, the girls were over the moon. On opening night, December 28, 1956, they planned to see the movie again, hoping to squeeze in two viewings before curfew. They wanted to make the best of their Christmas break and see the flick as many times as possible before going back to the drudgery of work and school. Patricia's 13th birthday was three days away, and they could not think of a better early celebration.

That morning was a typical one in the Grimes home. Barbara was up at around 8:00 a.m. to go to her part-time job in the mailroom of Wolf Furniture House at 4211 Archer Avenue. Patricia, called "Petey" by family and friends, got up a little later. The girls, who had always been close, were excited for that evening's festivities. Before Barbara left for work, they made a date to meet for lunch at a local dime store.

Speaking about Barbara's last day at work, the office manager at Wolf later told the *Chicago Tribune*, "She was quiet, as usual. Barbara seldom spoke unless spoken to. You would hardly know Barbara was around. She was so quiet."

Miss Plozek, an office manager at the business, described Barbara as a timid, nervous girl who was afraid to meet and talk with strangers. "We tried to let her work in the general office, accepting payments, but she was too shy," she explained.

After the girls met for lunch, Barbara headed back to work and Patricia went home to do chores. When she finished her house-cleaning, Patricia went for a milkshake with her brothers, Jimmy and Joseph. She then dropped in to the candy store to buy comic books with a girlfriend.

Patricia was home at 4:30 p.m., and Barbara came home from work around 6:00 p.m. Both girls had dinner with the family.

Lorretta Grimes, the family matriarch, was not so sure a trip to the movies was a good idea. It was a chilly night. Barbara had been ill, and she was still getting over a cough.

Life was tough for Lorretta. She was a divorcee with five children at home. As well as taking care of a household, she worked as a part-time clerk. What little she earned from her job supplemented the $35 per week in child support she was receiving from her ex-husband, truck driver Joseph Grimes.

The two sisters begged for permission to go to the movies and eventually wore Lorretta down. Too tired to argue with them, she gave them each $2.50 to spend on the movies and bus fare.

Patricia and Barbara left their home at 3634 South Damien Avenue in southwest Chicago's McKinley Park neighbourhood around 7:15 p.m. They walked the couple of blocks to the bus stop, where they caught the #62 bus. After that, it was a straight drive to the theatre.

A friend spotted the sisters buying popcorn at 9:30 p.m. between showings of *Love Me Tender*. Their pal, 15-year-old Dorothy Weinert, was sitting next to Barbara and Patricia. She last saw the girls when she left the theatre at 10:15 p.m. to make it home before her curfew. The sisters were still there when she left, wanting to savour every last minute of their idol.

The girls did not arrive home at 11:45 as promised, and at midnight there was still no sign of Patricia and Barbara. Lorretta sent her son Joey, 14, and his older sister, 17-year-old Theresa, to the bus stop to wait for the pair. Theresa and Joey returned home after three buses passed with no sign of their sisters.

Lorretta called the police at 12:30 a.m. to report the girls missing. She telephoned again at 2:00 a.m. because the sisters were still not home and she was worried sick. Patrolling police officers received a description of the missing girls and began to watch out for them.

Over the next few days the search for Patricia and Barbara ramped up, as there was still no sign of them. Hundreds of police officers were tasked with interviewing people and scouring downtown Chicago looking for the girls. Searches of abandoned properties and wooded areas yielded no new information. Chicagoans looked for the girls in backyards and dumpsters, diligently following the story in the news.

Joseph Grimes was devastated by the disappearance of his daughters and pleaded with his truck driving co-workers to help him search for them, begging them to keep an eye out as they went about their business.

Barbara was last seen wearing a yellow blouse, a grey tweed skirt and black shoes with white bobby socks. Over that outfit, she wore a dark knee-length coat with a grey scarf. Patricia was wearing blue jeans that came down to her shins, with a yellow sweater and black shoes with white socks. She wore a white scarf on her head, and her black jacket had white stripes on the sleeves.

A local bank teller, Roger Menard, 19, came forward to offer some information on the case. He said he had been at the late screening of *Love Me Tender* and was sitting behind the Grimes sisters. They were still sitting in their seats when he left the theatre, and he noticed them behind him as he walked northeast along Archer Avenue.

Roger said that while the Grimes sisters were behind him, he looked back and saw that a late-model green Buick had stopped beside the girls and that they chatted with the occupants of the car briefly before the car drove on.

At some point the girls passed him, and Menard witnessed another car pulling up beside them. Again, they chatted with what appeared to be two teenage boys inside. The girls walked on toward their bus stop and giggled as the car pulled away.

Others, including the bus driver himself, claimed the girls boarded an eastbound bus after the second showing of the movie let out. They got off the bus at Western Avenue at 11:05 p.m., half-way into their usual bus ride home. No one knows why they left the bus so far away from their regular stop.

Earl Zastro and Ed Lorden, another pair of teenage boys, claimed they had passed the Grimes girls at 11:30 p.m. at the corner of 35th Street and Seeley Avenue, just two blocks from their turn onto South Damien Avenue. The young men, who recognized the girls, said they appeared to be playing in doorways, jumping out and scaring each other as they walked, no more than a five-minute stroll from home. They had plenty of time to make their 11:45 p.m. curfew. What had happened to them in the last 500 metres (1,600 feet) of their walk home?

For the next week, there were several unconfirmed sightings of Barbara and Patricia Grimes. People claimed they had seen the girls walking along the streets of Chicago, eating at local diners, listening to music in a record store and travelling on transit buses and trains out of Chicago. Two weeks after their disappearance, the mother of a friend of Patricia's swore up and down that she had received a hang-up call from the younger Grimes girl.

Police started to wonder if the girls had run away. One bit of ridiculous gossip about the girls was that they were seen getting into a fancy dark car with a man who looked a lot like Elvis Presley. The more sensible rumour mill speculated that the girls had run away to meet Elvis.

Police also endured pranksters calling in false tips. Since each tip had to be taken seriously and cleared, this took valuable police resources away from the real search.

The thought that Patricia and Barbara had run away got more traction when, on January 17, 1957, a woman from Nashville, nearly 1,500 kilometres (930 miles) away, claimed she had seen the girls in that city and even helped them find an employment agency. The clerk at the agency ID'd the sisters from their photos, confirming the woman's tale. But no one else in Nashville made any claims that they had seen the Grimes girls.

By January 18, 1957, police had interviewed 10,000 people in the double disappearance, yet they felt no closer to finding Patricia and Barbara than they had been at the start of the investigation. Police wondered if someone was holding them against their will. Their parents continued hoping against hope that their daughters would be found alive.

Elvis Presley himself became involved in the case briefly on January 19, 1957. While making a gospel album for RCA Records at Radio Recorders in Hollywood, California, Elvis learned of the two missing fans. Patricia's and Barbara's fan club cards had arrived in the mail after they had vanished. Urged by police and moved by the story, Elvis took to the airways, on television and radio, and made a plea to the Grimes sisters to go home. An article in the January 20, 1957, edition of *The Times* of Hammond, Indiana, quoted Elvis as saying, "If you are good Presley fans, you'll go home and ease your mother's worries."

At around 1:00 p.m. on Tuesday, January 22, 1957, Leonard Prescott of Hinsdale, Illinois, was headed east on German Church Road to pick up a few things for his family when he saw something odd just off the road. It looked like two mannequins, like the ones he was used to seeing in department store windows.

Prescott continued on his way, but the scene kept nagging at him. After dropping off his groceries, he returned with his wife to the location, about 60 metres (200 feet) east of County Line Road. When they got out of the car for a closer look, they immediately realized the forms beside the road were two bodies. The couple hopped back into their vehicle and drove to the Willow Springs Sheriff's Department. Police arrived at the scene at around 1:35 p.m.

The area had been under deep snow until recently. When the weather warmed and the snow melted away, the bodies were exposed. It appeared the girls' bodies had been there for several days. Both of the frozen bodies were nude and were located just inside the guard rail and down a slight incline, only a few feet off the shoulder of the busy country road. It looked like someone had hastily dumped the bodies there and driven off.

Press got wind of the discovery, as did other lookie-loos who swarmed the site, parking their cars along the shoulder and milling around trying to get a peek at the bodies. Frustrated detectives had canvas tarps put over the bodies to preserve their dignity.

The girls were lying in a T shape in the tall brown grass. Coroner's office investigator Harry Glos told the *Chicago Tribune* that Patricia had three puncture wounds in her chest, perhaps from an ice pick. Barbara, whose head lay underneath her sister's torso, had marks and bruises on her face that may have been from a beating. Her nose was broken.

Reporters were all too happy to snap pictures of a distraught Joseph Grimes as police brought him to the site to identify his daughters. After his grim task, a reporter took a photo of the anguished father as he made his way back to a waiting police car. He was so weak from grief, two burly cops had to walk on either side of him, holding him up.

Like vultures descending on a fresh kill, reporters were present at 3634 South Damien Avenue as Lorretta Grimes heard the news from police that her girls were dead. The front page of the *Chicago*

Tribune on January 23, 1957, displayed a photo of the heartbroken woman sitting in her living room as a young friend of the girls' consoled her.

Comparisons were made early on to the unsolved murders of three Chicago boys only 15 months earlier. Robert Peterson, 14, John Schuessler, 13, and Anton Schuessler Jr., 12, went missing and were later found murdered and nude near the Des Plaines River on October 18, 1955. Their clothes were never found. Patricia and Barbara's clothing had disappeared as well.

There was controversy around the cause of death of both girls. The bodies were to undergo autopsies on January 23 but required thawing out before an examination could be completed. Remnants of their final meals and the popcorn in their stomachs indicated the sisters had died on the night they disappeared. These findings discounted all the apparent sightings of them after they'd gone missing.

The pathologist on the case, Cook County coroner Walter McCarron, listed the cause of death for both girls as murder, with shock and exposure as secondary contributors, but only because he could not pin down how they actually died. McCarron's findings did not address Barbara's broken nose and bruises, nor were the apparent ice pick wounds on Patricia's chest considered significant. He believed that post-mortem rodent infestation had created these injuries.

Harry Glos, the chief investigator of the Cook County Coroner's Office, told reporters later that the autopsy had found semen inside Patricia's body. He revealed that there had been milk in Barbara's stomach, but she had not had milk with her last meal at home. Harry also believed that evidence of a thin veneer of ice on the bodies proved the girls had been alive until January 7, more than a week after they had disappeared. These findings contradicted the popcorn present in the girls' stomachs. Glos felt the murderer was sophisticated and intelligent and had somehow known how to hide what he had done. Had the killer fed the sisters popcorn a week later to throw the timeline of their deaths into question? Coroner McCarron was livid that Glos had made these revelations public and fired him for insubordination and damaging the integrity of an investigation.

In Chicago, parents told their teenage girls they could not set foot outside alone, even during the day. Police had hoped to solve the case quickly, but that's not what happened.

One of the early suspects was Walter Kranz, a 53-year-old self-proclaimed psychic and steamfitter. He had phoned a tip line while drunk at a local tavern on January 15, 1957. He said that a vision told him the girls were in Santa Fe Park. Police had written him off as a crank after questioning him. But when the bodies were discovered, they were only 2.4 kilometres (1.5 miles) from Santa Fe Park. Two lie detector tests given to Kranz were inconclusive. Police later released him without charge.

Two days after the bodies turned up, so did another suspect—a 21-year-old drifter named Edward Lee "Bennie" Bedwell, who had an Elvis-like hairdo and sideburns. He came to investigators' attention after someone claimed to have seen him with the girls in a restaurant on December 30, two days after they had disappeared. After some intense questioning, Bedwell confessed, and police charged him with the murders. Bedwell later recanted his confession, but the district attorney proceeded anyway.

Later, a coroner's inquest determined that Bedwell had fabricated his confession, which did not match the evidence. It was believed the Cook County Sheriff's Office might have bullied him into it, holding him for three days in a motel room before he signed the typewritten confession despite the fact he could not read or write.

Over the years, multiple people have confessed to the crime, but there was never a conviction. Bedwell was the only man ever charged.

One young man the police looked into was 17-year-old Max Fleig. Max confessed during a polygraph examination to kidnapping and murdering the Grimes sisters. Since he was a juvenile, however, his polygraph was deemed illegal, and he was released. He later murdered another young woman and was caught and convicted in that case.

On December 28, 1962, on the sixth anniversary of the sisters' disappearance, a 40-year-old machine operator in California named Alfred Smith Lawless confessed to the murders. He blurted out his admissions while police were arresting him for drunk driving.

According to an article printed in the *Rock Island Argus* on December 29, 1962, Lawless said: "Six years ago today, I killed Barbara and Patricia Grimes, and I've been running ever since. I see visions of those two girls all the time. All I think about lately is how I left them to die, stripped and naked on that snowbank in the woods. For years I've been running. I just had to tell somebody."

Alfred's story did not hold up under questioning, though, and he did not possess the specific details of the crime that only the killer might know.

The case went cold and for years afterwards, cruel pranksters would call Lorretta Grimes and confess to the murders. Lorretta suspected one caller might have been the real killer when the man mentioned a deformity on one of the girls' feet, a fact unknown to most people. The same person called Lorretta back years later after another local girl was murdered, but the caller has never been identified.

A retired detective with the West Chicago Police Department, Ray Johnson, continues to write about the case, has appeared in several documentaries and runs an 1,800-member Facebook group dedicated to solving the cold case. The murders of Patricia and Barbara Grimes remain unsolved to this day.

Chapter 11

DARK WATER

Elisa Lam, a Canadian university student, was on vacation in Los Angeles when she disappeared from the infamous Cecil Hotel sometime between January 31 and February 1, 2013. The last known images of her were recorded by a surveillance camera inside one of the hotel's elevators. In the four-minute video, Elisa seems to be playing hide-and-seek with an unseen partner.

After her appearance on the security video, Lam's whereabouts were unknown for more than two weeks, until February 19, when a maintenance worker found Elisa's decomposing body in one of the four 3,800-litre (1,000 gallon) water tanks on the hotel's roof.

Thanks to the eerie video, the mystery surrounding Elisa's death spread virally, catching the attention of bloggers, podcast hosts and armchair detectives. There has been a lot of speculation around her death. Some believe she met with foul play, while others believe something supernatural happened. Still others think she simply died by suicide.

The daughter of emigrants from Hong Kong, Elisa Lam, known as Lisa to close friends, was born on April 30, 1991. Her parents, David and Yinna, ran Paul's Restaurant, a Chinese food establishment at 4621 Hastings Street, in Burnaby, B.C.

People close to Elisa said she was kind, considerate, compassionate, creative and sensitive. Although outgoing and fun, like many creatives, she would sometimes retreat within herself and occasionally suffered dark depressive episodes during which she would spend days alone.

She found solace in her little white dog and by blogging. Elisa's Instagram page and other writings indicate she was obsessed with F. Scott Fitzgerald's novel *The Great Gatsby*. She read and reread the book and collected various editions of it in English and other languages. Elisa's social media accounts and blogs speak to her love of travel, art, fashion and video games. She also posted a lot about French culture and how much she enjoyed the French language. Elisa blogged a few times about a serious boyfriend, but they had broken up sometime in 2011, two years before her death.

But amid the lighter fare on her social media accounts, there were brief glimpses into Elisa's darker mind. Both her Tumblr and Blogspot blogs had the same epigraph, a quote by *Fight Club* author Chuck Palahniuk that states, "You're always haunted by the idea you're wasting your life."

On May 8, 2012, she retweeted a story about the death of Maurice Sendak, author and illustrator of *Where the Wild Things Are*. The tweet included a quote attributed to the late writer that said: "I'm not afraid of annihilation. I'm not afraid of death. I just want to know more before I go."

There are some standout posts by Elisa about her ongoing struggles with depression as well. It appears she put a lot of pressure on herself to do well in school and felt she did not measure up academically.

On November 21, 2011, Elisa wrote in a Blogspot post: "Depression sucks. I have no control over my emotions. I will be angry for two minutes and then sad again. I will be happy for half an hour and then emotional again. So far all I've done is lay on my bed and watch episodes of Chopped. I'm just waiting for it to pass."

In a post titled "On Happiness," Elisa quoted author and notorious depressive Ernest Hemingway: "Happiness in intelligent people is the rarest thing I know." Elisa also said she would edit the post when her "brain function" improved, indicating she was getting some help.

Elisa was a student at the University of British Columbia and sought medical help for her depression through Student Health Services Psychiatry. She began seeing a psychiatry specialist at the Scarfe Free Counselling Clinic, who assessed Elisa and determined she had untreated bipolar disorder. The specialist prescribed medication to manage her emotional highs and severe depressive episodes.

In March of 2012, Elisa, feeling a bit better, wrote on Tumblr that she had gotten a part-time job. But the darkness was still dogging her. She wrote, "And if I weren't so lazy I would go learn how to do something . . . like coding or whatnot. I'm falling into a pattern of going on Tumblr and it's not giving me any joy actually. It's just something to do. Idling by."

On April 27, 2012, before going quiet online for three months, she said the following in a post titled "Worries of a Twenty Something": "I spent about two days in bed hating myself."

Like many people, Elisa often found herself pulled into the vortex of social media and mentioned needing a break from Facebook, admitting, "that might help." Elisa was on the right track. Numerous studies have indicated that reducing screen time and limiting social media usage does have positive effects on people's mental state.

In early January of 2013, a blog post indicated that Elisa had found a new boyfriend, whom she had fallen for quickly.

Later that same month, Elisa wrote about a planned trip south along the west coast from British Columbia down to California. She'd been to Ottawa previously and wanted to see the Golden State.

> *Planning, planning, planning for the West Coast tour . . .*
> *Sigh, turns out I won't be making as many stops as I'd*
> *like; Vancouver, San Diego, Los Angeles, Santa Cruz and*
> *San Francisco. I really want to stop by San Luis Obispo*
> *but alas . . . we'll see. Suggestions and meet-ups still highly*
> *appreciated.*

Just days before her trip was to begin, on January 18, 2013, Elisa and her boyfriend of only a few weeks broke up. Elisa wrote that her boyfriend had broken up with her while she was out at a function with friends. She was devastated and indicated in her writing that her instincts were to go home, but she chose to remain.

Four days after getting dumped, on January 22, 2013, Elisa got on a plane alone and headed south for her ill-fated California trip. She travelled around southern California for a few days by bus and train, even visiting the world-famous San Diego Zoo one day. Elisa seemed to be having fun hanging out by herself and doing what a shy but adventurous 21-year-old would do.

She stayed in touch with friends and family along the way and indicated she was happy to be travelling and seeing new sights. Elisa showed no signs of worry that someone was after her or that anything at all was wrong. If her recent breakup was on her mind, she didn't say anything about it publicly on her social media.

Elisa arrived in Los Angeles on January 26, 2013, and checked in to the infamous Cecil Hotel at 640 S. Main Street, now called the

Stay on Main. When the hotel opened in 1927, the owner, hotelier William Banks Hanner, had high hopes for it, but the area has since declined over the years. Most likely because of its proximity to skid row and its inexpensive rooms, the Cecil Hotel attracts a more transient clientele these days.

Travelling students like Elisa use the hotel as a crash pad, but so have other less savoury characters. Most notably, two serial killers have rented rooms in the Cecil. In 1985, the Los Angeles Night Stalker, Richard Ramirez, temporarily made his home there. In 1991, Austrian serial killer Johann "Jack" Unterweger made his way to L.A. and stayed at the Cecil while he brutally murdered three local sex workers. And the Cecil is rumoured to be one of the last places Black Dahlia victim Elizabeth Short was seen before her gruesome and still unsolved murder in 1947.

There have been several suspicious deaths at the hotel over the years as well. Since 1931 there have been at least 16 documented deaths from non-natural causes, including suicides, accidents or murder.

On January 31, 2013, the day before she was to check out of the Cecil and head to Santa Cruz, Elisa Lam disappeared. When she did not check out on February 1, 2013, the hotel's management became increasingly concerned. No one had seen her that day at all. Elisa was not in her room when they checked, but all her personal belongings were still there, including the medications she was supposed to take every day to manage her bipolar disorder.

Elisa was reported missing by the hotel staff. Using dogs, the LAPD searched the hotel's easily accessible areas, including employee-only areas like the basement and the roof. But there was no sign of Elisa.

The police called her family, who told them they had not heard from Elisa since January 31 either. It was unusual for her not to check in daily, especially since she was travelling alone. Elisa's parents hopped on a plane and came down from Vancouver to help look for her.

On February 6, L.A. police released a community bulletin, distributing it throughout the downtown L.A. neighbourhood. The flyer had two photos of Elisa as well as identifying information and a summary of her disappearance:

> **NAME:** *Elisa Lam*
> **DESCRIPTION:** *Female, Chinese (Canadian), black hair, brown eyes, 5'4", 115 lbs., D.O.B.: 04/30/91*
> **SUMMARY:** *Elisa Lam was last seen on January 31, 2013, at the Cecil Hotel at 640 S. Main Street in downtown Los Angeles. Lam was traveling alone from Vancouver, Canada, and arrived in Los Angeles, California, on January 26, 2013. Her final destination was Santa Cruz, California. She takes public transportation including Amtrak and buses.*
> **LAST KNOWN ADDRESS:** *640 S. Main Street in downtown Los Angeles*
> **LANGUAGE SPOKEN:** *English (Fluent), Cantonese*
> **ADDITIONAL:** *Possibly suffers from mild depression. Anyone with information concerning this case is asked to contact Detectives at the Homicide Special Section, Robbery-Homicide Division.*

A local bookseller remembered Elisa buying books, records and other gifts for her parents and her sister a day or so before her disappearance. Elisa had stood out to the store's owner because she had been struggling with the cumbersome bags of gifts as she left the store. She had been chatty and seemed in good spirits.

For two weeks, there were no leads and no sightings of Elisa. On February 14, the LAPD released the infamous video of Elisa in the elevator at the Cecil Hotel on the night she disappeared.

It immediately went viral across the Internet, gaining millions of views.

The quality of the video is low resolution, and it is not time-stamped. In the first frames of the video, the elevator door opens and Elisa glides in. Employing one odd flowing movement, she bends over and pushes all the buttons on one side of the control panel. She's wearing a red hoodie, a green Alexander Keith's beer T-shirt, knee-length black shorts and open-toed sandals.

Elisa stands up and backs into the corner of the elevator farthest from the door. She stands there looking straight ahead for a moment. The young woman then walks cautiously to the door and quickly steps a single foot into the lobby, poking her head out and rapidly looking both ways. She slides back inside the elevator, presses herself flat against the left wall and then slithers into the corner near the control panel, as if she's trying to hide.

As the video progresses over four minutes, Elisa goes in and out of the elevator multiple times. She pushes buttons and waves her hands about as if gesturing at someone in the hallway. Her hand movements don't seem quite right somehow. She finally leaves the elevator, and the door closes. The elevator door opens twice as though someone is pushing the call button, but Elisa never comes back into the frame. The video ends on a closed door.

Everyone who watched the video online seemed to have a theory about what was going on with Elisa in the video, but there were still no new leads. Some people believed she was playing hide-and-seek with a person who later abducted her. Others have suggested she was interacting with one of the hotel's many "ghosts." Some speculated that Elisa's odd hand gestures were indicative of someone who had taken MDMA, PCP or some other party drug. Some thought they saw someone having a psychotic break.

Five days after the video's release, there were still no leads for investigators to go on. On the same day, February 19, 2013, hotel guests began calling the front desk, complaining of low water pressure when attempting to shower.

A maintenance worker went to the roof to check on the state of the four large water tanks that serve the 600 rooms in the old 19-floor brick structure. In one of the tanks, only three-quarters filled with water, the maintenance man found a black-haired woman's naked body, floating face down. Her clothes and hotel key floated next to her. He was aware of the missing woman and immediately knew he had found Elisa Lam.

The police secured the scene and began gathering evidence. The Los Angeles Fire Department spent the day draining the water from the tank and then carefully removed the body. Helicopters that belonged to L.A. news organizations buzzed around the hotel's roof, jockeying to get the best shots of the body recovery.

Although the fire department and the Department of Public Health told the press that Elisa's body posed "no biohazard concerns" because of the chlorine present in the city's water, people staying at the Cecil were disgusted. The thought of having shared water with a corpse was too much for some to bear. Some claimed the water had tasted funny. Many of the short-term guests checked out right away, as did a few long-term residents.

As news of the body's discovery broke, a new level of interest in Elisa Lam took hold on the Internet. People watched and rewatched the now notorious elevator video for clues to her death.

At autopsy, Elisa's body showed signs of moderate decomposition consistent with her having died on the day she disappeared. She showed no signs of damage to her larynx or hyoid bone or petechial hemorrhaging in her eyes that would have indicated strangulation. She showed no signs of recent intercourse or any indications of assault, sexual or otherwise. Elisa had water in her lungs. Her cause of death was determined to be accidental drowning, with mild bipolar disorder as a contributing factor.

Toxicology tests of Elisa's blood were interesting more for what they did not contain. There were no traces of illicit drugs in her system. There was a minimal quantity of alcohol present, equivalent to a blood alcohol content of 0.02, indicating she may have had a drink earlier on the day she died. She was not drunk.

Elisa was taking a few different drugs, psychiatric and otherwise. A Reddit post outlined the drugs police discovered in her hotel room that she had prescriptions for:

- Dexedrine: 20 milligrams (a stimulant prescribed for ADD/ADHD and narcolepsy)
- Lamictal: 100 milligrams (an anticonvulsant and mood stabilizer prescribed for epilepsy and bipolar disorder)
- Seroquel: 25 milligrams (an atypical antipsychotic prescribed for schizophrenia, bipolar disorder and major depressive disorder)
- Effexor: 225 milligrams (an SNRI antidepressant prescribed for major depressive disorder, generalized anxiety disorder, panic disorder and social phobia)
- Wellbutrin: 300 milligrams (an atypical antidepressant prescribed for depression and smoking cessation)

There were two over-the-counter medications as well. Police found a bottle containing ibuprofen, a common anti-inflammatory and pain reliever, and some pseudoephedrine, more commonly known by the brand name Sudafed, a nasal and sinus decongestant.

Elisa's blood samples indicated she had taken at least one antidepressant the day she vanished. She had taken her second antidepressant and mood stabilizer recently, but not that day. She had not taken her antipsychotic recently.

According to an article on healthline.com, reviewed by Alan Carter, PharmD, in 2019, the usage of antidepressants without an antipsychotic in people with bipolar disorder can cause a manic episode and possibly lead to psychosis. This could explain Elisa's bizarre behaviour in the elevator. Four main symptoms commonly associated with a psychotic episode are hallucinations, delusions, confused thoughts and a lack of insight and self-awareness.

The British National Health Service says, "Someone who develops psychosis will have their own unique set of symptoms and experiences, according to their particular circumstances."

Elisa was, in all likelihood, suffering a psychotic break that night in the elevator. That she appeared to be playing hide-and-seek, and talking with someone who wasn't there, indicated the possibility of hallucinations or delusions and would also explain her odd hand movements.

People have questioned how Elisa got onto the roof and how she ended up in the water tank. The reality is not as mysterious as many think, even though all roof access is unmarked. It was widely misreported that there was only one locked and alarmed door leading to the roof, leading people to believe Elisa met with foul play.

In truth, there were several ways to access the roof. There are fire escapes on three sides of the hotel that lead to the top of the building and are accessible from unlocked windows. As there were no reports of the roof access door alarm going off the night she disappeared, it's believed Elisa used one of these fire escapes to get onto the roof.

Contrary to other false reports, there is also more than one way to access the top of the water tank that Elisa drowned inside. Press photos taken as the fire department recovered Elisa's body tell the tale. Elisa could have used the pipes and the small ladder attached to make her way onto the top of the tank. She might also have crawled up on top of the elevator wheelhouse and jumped down to the tank, which was only a metre (just over 3 feet) below. Either would not have been a difficult task for the relatively fit 21-year-old woman.

Once she had opened the top of the tank and dropped down into the water, reaching the top of the tank to extricate herself would have been impossible. At some point, Elisa removed her clothing, grew tired and drowned.

Only Elisa could explain why she felt compelled to climb onto the roof and into the tank. Perhaps in her altered state, the idea of going for a swim in the tank seemed like a good idea, or maybe she was still playing hide-and-seek with an imagined partner or, worse, believed someone was chasing her. Elisa's psychosis would have made it impossible for her to understand that going into the tank was a bad or even dangerous idea.

We will never know the entire story of what happened to Elisa Lam, but had she not been alone on her trip, she would most likely still be alive.

Chapter 12

THE UNKNOWN MAN

On November 30, 1948, a local jeweller, John Bain Lyons, and his wife were out for an evening stroll along Somerton Beach in Glenelg, a suburb just 11 kilometres (7 miles) southwest of Adelaide, Australia. Near the stairs leading down onto the beach, the couple noticed a well-dressed man in a relaxed pose lying on the sand. He had his head gently propped up against the seawall. His crossed legs pointed toward the sea.

Mr. and Mrs. Lyons were about 20 metres (66 feet) away, according to the coronial inquest, and thought the man might be dead. They were relieved when they saw him lift his arm briefly. Almost immediately, it fell limply back down to his side. It appeared as though he had been trying to light a cigarette but was too weak. Thinking the man was just drunk and celebrating the first day of the Australian summer 24 hours early, the couple walked on.

Lyons went out for a swim early the next morning. As he came out of the water, he glanced up the beach and noticed the man lying in the same spot in the same pose he and his wife had seen the day before. This time, two other men with a horse, trainee jockeys, were standing near the man, poking at him. Lyons joined them, and when they found they were unable to rouse the man, Lyons called the Brighton police at 6:35 a.m. The man was dead.

The dead man was overdressed for the beach, wearing a fawn-coloured suit with a shirt and tie, complete with a freshly pressed double-breasted jacket and brown shoes. He was, however, missing a hat, which was customary at that time. An unsmoked cigarette lay on the suit's lapel, possibly the same one Lyons had seen the man attempting to light the day before. The man had a serene look on his face.

At 6:45 a.m., the police arrived and checked on the unresponsive man. They could see no signs of violence at all. There was no blood, nor did his body show signs of being beaten, shot or stabbed. Police had the man removed from his resting place and taken to the hospital. There Dr. John Barkley Bennett officially pronounced the man dead. The doctor could find no immediate cause of death but presumed it to be heart failure occurring at approximately 2:00 a.m. that morning.

The first order of business after declaring someone deceased is the notification of next of kin. But first, one has to know the identity of the dead person. Authorities looked through the man's belongings and found that the stranger had no identification of any kind with him. He was not carrying a wallet, and he had no money in his pockets.

The man's suit was much too heavy for the weather in that area at any time of year, indicating he had come from a colder climate. Perhaps he had intended to make his way to that specific beach for some reason known only to him and died there.

His trousers were torn slightly in one spot and crudely repaired with orange thread. The man also wore a white dress shirt under a brown knitted pullover, and the tie cinched neatly around his neck was red, white and blue. His underclothes consisted of a sleeveless undershirt and jockey shorts. His brown shoes looked freshly polished. It was as though he had dressed himself for his own funeral.

Even more strange was the fact that every manufacturing label was missing from all articles of his clothing. Those labels would have given investigators a lead on the man's identity. It appeared someone had gone to great lengths to make his identification difficult.

The possessions found in his pockets were a bit more helpful. He was carrying a railway ticket to Henley Beach and a bus ticket to North Glenelg. The two ticket stubs aided in tracking the man's movements before his death but led quickly to more dead ends.

Clues to his possible nationality came from the other items he was carrying. There was a packet of Wrigley's Juicy Fruit gum, made in the USA. A package of British-made Army Club cigarettes in his pocket contained seven American-made Kensitas cigarettes. He had a packet of matches made by Bryant & May, a British company, an unremarkable handkerchief and an American-made metal comb.

The last thing found in his watch fob pocket was a small piece of paper that appeared to have been torn from a book. It was rolled up tightly and would have been easy to miss. On the paper were the words *Tamám Shud*, written in a Middle Eastern–looking font. From Persian, the phrase translates eerily to "it is ended."

While police tried to track down information on the man based on his personal items, Dr. John Matthew Dwyer, a pathologist, went to work trying to determine the man's cause of death and get as much information possible from the man's body. As a police constable looked on, Dwyer noted his findings.

There were no marks on the man indicating foul play or physical violence.

The clean-shaven, physically fit stranger measured 180 centimetres (5 feet, 11 inches) tall and was between 40 and 50 years old. He had grey eyes and coarse, wavy, mousy ginger hair that was greying behind his ears. There were nicotine stains on his fingers. He wore no jewellery, and the absence of a wedding ring indicated he might be single.

The man was missing nine top teeth and another nine from the bottom, mostly from the back. He had three scars on his left wrist, another crescent-shaped scar near his left elbow and a 2.5 centimetre (1 inch) scar on his upper left forearm. He had no tattoos. His feet were size eight, and his toes were jammed and mashed together as though he had often worn pointed shoes. The man's fingernails and toenails had recently been clipped.

The way his ears looked was a distinguishing feature. In 98 to 99 percent of the population, the cavum (the hollow leading to the ear canal) is larger than the cymba (the hollow directly above the ear canal). The stranger's cavum was smaller than his cymba in both ears, a genetic abnormality that investigators were hopeful might assist them in determining his identity.

As well as multiple photographs taken from various angles, a plaster cast—a death mask—was carefully made of the man's face to preserve a three-dimensional representation of him. A photo was also taken of the mask to provide investigators with something to show people potentially connected to the victim without having to share a gruesome photograph of a dead man.

The autopsy results showed the man's heart was normal but contracted, and his lungs were dark and congested. His pupils were small and about the same size. The doctor remarked that certain drugs might be associated with a contraction of the pupils.

There were remnants of the man's last meal in his stomach, including potato and bits of a pastry, a savory turnover of sorts. There was also blood, suggesting to Dr. Dwyer that there might be poison present. He looked for signs common in other types of poisoning but could not determine what the substance was. Dwyer sent liver and muscle samples off for testing at the government labs. To be thorough, he included samples from the stranger's stomach, urine and blood.

Deputy government analyst Robert James Cowan completed the testing. He could not find any evidence of common poisons, and in a report issued by the Taman Shud Case Coronial Inquest, Cowan was quoted as saying, "If he did die from poison, I think it would be a very rare poison. I mean something rarely used for suicidal or homicidal purposes." Although Cowan's opinion leaned toward natural causes, there was still evidence in the body's tissues that suggested poisoning.

In the same report, Dr. Dwyer, who respected Cowan's findings, said, "There are changes which could occur, particularly with certain quick acting barbiturates. There are other poisons which do come into the picture which would be decomposed very early after death. In support of my statement concerning the disappearance of certain barbiturates, I can put in an extract from a book dealing with the matter."

The official cause of death was determined to be heart failure due to suspected poisoning. Investigators, however, did not believe the poisoning was accidental and had to decide whether the stranger had poisoned himself or someone else had done it to him.

On January 11, 1949, police called around to all local hotels, dry cleaners, bus depots, train stations and anywhere else with a lost property office and asked them to keep an eye out for any unclaimed property that might have belonged to the man.

On January 14, detectives were sent to the Adelaide Railway Station to look at a suitcase. It had been in the station's cloakroom since November 30, the day before the stranger turned up dead. The manufacturing label of the case was missing, and there were no identifying marks or tags, much like the dead stranger's clothing.

As well as the dates, other things matched the suitcase to the dead man. There was a tin of brown shoe polish like that used on the shoes found on the man's body, and a twist of Barbour's brand orange-coloured thread, which seemed to match what they had seen on the man's trousers. When compared using a microscope, it was determined the two pieces of thread matched.

Numerous items of clothing that fit the man's body were inside the suitcase. These included two more sleeveless undershirts, two pairs of underpants and a single pair of long pants (recently dry cleaned) with sixpence in one pocket (the only cash found in all his belongings). There was also another sports coat, other shirts and pyjamas, all with the tags torn out. The suitcase contained grooming sundries that a travelling man might take with him, but nothing outstanding.

There was a laundry bag with the name *Keane* written on it, as well as one sleeveless undershirt that bore the name *Kean*, without the last *e*. Many believe the name *Keane* or *Kean* was an alias or a red herring left behind to throw investigators off the real trail. The name has, thus far, led nowhere.

By February 1949, there were no less than eight possible identifications of the body. None turned out to be accurate, as the individuals turned up either alive or deceased somewhere else. Australian authorities failed to identify the man using his fingerprints, so they sent copies of the prints to the United Kingdom and the United States. Neither Scotland Yard nor the FBI had the man's fingerprints on file. Australian officials were no closer to identifying the man than on the day Lyons and the pair of jockeys had discovered him.

After he had been lying in refrigeration for months, awaiting identification, the authorities buried the unknown man on June 14, 1949. Captain E.J. Webb of the Salvation Army led the service, which was held in secret to keep the lookie-loos away. Thanks to media reporting on the case, the public had become fascinated with the mysterious stranger.

The man's casket was encased in concrete to keep it as intact as possible in case some relative identifies him one day and wishes to repatriate his remains to wherever they belong.

A donated stone placed at the head of his grave bears the following inscription:

HERE LIES THE UNKNOWN MAN WHO WAS FOUND AT SOMERTON BEACH 1st DEC 1948

A coroner's inquest into the man's death began three days after they buried him. The coroner's final comments before adjourning the inquest did not provide closure and left the matter open, pending more evidence and identification of the stranger.

Coroner Thomas Cleland wrote: "The evidence is too inconclusive to warrant a finding. There is no evidence as to who the deceased was. Although he died during the night of November 30–December 1, I cannot say whether [the poison] was administered by the deceased himself or by some other person."

Police put out a public appeal to find the book from which the *Tamám Shud* phrase had been torn. Literary scholars informed them that the paper had come from the last page of a copy of the *Rubáiyát of Omar Khayyám*. The book was an English translation of quatrains attributed to "the Astronomer-Poet of Persia," Omar Khayyam, who lived between 1048 and 1131. The book had been popular since its first translated printing in 1859. The man's clear understanding of the final sentence, using it as a suicide note of sorts, led police to believe he was well educated. Investigators rifled through copies of the tome in bookstores and libraries trying to find the page that matched the tiny scroll, but found none.

Hearing about the unnamed man and the search for the book jogged the memory of Adelaide chemist Ronald Francis. (The name was a pseudonym.) He recalled his brother-in-law finding a copy of *The Rubáiyát* close to the date that the body turned up. He had discovered it in his unlocked car, parked near Somerton Beach. The book was still in his brother-in-law's glove box.

Francis retrieved the book and took it into the Adelaide police station on July 23, 1949. It was a rare first edition of Edward Fitz-Gerald's translation of *The Rubáiyát of Omar Khayyám* that had been published in 1859 by Whitcombe and Tombs in New Zealand. The back page was torn in a way that did not quite match the scroll found in the man's pocket. The scroll was smaller, indicating that perhaps something more had been discarded. Experts analyzed the paper and the book together and determined the two did match. Police were comfortable that the scrap in the stranger's pocket belonged to the book.

The found book actually raised more questions than it answered. On the back page of the book there was a code written in pencil. The second line was crossed out.

WRGOABABD MLIAOI WTBIMPANETP
~~MLIABOAIAQC ITTMTSAMSTGAB~~

It appeared to be an encrypted message. Leading amateur code breakers, military experts, astrologers and occultists have tried to decode the letters without success. The sample of this particular code is too small to break using ordinary methods.

Near the cypher, there were two phone numbers. One led nowhere, but the second belonged to a nurse in her 20s who lived near Somerton Beach. Reports call her "Jestyn," but police have kept her true name private to maintain her anonymity. Jestyn denied knowing the man. However, when she was shown his photo, she became faint. Police then realized she was not being forthcoming with them.

After some prying, Jestyn admitted to having given a copy of *The Rubáiyát of Omar Khayyám* to a man she knew as Alfred Boxall in the year before the stranger appeared dead on Somerton Beach. Police managed to track Boxall down. He was alive and well and all too happy to show police the copy of *The Rubáiyát* that Jestyn had given him. Had she given away more than one copy of the book to people?

The police had hit another dead end.

To explain the uncrackable code and the pains he had taken to conceal his identity, some believe the stranger was a spy from either the U.S. or Russia. Perhaps he was murdered, one of the early casualties of the burgeoning Cold War between the two superpowers. But why was he in Australia?

Some have surmised that the Somerton man was Jestyn's rejected lover, who may have killed himself on that beach because it was a special place for the two of them. However, it is still unclear why she would deny knowing him.

Jestyn had a son born in July of 1947. Amateur researchers claim this man shared the same odd ear shape as the Somerton man. Jestyn herself died in 2007, and her son died two years after her. Neither of them is around to answer the questions that all the people trying to solve the case would like to ask.

Jestyn's son did have a daughter. Perhaps, if the stranger is ever exhumed and the DNA of Jestyn's granddaughter and the Somerton man match, we will have some more answers.

Chapter 13

THE DYATLOV PASS
INCIDENT

One of the most enduring mysteries of modern times began in 1959, in the Northern Ural Mountains on Kholat Syakhl, which translated from the local Mansi dialect, means "Dead Mountain." In this cold case, a group of nine hikers on a skiing expedition from the Ural Polytechnic Institute in Yekaterinburg, Russia, died on the mountain that February under mysterious circumstances. The site was later named Dyatlov Pass in memory of the group's leader, 23-year-old Igor Alekseyevich Dyatlov.

The skiing expedition, which was scheduled to last for two weeks, was undertaken by 10 experienced people, two women and eight men. The group arrived after travelling by train to Ivdel on January 25. From there, they headed north into the mountains by truck, arriving at the settlement at Vizhay, where their challenging trek to Mount Otorten was to start on January 27. On January 26, 1959, Igor Dyatlov sent his last message to his family on the back of a postcard addressed to his father in Pervouralsk.

Hello everyone.

Today, 26, we leave on the route, we arrived well.

On February 12–15 I will visit Sverdlovsk. I probably will not go home, so let Rufa bring linen to our room for a trip to Penza.

From there I will return on March 5–7.

Greetings, Igor.

Early during the first day of hiking, the 10th member of the group, Yuri Yudin, a 21-year-old geologist, became ill. Yudin was having a severe attack of radiculitis, a pain that radiates along the nerve, caused by inflammation at the root of its connection to the spinal column. Yuri had suffered from the condition since he was a boy and had been able to overcome attacks on expeditions in warmer weather. The cold and relentless winter winds exacerbated the ailment, leading Yuri to make the tough decision to leave the group behind. On January 28, Yuri returned to Vizhay with the sled and driver the group had hired to haul their gear. This choice saved Yuri's life. He would never see his comrades again.

Dyatlov and his crew failed to send a telegram as they had promised on their return to Vizhay, which they claimed would be no later than February 12. On February 21, using helicopters, the Soviet army began a search of the group's planned route.

One group flew into the area that had been the ultimate destination for Dyatlov and his group. It quickly became apparent they had not made it there at all. Mansi locals, student volunteers and soldiers searched for the missing hikers at key points along their planned route.

On February 25, a group led by Boris Slobstov found ski tracks they believed belonged to Dyatlov. The next day they found a badly shredded tent that had belonged to the hikers. Slobstov recognized it right away because he had aided in building the long tent three years prior.

The tent, flattened and partially buried in snow, held valuable clues, including diaries belonging to the expedition members, chronicling what had gone on during the trip, as well as cameras filled with undeveloped film. But these items gave few hints about what appears to be a violent end to the expedition, the details of which still remain unexplained.

The official report written upon finding the tent states:

> *Camp site is located on the northeast slope of mountain 1079 (Kholat Syakhl, red) at the source of river Auspiya. Camp site is located 300 meters from the top of the mountain 1079 on a slope of 30°. Camp site consists of a pad of flattened snow, on the bottom are stacked 8 pairs of skis (for tent support and insulation, red). Tent is stretched on poles and fixed with ropes, at the bottom of the tent 9 backpacks were discovered with various personal items, jackets, raincoats, 9 pairs of shoes. There were also men's pants found, and three pairs of boots, warm fur coats, socks, hats, ski caps, utensils, buckets, stove, ax, saw, blankets, food: biscuits in two bags, condensed milk, sugar, concentrates, notebooks, itinerary and many other small items and documents, camera and accessories to a camera.*

It appeared as though someone had slashed the tent in multiple spots on both sides from the inside. The fact that the hikers had fled, leaving most of their cold-weather survival gear and even their footwear, caused great concern. No one would have survived long in the cold Russian winter without insulated clothing, let alone shoes.

The film rolls from the six cameras found in the tent were developed and pored over by investigators. The snaps showed a group of young people having an adventure. The first photos depicted pleasant beginnings. Warmly clothed and well equipped, the group smiled and joked with one another as they met locals in the various settlements. As the photographic timeline progressed, the locations looked more and more remote. The winter weather deteriorated and the snow got deeper, and travel became more strenuous. One of the final photos taken was a haunting snap of some group members as they skied single file into a sky darkened by a nasty blizzard.

The recovered diaries give a detailed account of the group's arrival at the alpine area's lowest point on January 31, 1959, where their climb began in earnest. The group cached equipment and provisions for their return trip in the forest on a platform they set up high above the ground. Then they headed farther up onto the mountain and through the treacherous pass the next day.

According to the diaries, the group was late beginning on February 1, 1959, only making it around 4 kilometres (2.5 miles) before the weather forced them to stop at 5:00 p.m. Rather than turn back and lose a day, they erected their tent in the shadow of the mountain in a spot they felt would be out of severe weather along the slope of Kholat Syakhl. They were only 16 kilometres (10 miles) from their destination, Mount Otorten.

The group cooked and ate their last dinner in the tent between 6:00 and 7:00 p.m. At some point soon after dinner, something terrible happened. The occurrence was life-threatening enough to send the experienced hikers slashing their way out of their tent, leaving their coats and shoes behind.

Just before noon on February 27, near the remains of a small fire beside a large cedar, about 1.5 kilometres (1 mile) from the tent, searchers found the first two bodies. They were Yuri Krivonischenko, 23, and Yuri Doroshenko, 21.

One of the mountain rescue team members, Boris Slobstov, later wrote that the remains of a fire were discovered near a cedar tree. Approximately 3 metres (10 feet) from the fire lay the frozen, unclad body of Yuri Doroshenko. His hand was burned and there were cedar branches under his corpse. Close by, also frozen, was Yuri Krivonischenko's body.

Krivonischenko was dressed in badly torn long johns, with a sock on his left foot and his right foot bare. A sock matching the one on his left foot lay burned near the fire. He had numerous cuts, abrasions and bruises on his body, as well as evidence of burns.

Doroshenko also had odd injuries on his body. The hair on one side of his head was singed and burned. He too was dressed lightly in a button-up shirt, socks and torn long johns. The soft tissue of his right cheek was covered with grey foam. There was more of the grey foam, perhaps caused by fluid in the lungs, in his open mouth.

The cause of death for both Krivonischenko and Doroshenko was hypothermia. Some have claimed that a hypothermic end-stage behaviour called paradoxical undressing was responsible for the lack of warm clothes. However, it was later discovered that both men's clothes had been cut off their bodies after death and someone had taken the clothing away. Some of the less damaged items were found on the bodies of other expedition members who died. It is possible that the longer surviving members of the expedition removed items of clothing from their dead comrades in an effort to get more warm clothing. Other bits and pieces were in the snow nearby, and some of the clothes were never found. Someone, or something, had also moved both of the men post-mortem. But why?

Thanks to broken branches 5 metres (16 feet) up the cedar tree, it was apparent that the men had climbed up the tree for some reason. Were they trying to look at something? Back toward the tent? Had they become lost somehow? Why did they leave the tent in the first place? Were they trying to get away from something on the ground by taking refuge in the tree?

Just over 300 metres (980 feet) away from Krivonischenko's and Doroshenko's bodies were the remains of the group's leader,

Igor Dyatlov. All that was visible above the snow were Igor's hands, balled into fists. He had odd socks on his feet but was wearing more clothing than the previous two men.

He too was covered in bruises, scratches and cuts, including mysterious bruises on his knees and ankles. Injuries to his hands were consistent with signs he may have been in a violent fistfight in the hours before his death. The location of his body indicated he might have been returning to the tent when he perished. Dyatlov's cause of death was also determined to be hypothermia.

The body of one of the group's two female hikers, 22-year-old Zinaida Kolmogorova, was found 330 metres (1,080 feet) closer to the tent than Dyatlov. She was lying face down in the snow with her head pointed toward the tent. On her feet were three pairs of socks but no shoes. Zinaida had multiple layers of clothing on.

She was in the fetal position, which is typical for hypothermic death. However, she was the only one in the expedition found in this pose. She might have come from the area near the cedar where the bodies of Krivonischenko and Doroshenko lay, and been attempting to make her way back to the tent when she succumbed.

Kolmogorova had many bruises, cuts and abrasions on her face and hands and had suffered frostbite. There was a large and angry bright-red bruise on her lower back on the right side, measuring approximately 6 by 30 centimetres (2.5 by 12 inches).

The autopsy report on Zinaida's corpse states she died of hypothermia exacerbated by the injuries she had received, which may have been caused by a fall. In the conclusion of the autopsy report, the last sentence stated that Zinaida's cause of death appeared to be violent and accidental.

It was not until March 5 that the body of Rustem Slobodin, 23, was found 480 metres (1,570 feet) away from the first pair discovered near the cedar. He was buried face down under 50 centimetres (20 inches) of snow and had a single felt boot on his right foot.

Rustem wore a long-sleeved undershirt and another shirt underneath his sweater. He wore two pairs of pants and four pairs of socks but was still underdressed.

His cause of death was later determined to be hypothermia, but he showed multiple bruises and abrasions, particularly about his face and head. The left frontal portion of his skull was fractured, possibly from being hit with a blunt instrument. There were angry bruises on one of his legs, some skin was missing from his forearm, and his hands had bruises on them in the same way that Dyatlov's did, indicating a possible fight. Investigators believe Slobodin's body was also moved after his death.

Authorities expanded their searches of the area, looking for answers to what had happened. All of March and April passed with the remaining hikers still missing. On May 3, 1959, clothing was found in a ravine 75 metres (245 feet) from the cedar where Krivonischenko and Doroshenko had died. It was on the side of the tree leading away from the shelter of the tent.

The searchers began digging in the snow, and two days later, they found another body, this one in a creek at the bottom of a ravine. They recovered three more bodies nearby.

The only recognizable corpse was that of the second female hiker, Lyudmila Dubinina, 20, the youngest expedition member. She was lying on her stomach with her knees in the water. She seemed to have been crawling up the bank when she died. She was wearing a sweater that had belonged to Krivonischenko, along with underwear beneath two pairs of pants and two pairs of long socks, with a third sock on one foot. The outer pair of pants was burned by fire and had then been ripped. She also wore a small hat.

Dubinina's body was severely damaged. Her nose had been broken, and most of the flesh on the lower part of her face was gone. Her tongue and eyeballs were missing, and it appeared they had been removed after she died.

The autopsy report concluded that Dubinina's death was caused by massive bleeding into the right ventricle of her heart, exacerbated by multiple bilateral rib fractures and internal bleeding into her abdomen and chest. One or more powerful blows to her chest caused her injuries. The report stated they could have resulted from a fall from a great height, or she might have been thrown.

Semyon Zolotaryov, whose body lay near Lyudmila's, was also severely injured. He wore a long-sleeved shirt and black sweater underneath a coat with the top two buttons undone. On his head, he wore two hats. A short scarf was around his neck. He was also wearing light leather shoes that would have protected his feet from the cold. His hands and legs were underwater in the creek, causing some of his skin to slough away.

Semyon had an open wound on the side of his skull, and his eyes were also missing. He had five broken ribs on his right side, resulting in a condition called flail chest, an excruciating injury that makes breathing difficult. The badly broken ribs also caused massive bleeding into his chest around his lungs. Like Lyudmila, Semyon's brutal injuries could have been caused by falling or being thrown, or by something squeezing him hard enough to break his bones.

Twenty-four-year-old Aleksander Kolevatov's body was also in the creek near Semyon and Lyudmila. The young man was wearing a sleeveless shirt, a long-sleeved shirt, a sweater, a fleece sweater, an unzipped ski jacket and no shoes. His neck was deformed, and his nose was shattered. He had a large open wound behind his left ear. The pathologist who performed the autopsy on Aleksander's body had trouble settling on a cause of death, vacillating between hypothermia and violence.

The final hiker found was 23-year-old Nikolay Thibeaux-Brignolle. He was the most appropriately dressed of all the dead hikers. He was wearing warm clothes. He even wore felt boots called *valenki*, which were typically worn in the Siberian winter. That he and Aleksander were both dressed for the weather was interesting. It indicated they might have already been outside the tent when the event sent the others fleeing into the cold.

Nikolay's arm and lip had bruising. The injury that had killed him was a massive skull fracture that led to a fatal brain bleed. The cause of the wound, however, was mysterious. Like Lyudmila's and Semyon's injuries, it appeared to have been caused by extreme force, perhaps from a fall or a blunt force instrument. Or something may have thrown him.

More than 60 years have passed since the Russian rescue team recovered the last members of the Dyatlov expedition. Some have surmised that the group were victims of a crime. Perhaps they stumbled onto a Soviet Special Forces secret operation and were murdered to keep them quiet. Another theory posits that police mistakenly murdered the hikers after they were misidentified as escapees from the gulag. Yet another theory is that the hikers died at the hands of local Mansi hunters, upset that they were in the area. There have been thoughts that a massive snow slab or avalanche might have buried them, but this doesn't account for searchers finding the tent only partially buried and slashed from the inside.

The theories that are the most fun to consider involve the paranormal. Some conspiracy types claim they see a UFO in a photo at the end of the roll of film in Aleksander Zolotaryov's camera. Others think it looks like an unfocused, unintentional misfire.

Another far-out theory is that there was an attack on the tent by a yeti or an abominable snowman. Is this what caused a group of educated and experienced hikers to run off into the Siberian night in so little clothing? Some say that Lyudmila Dubinina's missing tongue is proof that they were killed by some flesh-hungry monster that chased the group down, murdering a few of them while tossing the others around like rag dolls.

In early 2021, an article appeared in the journal *Communications Earth and Environment* claiming the group was killed by an avalanche. A group of Swiss scientists based in Lausanne revisited the mysterious calamity and, after examining weather and other environmental factors in the area, determined that a small but deadly avalanche was the event that killed a number of the students. They posited that the others in the group, who survived the avalanche, died from exposure afterwards, when their camp was destroyed. This would account for some of the blunt force damage found on some of the bodies. Despite the scientific study, many people are still skeptical about the explanation.

After all these years, no single explanation seems to explain how this group of people died so violently on this ill-fated ski trip.

PART THREE
The Madness of Crowds

Sometimes murder and mayhem are driven by
one sick mind; other times it is a group effort.

Chapter 14

NORTHERN RAMPAGE

The murders of an Australian man, Lucas Fowler, and his American girlfriend, Chynna Deese, near Liard River Hot Springs, British Columbia, in mid-July of 2019 were horrific. The couple had been shot to death and their bodies left behind in the van they'd been travelling in.

As police were trying to figure out who killed the pair, a much-loved botanist and university lecturer at UBC in Vancouver, Leonard Dyck, also turned up dead four days later, having been shot to death near Dease Lake, British Columbia. His SUV was missing, and the burnt-out husk of a camper truck belonging to a young Vancouver Island man was found nearby. On their way north for work, the owner of the vehicle and his friend had failed to check in with family for days and were now considered missing. Were the two young men also victims, police wondered. Or were they suspects?

Although the RCMP initially stated that the murders of the couple and the botanist were not connected, it quickly became apparent that they were. Investigators also quickly determined that the two missing young men were not victims but the perpetrators of the crime. This triggered a massive manhunt and intense investigation across four provinces and one territory as Canadians watched events unfold in their news feed over the next three weeks.

Chynna Noelle Deese, 24, was from Charlotte, North Carolina, and was the youngest of four siblings. She had two brothers and a sister and had graduated from Myers Park High School in 2013 before going off to college. She graduated from Appalachian State in 2017 after studying psychology and business. Chynna's friends and family described her as having an infectious smile, and said she was kind and considerate of others. According to her obituary, in her spare time Chynna volunteered at Joni and Friends, a Christian-centred organization that offered family retreats for individuals affected by disabilities.

Chynna also had an adventurous spirit and she frequently travelled, visiting 13 countries in Asia, South America and Europe. She paid for her trips by working at non-profits and hostels in the countries where she was visiting. On one of her trips to Croatia after college, she picked a temporary job at a hostel, where she met a good-looking tall, blond and bearded man named Lucas Fowler. Fowler was from Sydney's Hills District, Australia, and was the son of New South Wales police chief inspector Stephen Fowler.

Lucas was the youngest of the four Fowler children. He shared Chynna's adventurous spirit and loved to spend time outdoors in nature, camping or riding his dirt bike. A year younger than Chynna, Lucas was in the middle of a two-year-long backpacking trip around the world when they met. The pair clicked right away, and it was clear to everyone around them that they had fallen deeply in love.

After they met, Chynna and Lucas travelled to the United States, where they borrowed her dad's 1996 Land Cruiser for a trip around the country. The couple's adventures took them west into the Rockies and then into Yellowstone National Park. After that, they travelled south along the west coast to San Diego, where they crossed the border into Mexico and briefly toured Central America.

Chynna and Lucas made it back to Charlotte for the holidays in 2018 and spent two months with the Deese family that winter. It was evident to everyone who saw Lucas and Chynna together that they were a true love match.

When Lucas's temporary U.S. visa ran out in January of 2019, he decided to head to Fort Nelson, British Columbia, where he snagged a job at a local ranch. Canada was not nearly as far away as Australia, and working there allowed him to remain closer to Chynna.

Over the next few months, Chynna worked hard and saved her money. She planned to join Lucas in B.C. in July for a 25-day vacation. They were going to tour around Northern British Columbia in a beaten-up 1985 Econoline van that had been given to Lucas by his boss. Lucas had great mechanical skills and resurrected the old Chevy, which had not run for many years.

In early July, Chynna was packed and ready to go, but the work boots she'd bought for Lucas wouldn't fit into her luggage, so she decided to wear the massive size 12 boots onto the plane. A CBC News article reveals that one of Chynna's mother's last memories of her daughter is of her stomping through the airport wearing Lucas's too-big boots.

When Chynna arrived in Canada, the couple spent a week around the ranch before heading off on their road trip. On July 13, 2019, in a photo sent to their families, Lucas Fowler and Chynna Deese can be seen in Lucas's van, beaming as they left Hudson Hope, B.C., for their trip north to Alaska.

In a 17-minute surveillance video from Sunday, July 14, the day after the couple's departure, Lucas's van is seen pulling into a gas station. Lucas, his long hair in a ponytail, wearing long pants and a T-shirt, can be seen pumping gas into the two-tone blue van. Chynna, wearing a loose grey T-shirt, cut-off jean shorts and sandals, diligently cleans the windows all around the van and then embraces Lucas before she heads inside the convenience store. Lucas follows her when he's done pumping gas. After a few minutes, they exit the store together. Chynna has an armful of treats for the road and can be seen drinking from a massive cup. The pair climb back into the vehicle, and with Lucas driving, the video captures them as the van pulls away.

Hours later, the van broke down on Highway 97, which is about 20 kilometres (12 miles) south of Liard River Hot Springs. Although passersby offered to help or call the RCMP, the couple refused and seemed to have a handle on their situation.

CTV News reported that Alandra Hull, a road maintenance worker, drove past the couple at around 7:00 p.m. and was one of the last people to see Lucas and Chynna alive. Hull said they were standing near their broken-down van and were having a conversation with a bearded man, a tourist named Charles Ray. Ray had pulled over, offering help. The couple told him they planned to call a tow truck, but there was no cellphone coverage in the area. Charles was headed in the other direction to camp and would be further out of cell range, but planned to check on them in the morning.

The next day, at 6:20 a.m. on July 15, 2019, a tow truck driver saw a blue van on the side of the road and noted that the back window was smashed out. He quickly pulled over when he saw two bodies, a tall, bearded blond man and a blond woman, lying in a ditch not far from the van. Other passersby stopped to assist the tow truck driver in calling for help. One person drove back toward town until he had cellphone reception and called the RCMP at 7:22 a.m.

When police arrived to investigate, they found Chynna and Lucas lying 5 metres (16 feet) apart; they had been shot to death.

The couple had multiple entrance and exit wounds and had been shot from behind, execution style.

Police searched the crime scene and surrounding areas. They found unspent and spent casings with headstamp numbers 101 and 75. The number 75 is a date stamp that indicates the ammunition was manufactured in 1975, and the number 101 refers to the factory where the bullet was produced. The seized ammunition was determined to be from a firearm commonly referred to as an SKS, a nonrestricted semi-automatic rifle.

The RCMP Major Crimes Unit was brought in from Prince George and set about the task of identifying the dead couple and figuring out who had killed them and why. Over the next day, the bodies were identified and their families notified. Later, their names were released to the public at a press conference along with a plea from investigators for information. The RCMP said they believed there was little risk to people travelling in the area and confirmed the murders were not linked to any other crimes they were investigating at that time.

Four days later, on Friday, July 19, 2019, at approximately 7:19 a.m., 60 kilometres (37 miles) south of Dease Lake, more than 460 kilometres (290 miles) away from the double murder, the RCMP responded to a vehicle fire on Highway 37.

When police arrived on the scene, they found the truck completely gutted by fire. Responding officers found a burned licence plate, which was determined to be from a Dodge pickup truck the same make and model of the vehicle that was smouldering just off the road. The truck was registered to a 19-year-old man named Kam McLeod from Port Alberni, British Columbia.

That same morning, at about 8:30 a.m., a highway worker stopped at the fire scene where RCMP were investigating. He advised a Dease Lake RCMP officer about a deceased man he had just discovered approximately 2 kilometres (1.2 miles) south of the current investigation. The dead man was much older, shorter and stockier than Kam McLeod. Police could see he had suffered injuries to his head and body, including bruises and burn marks. Initially, the man's cause of death was unknown. The police did not release any further details about the man's injuries out of respect for his family.

The RCMP Major Crimes Unit was deployed to support the Dease Lake RCMP and the North District Major Crimes Unit with the investigation as they tried to determine how the vehicle registered to Kam McLeod was related to the discovery of the unknown man's body. Since Kam was nowhere to be found, a search warrant was drafted to allow police to search the burned truck.

Later that day, a family member of Kam McLeod told the RCMP that Kam and his friend, 18-year-old Bryer Schmegelsky, had left Port Alberni on Vancouver Island on July 12, 2019, telling their families they were on the way to Whitehorse in Yukon to look for work.

The two young men had last been seen in McLeod's red and grey Dodge pickup with a camper on the back, travelling south from the Super A general store in Dease Lake at around 3:15 p.m. the day before. Their families confirmed they had not heard from them in days.

A description of the two men was released to the public. Police wanted to know if they were okay, since they now appeared to be missing and may have information about the older man's death. The police released the following descriptions, as reported in a July 24 Global News article:

Kam McLeod:
6 foot 4 or 1.93 metres tall.
Weighing approximately 169 pounds or 77 kilograms.
Having dark brown hair and facial hair.
Having brown eyes.

Bryer Schmegelsky:
6 foot 4 or 1.93 metres tall.
Weighing approximately 169 pounds or 77 kilograms.
Having sandy brown hair.

Schmegelsky's and McLeod's families and friends told investigators they did not believe the boys were involved in the murder of the man near Dease Lake. They thought the two most likely were now victims as well.

On July 22, 2019, with the hope of identifying the Dease Lake murder victim, police released a composite sketch, which revealed him to be a kindly looking older, bearded man.

After 5:00 p.m. that same day, Helen Dyck called the police and reported that she believed the composite sketch was her husband, Leonard Dyck. She said she had not heard from him since he'd texted her on July 18. She hadn't been worried because she presumed he was out of cellphone range after his last text.

Leonard Dyck was a 64-year-old botany lecturer at the University of British Columbia. He left his Vancouver residence on July 16 to go on an outdoor research trip in his silver Toyota RAV4, which he slept in on his long drives. Leonard's last gas purchase was made on July 18 at 7:46 p.m. The store was located about 20 kilometres (12 miles) away from where his body was discovered.

Dyck, the oldest of five children, was born on July 9, 1955, and had grown up in Abbottsford, B.C. As a young boy, Leonard developed an interest in art, music and travel. But he also loved the natural world and studied marine biology and botany at university. He became an academic at UBC after earning his PhD. He was described by friends and family as a gentle guy who loved to sing and play guitar.

Earlier in the afternoon of July 22, after hearing about the search for Kam McLeod and Bryer Schmegelsky, along with details of the recent murders, a witness came forward and provided a statement to the RCMP. The witness knew McLeod and Schmegelsky and believed the boys may have been involved in the murders. This conflicted with original witness statements from people who knew the pair.

A search of the burned truck turned up a burned metal ammunition container. Even though it was severely damaged, the numbers 7.62 and 19-75-101 could be identified on the canister's top. Furthermore, multiple burned ammunition rounds with headstamp numbers 101 and 75 were seized from the truck. Police also seized a gas nozzle from a jerry can near the burned truck.

The RCMP began putting the pieces together and held a press conference to update the public. Investigators said that on July 12, 2019, Kam McLeod and Bryer Schmegelsky left Port Alberni, British Columbia. On the same day, they legally purchased one SKS semi-automatic rifle and a box of 20 rounds of Winchester 7.62 x 39 mm ammunition using Kam McLeod's possession and acquisition licence in Nanaimo, B.C.

Social media and news stories across the country soon began speculating on the whereabouts of the two young men, who appeared to be responsible for three senseless murders.

Police pieced together a timeline for Kam McLeod and Bryer Schmegelsky by tracing their bank card information and 984 hours' worth of surveillance footage from their trip. The evidence, along with their travel timeline, put the young men in the right places at the correct times to have committed the cold-blooded murders. Police discovered that after the murders of Lucas and Chynna, the pair had continued north into Yukon before turning back toward their fateful encounter with Leonard Dyck.

On July 19, 2019, the day of Leonard's murder, surveillance video showed McLeod and Schmegelsky purchasing gas and other items, including a crowbar and electrical tape, at a Vanderhoof hardware store. They arrived at the store driving Leonard's RAV4.

Afterwards, they quickly headed east, covering a lot of ground in a short period of time.

On July 20, they bought gas in Fairview, Alberta. The next day they were in Meadow Lake, Saskatchewan, and then hours later in La Ronge, and a day later, they were in Thompson, Manitoba.

On July 22, 2019, at around 2:30 p.m., a band constable from Split Lake, Manitoba, was at a check stop near an entrance on Highway 280. A silver SUV occupied by two tall, slim young men pulled up to the check stop. The men said they were camping in the area, and the officer allowed them to continue on their way. The following day the band constable recognized McLeod and Schmegelsky after seeing the photos in the latest RCMP report.

On July 23, 2019, at around noon, Major Crimes investigators learned that a burned RAV4 had been located in Gillam, Manitoba, the day before. The search for the suspected murderers turned its focus on Gillam, a small, remote community of 1,200 people more than 1,000 kilometres (620 miles) north of Winnipeg, near Stephens Lake. Somehow, the two young suspects eluded police for days even though Gillam was a small community and it would have been difficult for two strangers to hide there unnoticed.

The communities in Northern Manitoba were kept in a state of suspense and fear for another two weeks as police continued looking for the men. On July 29, 2019, police located several items belonging to the suspects in the Sundance area, including hundreds of rounds of ammunition. On August 1, 2019, McLeod's backpack was also located, containing a full box of ammunition along with McLeod's wallet, identification and clothing.

Then, on August 2, 2019, police located a damaged boat along the Nelson River, leading some to speculate the pair had fled across the river, although this later proved to be untrue. An underwater search conducted where the boat was found did not uncover any additional items linked to the suspects.

Finally, on August 7, 2019, police located two deceased bodies approximately 8 kilometres (5 miles) away from the burned RAV4. Police seized two SKS semi-automatic rifles near the dead men and two spent cartridges. These rifles were examined by the firearms lab and were determined to be the same guns used in the Liard River and Dease Lake homicides. One of the two guns was the same one purchased by McLeod and Schmegelsky back on Vancouver Island.

Police recovered a digital camera where the bodies of McLeod and Schmegelsky were located. The camera, determined to be Leonard Dyck's, contained six videos and three still images. In the videos, McLeod and Schmegelsky took responsibility for all three murders. They also described their intent to die by suicide and their wish to be cremated.

The RCMP Behavioural Analysis Unit (BAU) conducted a review of the videos but claimed afterwards they did not contain any information regarding the motive for the murders, nor did they provide any further details about the crimes.

Everyone, including the friends and families of the killers, has been left to speculate on the motives of the young men. Bryer Schmegelsky's dad, Alan, spoke to the press during the manhunt and was just as confused as anyone, claiming they were just regular kids. Some websites have suggested the RCMP is holding back information because the two killers might have identified with a specific group, and authorities don't want to give any publicity to radical fringe groups or ideas. People have posted photos of Bryer in military garb, holding weapons and in possession of Nazi memorabilia. Others have suggested they were incels. But after their murderous summer trip through western Canada, the only two who know why any of the murders happened are dead.

Chapter 15

THE UFO CULT

On March 26, 1997, police found the bodies of 39 members of a religious UFO cult known as Heaven's Gate in an 830 square-metre (9,000 square foot) home in Rancho Santa Fe, a San Diego suburb. All, including the group's leader, Marshall Applewhite, had died in a ritualistic act of mass suicide. The headline on the cult's website, which remains online today, stated, "Hale-Bopp brings closure to Heaven's Gate." Over the following weeks, as investigators probed what happened in the home, the story of the Heaven's Gate cult emerged, each detail weirder than the next.

Human beings have always been fascinated by what we observe in the night sky. We have been giving names and meaning to the twinkling shapes overhead for thousands of years. Rare sightings of objects in the sky, like comets, were considered to be bad omens: a sign that the gods were displeased. Ancient civilizations blamed comets for many misfortunes, including plagues, crop failures, fires and the downfall of empires.

Our scientific understanding of astronomy has been a more recent development. With the advent of more powerful telescopes and other means of analysis, we understand that a comet is simply a massive, dirty ball of ice hurtling through space on a predictable orbit around our sun. As a comet approaches the sun, it begins to melt and gases and dust trail behind it, creating what is commonly called a tail.

Even with all the scientific knowledge available, in 1910, when Halley's comet was due to pass, some people were fearful about what might happen when it came close to the Earth. Many worried people bought "comet insurance" and "anti-comet pills" from con artists who had whipped them into a panic, claiming deadly gases from the comet would envelop the planet and destroy those who left themselves unprotected. But Halley's comet passed then, and again in 1986, without incident.

Independent of one another, in July of 1995, two astronomers, Alan Hale and Thomas Bopp, discovered a new comet with a 30-kilometre (19 mile) radius. It was much larger and brighter than Halley's comet, and in May of 1996, the newly named Hale–Bopp comet became visible to the naked eye. As Hale–Bopp made its way across the night sky, people with unusual beliefs came out in droves. Some of them believed Hale–Bopp was a special message to the universe, while others felt it was a sign that otherworldly beings were visiting us.

In 1996, as Hale–Bopp was high above Earth, the comet became a popular topic on late-night radio host Art Bell's nightly talk show, *Coast to Coast AM*. Bell broadcast from his double-wide trailer in the high desert in Pahrump, Nevada, not far from the mysterious and storied Area 51. The nightly program was an excellent place for supernatural and paranormal nerds to get their fix of weirdness. Art Bell's show covered conspiracies around the Hale–Bopp comet on multiple programs.

One of the call-in guests on Art Bell's show on November 14, 1996, was Chuck Shramek, an amateur astronomer, conspiracy theorist and radio announcer on KTRH out of Houston. Among his many weird beliefs and conspiracy theories, Shramek claimed the government was performing experiments on humans using chemtrails from aircraft. He was also a moon landing denier and once reported that Jackie Onassis was secretly married to Captain Kangaroo for almost 12 months.

Art and his guest, political science professor Courtney Brown, a proponent of remote viewing, talked with Shramek about a photo he had taken that evening, which he claimed showed a "Saturn-like object, near the comet." Shramek claimed the government's lack of public photographs of the Hale–Bopp comet indicated they were hiding something they felt "might disturb people." According to his observations, Shramek felt the object could be three to four times the size of Earth.

Art and Professor Brown looked at the photo and stated that others in their community reported seeing a similar thing near the comet. Brown said he and three pairs of remote viewers began probing the "anomalous object." Brown claimed the remote viewers saw a humongous vehicle near the comet that was under intelligent control and contained both natural and technological structures. He further claimed a message was being sent directly to a "main guy" on Earth from beings within the object. That "main guy" could have been President Clinton, but Brown and the remote viewers were not sure. The vehicle, the professor said, was on a mission to awaken humanity to a new level of consciousness.

The mainstream media picked up the story, and expert astronomers from NASA and the Jet Propulsion Lab went to work debunking the photos while conspiracy theorists cried cover-up. Art Bell had Shramek back on the show on December 6, 1996, this time with alleged UFO abductee and author Whitley Strieber.

They spoke again about the object near the comet and insisted the government was trying to suppress the "important" information they felt the masses were entitled to know, using circular reasoning to reinforce their claims with the show's audience.

Hale–Bopp and its "companion" became regular fodder for Art Bell's show over the next few months. People came out of the woodwork with wild theories about the object they perceived near the comet, while others claimed to be deciphering messages coming from the extraterrestrials who were riding aboard the object.

One of the people following the story closely was Marshall Applewhite Jr., the leader of the Heaven's Gate cult. He was obsessed with the story. Applewhite believed the message from the alien craft was the one he and his group had been waiting for. According to Applewhite, he was the "main guy" the beings were referring to, not Bill Clinton. Applewhite then began to formulate a plan that would ultimately lead him and 38 of his followers to take their own lives.

The chatter from Art Bell, his guests and conspiracy theorists on the Internet perfectly fit Applewhite's belief in a coming apocalypse. In the months leading up to Art Bell's show on Hale–Bopp, Applewhite had released two videos that he had transcribed and posted on the Heaven's Gate website. These videos featured a wild-eyed Applewhite staring into the camera and warning that the Earth was about to be "recycled." He also said he and his group would be leaving soon and implored others to do the same to "save" themselves.

Marshall Herff Applewhite Jr. was born on May 17, 1931, in Spur, Texas, to Marshall Sr., a Presbyterian minister, and his wife, Louise. They were a devoutly religious family. Marshall Jr. wanted to follow in his father's footsteps and become a minister himself, and obtained a degree in philosophy in 1952. Applewhite later pursued a master's degree in music, from the University of Colorado, then embarked on a career in academia.

Even though Applewhite was married, he struggled with his sexuality and had numerous affairs with men over the years. He and his wife divorced in 1968, much to Applewhite's and his family's shame. Then, in 1970, Marshall was fired from the University of Houston, and his life spiralled downward for the next year. After the death of his father, Marshall Sr., in 1971, depression overtook Marshall Jr. He reached out for help and checked himself into a psychiatric hospital. It was there that he met his spiritual partner, a pediatric nurse named Bonnie Nettles.

Applewhite and Nettles shared spiritual and philosophical views and bonded over their mutual interest in UFOs, Biblical prophecy and paranormal subjects like spiritualism and reincarnation.

Marshall and Bonnie began spending all their time together, reading Scripture and talking about religion, the occult and the paranormal. The two had been through a lot of trauma in their lives, and although they were not sexually intimate, there was a strong connection between them. Soon they began to believe they were on Earth for some divine purpose. They felt their "next level" minds had been given to them to carry a message to a fortunate few, who would follow them as they fulfilled Biblical prophecies.

The odd couple began calling themselves "the Two," after the two witnesses mentioned in the Book of Revelation. Once out of the psychiatric hospital, the pair rented a car using a stolen credit card and took off for Canada. There they travelled across the country, spreading their strange message of salvation. While travelling, the couple was caught and convicted of credit card fraud, which earned each of them a brief stint in prison.

With the time afforded him in prison, Applewhite redefined the basis of his New Age theology. He decided he was a higher life form than the other humans he dealt with daily. He believed he was sent to Earth from beyond the stars by a divine entity. He began to talk about aliens and UFOs, prophesizing that someday

soon, a sign would appear to prove his divinity. He and his followers would then be taken in a spacecraft far away from the backward
folks on Earth.

To transcend their lowly human existence, Applewhite and Nettles took on a series of paired names. They called themselves Guinea
and Pig, Nincom and Poop, and Bo and Peep. The monikers they
finally settled on paid homage to Applewhite's musical education.
They decided to call themselves "Ti" and "Do" from Rodgers and
Hammerstein's timeless classic song "Do-Re-Mi" from *The Sound
of Music*. Applewhite would be Do (*doe*), and Nettles was Ti (*tea*).

Over the next few years, Applewhite and Nettles began gathering followers through speaking engagements on the subject of
"human individual metamorphoses," which attracted New Age
believers from all over North America. The group used a recruit-
ment poster as a selling tool for their lectures in 1975 and 1976.
Documents preserved on the Heaven's Gate website succinctly
encapsulate the focus of their talks. Applewhite and Nettles dis-
cussed UFOs, why the two of them came to Earth and when they
would leave.

The couple claimed they had come from a "level above human"
and took human physical form to educate the people of Earth
about how and when they would be able to ascend to the next
level themselves. They claimed they did not represent any religious
organization and were not recruiting members, although they
invited anyone interested in physical realms beyond their earthly
existence to attend.

When Applewhite and Nettles acquired a convert, they would
pair the person with another believer and send them off to preach
to others, helping them spread their message farther and faster.
After gathering a core group between 1975 and 1976, Applewhite
and Nettles ordered the followers into seclusion to prepare for their
mission. Applewhite told members they could not communicate

outside the group, especially with earthbound family members, who would distract them from their ultimate mission. Isolation from friends and family is a classic tactic used by cult leaders to remove outside influence and brainwash followers. And for Applewhite, it worked well as a way to control his group.

In 1985, Bonnie Nettles died of liver cancer. Applewhite told the rest of the group that Ti had chosen to go on ahead; her "vehicle" had broken down and had been left behind. He assured the group she would be there to welcome them when it was time for them to go. From that point on, Applewhite was the sole leader of Heaven's Gate.

Over the next 12 years, the Heaven's Gate followers remained secluded, giving Applewhite ample time to brainwash them further. In 1992 they produced a series of videos called "Beyond Human—The Last Call," which they hoped to broadcast via satellite TV. The videos outlined their mission and were meant to attract more members to their group. The theories postulated in the videos contained a mix of weird philosophy, pop psychology, science fiction and odd interpretations of verses from the Book of Revelation. In the introduction to the series of videos, the group claims to call itself Total Overcomers Anonymous, because of their "desire to overcome all aspects of the human kingdom."

On October 23, 1993, while trying to attract the numbers required for their final mission, the group published a pamphlet titled "Total Overcomers Classroom Admission Requirements." The pamphlet made it clear that Applewhite expected "total commitment" from anyone who joined the group.

This pamphlet is full of red flags for anyone who has an understanding of how cults work. Some of the most concerning passages included the following:

Potential members were to obey without question. Initiates were told they had to relinquish personal possessions because they would not need them anymore, that personal items would hold them back spiritually. Those possessions, of course, were turned over to the cult. Past relationships and connections with family and friends also had to be severed prior to joining the cult, with Applewhite citing the same reasoning. Initiates were assured that their families would be looked after by the higher beings in the Next Level.

All addictions, physical or psychological, were to be left behind, as they were of the human world.

The suppression of sexual desire, an area where Applewhite himself had struggled mightily, was paramount to the group. Applewhite arranged for a Mexican doctor to surgically castrate him and seven other men in the group to assist in their goal to remain celibate. Members were also discouraged from adhering to a specific gender, which Applewhite said did not matter in the Next Level. All members of the group began dressing in a similar androgynous way and even adopted similar hairstyles.

Upon joining the group, followers had to rename themselves, essentially erasing their past lives. They adopted bizarre names, all ending in -ody. Applewhite claimed their new names were more befitting of space travellers. He was now in complete control of his followers.

In January of 1997, after hearing about Hale–Bopp and its companion object on Art Bell's show, Applewhite began planning for the group's departure. That same month, one of the group members, a man named Rio DiAngelo (known as "Neody"), felt compelled to leave because he had work to do in the outside world before embarking on the journey to the Next Level. DiAngelo became a web designer and stayed in contact with the group via email, never entirely cutting off contact. That left 39 members of the cult, consisting of Applewhite and his 38 recruits. Of those remaining with Applewhite, 21 were women and 17 were men, ranging in age from 26 to 72.

Despite the fact that reputable scientists had quickly debunked the photos on Art Bell's website that claimed to show Hale–Bopp's mysterious companion, Applewhite carried on with his plans. The cult members began recording their goodbye messages on video and prepping for their departure. Their faces in the videos seem joyous, and their parting words were thoughtful.

A public message was also released on the Heaven's Gate website:

> *Whether Hale-Bopp has a "companion" or not is irrelevant from our perspective. However, its arrival is joyously very significant to us at "Heaven's Gate." The joy is that our Older Member in the Evolutionary Level Above Human (the "Kingdom of Heaven") has made it clear to us that Hale-Bopp's approach is the "marker" we've been waiting for—the time for the arrival of the spacecraft from the Level Above Human to take us home to "Their World"—in the literal Heavens. Our 22 years of classroom here on planet Earth is finally coming to conclusion—"graduation" from the Human Evolutionary Level. We are happily prepared to leave "this world" and go with Ti's crew.*

Hale–Bopp would travel closest to Earth on March 22, 1997, so on March 21, the group celebrated their impending "graduation" with their last meals. As the comet glowed in the sky above them, the group ordered identical takeout meals from a nearby Marie Callender's restaurant in Rancho Santa Fe. They feasted on turkey pot pie, blueberry cheesecake and iced tea.

No longer privy to all that was unfolding at the house, Rio DiAngelo became concerned when he hadn't heard from anyone in the group on Monday, March 24, 1997. They were always prompt in replying to his emails. That's when he began to suspect that his friends might have moved on to the Next Level without him. Two days later, Rio's fears were confirmed when he received a FedEx package that contained a video and letter. The letter, later released on the Heaven's Gate website, said, "By the time you read this, we will have exited our vehicles."

DiAngelo left work and went to the house in Rancho Santa Fe, knowing what he would find there. Holding a shirt doused in cologne to guard against the strong smell of death in the house, DiAngelo entered, recording on a video camera the eerie sights as he went from room to room. He later claimed he was envious of the group, who had all completed their missions.

Every member of Heaven's Gate was dead. Each of them was found lying on a bed or cot, face up, dressed in identical long-sleeved shirts and black sweatpants. They all wore black Nike shoes with white highlights and the swoosh logo on the side. Each person wore an armband with a patch that read "Heaven's Gate Away Team."

It was later determined that the group had worked in shifts, over three days, to complete their group suicide. Two groups of 15 people, one on Saturday and one on Sunday, took their lives first. On Monday, the last nine members of the group ate a concoction laced with between 50 and 100 phenobarbital pills and vodka, and placed plastic bags over their heads. As each group of people died, the remaining followers removed the plastic bags from their heads and put purple shrouds over their faces. The final two women to kill themselves were found with the plastic bags still over their heads.

After his discovery, DiAngelo made an anonymous 911 call, and Encinitas sheriff's deputy Robert Brunk arrived at 18241 Colina Norte and discovered the 39 bodies. It did not take long before the media caught wind of the story, and news helicopters began buzzing around the house as police carried out body after body.

For months afterwards, the media were on fire with stories about the cult's mass suicide. News organizations obtained the video DiAngelo had made after discovering the suicide, which was shared online for all to see. Later, two former members of the group also died by suicide.

Ten years after the suicides, Rio DiAngelo, still a believer, released a book called *Beyond Human Mind: The Soul Evolution of Heaven's Gate*. Now, more than 20 years later, DiAngelo and other former members of the group claim they are still, somehow, in contact with the Heaven's Gate Away Team.

Chapter 16

COLONIA DIGNIDAD

The full scope of the atrocities committed at the hands of Adolf Hitler and his army of Nazis during World War II are well documented. News reports from former occupied Europe displayed photos and film of the organized genocide perpetrated by the Führer and his goons. As Allied forces were almost on his doorstep, Hitler killed himself, dying by suicide beside his bride, Eva Braun. A few of the Führer's closest adherents followed his lead and also died by suicide. Yet some of his followers, deciding they were not yet done with life, chose to escape from Europe, skittering away rather than facing the music for their horrendous war crimes.

If a member of the Nazi party had the means, clandestine escape routes, called ratlines, were available to them. Switzerland, Italy and even the Vatican helped smuggle Nazi war criminals out of Europe to countries without extradition treaties. But it was Spain that harboured many of them until they could secure passage to Nazi havens in South America. Countries like Argentina, Bolivia, Brazil,

Colombia, Ecuador, Guatemala, Mexico, Paraguay and Peru saw an influx of German-speaking Europeans in the years after World War II. Money spoke louder than their fraudulent paperwork, so they were allowed to immigrate and began living quiet lives.

Chile also gained its fair share of blond-haired and blue-eyed immigrants postwar. As the years passed, some Nazis decided that residing in more remote areas was the best way to avoid detection by the groups of dogged Israeli Mossad agents who scoured the globe looking for the men responsible for the Holocaust who had slipped away.

Around 1961, a group of German immigrants, led by a charismatic preacher named Paul Schäfer, purchased an unused farm on nearly 5,000 hectares (12,300 acres) deep in the Andes, 380 kilometres (240 miles) south of Santiago, Chile's capital city. They called their new community, purchased with funds from tithes collected back home in Germany, "Colonia Dignidad," or Dignity Colony. The colony proliferated, bolstered by Chileans attracted to the group's disciplined and community-focused way of life. The legal name for the group in Chile was Sociedad Benefactora y Educacional Dignidad, or, in English, Dignity Charitable and Educational Society.

The Germans, called Los Alemanes by the locals, built their agricultural community with the idea of doing good works. They wanted to educate the 20,000 Chileans in the nearby villages about European ways of life and to preserve German culture while following Christian ideals. They gave residents jobs and brought in trade goods. The group provided free hospital services, built an elementary school and, later, erected a European-themed restaurant that served Bavarian food to the homesick Germans. The colony was far enough away from any other major towns or cities that they were self-sufficient. They even built themselves a hydro-electric power station that operated small factories and mills. The colony thrived, and members lived the kind of life they wanted to without attracting too much attention.

As with many cult leaders, Schäfer had a dark past. Paul Schäfer was born in Troisdorf, just south of Cologne, on December 4, 1921. He joined the Hitler Youth and had dreams of becoming a member of Hitler's elite Nazi SS, but his glass eye prevented him from achieving his goal. Schäfer was also a bit of a klutz. He'd lost his eye when he slipped while attempting to untie his shoelace with a fork. The German army still let him join, despite his infirmity. Corporal Schäfer served as a Luftwaffe medic and was stationed in France during the war.

In the early postwar years, Schäfer began preaching the Christian gospel after meeting Hugo Baar. Baar was a minister of a Calvinist religious sect called the Evangelical Free Church in Salzgitter-Bad. Church elders ousted Schäfer, however, after discovering he was sexually abusing two of the young boys he was ministering to. The young one-eyed preacher then roamed about Germany with a guitar, preaching sexual abstinence and gathering fresh followers thanks to his magnetic personality and talent for public speaking. He used donations from his followers to open an orphanage in Siegburg, near Bonn. Once again, however, it was discovered that he was sexually abusing two little boys under his care. This time the police were called. But before the law could take Schäfer into custody, he fled with a group of his followers and the cash he had collected for the orphanage.

Through friends, Schäfer met the Chilean ambassador to Germany, who, unaware of the abuse allegations, invited Schäfer and his followers to make a home in Chile. Schäfer, of course, accepted, and the group moved to South America.

In its first few years, Schäfer's colony, whose architecture resembled the Bavarian villages seen in the Alps, quickly earned a reputation as a bastion of authentic German culture. From the outside, it appeared to be a benign European settlement, but there were rumours of darker goings-on inside the compound, which had high fences, barbed wire and even a watchtower reminiscent of the Nazi camps. Although outsiders were not aware of the colony's Nazi connections, Colonia Dignidad remained an attractive destination for those with far-right-wing ideas. Hard-core Nazis saw the location as a safe place to perpetuate the fascist ideals that were now out of favour in Europe.

Among those rumoured to have spent time at the colony are highly decorated former Luftwaffe flying ace Hans-Ulrich Rudel, known as "the Eagle of the Eastern Front," and SS officer Walther Rauff, a one-time aide to Reinhard Heydrich, who was thought to be responsible for 100,000 Holocaust deaths by implementing mobile gas chambers. Some reports even have the top Nazi doctor at Auschwitz, Josef Mengele, nicknamed "the Angel of Death," visiting the colony as late as 1979.

Colony members gave up everything to be a part of Schäfer's group. The Chileans wanted to stay at Colonia Dignidad because life in Chile was tough and they liked the structure and security the organization provided. Many of the German settlers knew that going back to Europe meant having to face a war crimes tribunal, so they had few choices but to stay in the settlement. They were stuck, and Schäfer knew it.

German was the only language acceptable in the colony, and Chileans who wanted to join had to learn the language too. Once in the settlement, contact with outsiders and smoking and drinking were not allowed. Schäfer also dictated that a colonist's hard work was to be done without financial payment. The salvation of one's soul was the only remuneration. Schäfer and his goons forced their able-bodied followers to work 14-hour days and ruled over them by fear. Followers were warned to present a happy face to any outsiders lest they incur harsh punishment, including electrical shocks and psychoactive drugs, which were forcibly administered to make followers more agreeable. Anyone who saw another person breaking the rules was encouraged to turn the sinner in to Schäfer. Knowing about an infraction and not admitting your knowledge of it brought punishment just as swift and brutal as the lawbreaker's.

In a few years, the colony grew to 350 people. Rumours began spreading that adult members had kidnapped as many as 40 of the group's 100 children from Germany so Schäfer and the other adults could sexually exploit them. German authorities were powerless to investigate these crimes in Chile. Some reports say children, mostly adopted orphans, were "imported" by Schäfer and his followers for years after their arrival in the area.

Sexual oppression was Schäfer's main route to domination. He prohibited family, friendships or sexual relationships within the colony and forbade sexual intercourse in any form within the grounds of Colonia Dignidad. Since sex was forbidden, importing children from Germany was the only way they could acquire new members. Within the colony, husbands, wives and children all lived separately. The boys and girls also lived separately, with the boys' residence located suspiciously close to Schäfer's.

To create order in the colony, Schäfer instituted a complex ranking system. He put himself at the top of the large family, calling himself "the Permanent Uncle." Each rank, divided by age and gender, had its own emblem and even a flag. The colony members moved up the ranks at age 6, at 15 and again in their mid-30s. They graduated to the group of elders of the same gender at 50.

Outside influences like books, films, radio and television were strictly prohibited. The only communication equipment on the property was a shortwave radio that ran between the commune and an office they established in a Santiago mansion they had purchased. The mansion was the group's public face, and propaganda about life behind Colonia Dignidad's walls was created there. From the mansion's headquarters, Schäfer's organization supported various fascist causes, including the Partido Nacional Socialista Obrero de Chile (the National Socialist Workers Party of Chile), whose emblem was none other than the familiar red Nazi flag with a swastika in the middle.

Schäfer pressed former SS members who were living in the compound to provide security for the colony, putting to use their experience in overseeing concentration camps. The security force for the compound was also well armed. German shepherd guard dogs kept people out and members of the settlement inside. If anyone ran off when working in the fields, the dogs gave chase.

In 1966, a young man named Wolfgang Mueller escaped from the colony and revealed what he had seen inside. Mueller had tried to escape twice before but had failed. He claimed that, along with other young men in the colony, he was repeatedly beaten, drugged and raped by Schäfer while being held in a tiny cell. Mueller, who had been brought to Chile as a child, also stated that the abuse had started back in Germany when he was only 12 years old.

As well as speaking to the authorities, Mueller talked to the press, which enraged Schäfer. Schäfer ordered that his followers find out where the police were keeping Mueller. He wanted them to bring him back to shut him up permanently. After colony members orchestrated a violent raid on a Santiago safehouse, looking for him, Mueller fled back to Germany. Despite Mueller's public disclosures, Chilean authorities took no further action against Schäfer and his followers, and the colony was allowed to continue.

In 1970, Chileans democratically elected the country's first socialist president, Salvador Allende. He promised to look into the influx of Germans into the country after World War II and hinted at making trouble for people living at Colonia Dignidad. Schäfer and the other fascists who had hidden away in Chile knew the new government might upset their way of life, and they decided they had to act.

Colonia Dignidad threw their support behind the right-wing extremist terror organization Patria y Libertad and kept the leaders of the party hidden on the premises for protection. Patria y Libertad worked at destabilizing and delegitimizing Allende's rule through propaganda aimed not only at the people but also at generals in the Chilean army who were already unhappy with their new left-leaning president. Their tactics worked, and in 1973, the Chilean Armed Forces (the Army, Navy, Air Force and Carabineros) overthrew Allende's government in a violent coup. At the end of it, President Allende lay dead from an apparent self-inflicted rifle wound. Questions still remain about whether he died by suicide or was assassinated.

Generalissimo Augusto Pinochet, commander-in-chief of the Chilean army and admitted lead plotter in the coup, was installed as Chile's leader. The dictator and his extreme right-wing government, with whom Colonia Dignidad had built deep ties even before the coup, were much more acceptable to Schäfer and his group.

Pinochet had his own secret police intelligence organization, much like Hitler's Gestapo, called DINA, the Dirección de Inteligencia Nacional, or, in English, the National Intelligence Directorate. The DINA set about immediately creating a secret network of torture and detainment camps to deal with Pinochet's detractors. People who were vocal about the Chilean dictator began to disappear in droves.

Thanks to their previous relationship, Pinochet quickly identified the compound at Colonia Dignidad as uniquely suited to deal with the leftist dissidents still speaking out against him after the recent coup. DINA operatives knew that with experienced Nazis in charge, their work in handling Pinochet's detractors would be efficient and effective. Operating out of a house in nearby Parral, DINA agents would abduct dissenters and bring them to Colonia Dignidad for brutal torture sessions and indefinite detainment.

Pinochet visited Colonia Dignidad himself in 1974 and was impressed with the operations there. Over the years, the DINA and Schäfer's monsters tortured more than 300 opponents of the Pinochet regime in Colonia Dignidad's underground dungeons. As many as one-third of the people taken to the compound did not live to tell anyone about their experiences. Those who did survive carried not only terrible physical scars but deep psychological and emotional wounds as well. Those who made it out alive, including children sexually abused by Schäfer and some of his followers, all had stories to tell.

In 1977 Amnesty International intended to release a 60-page report called *Colonia Dignidad – deutsches Mustergut in Chile – ein Folterlager der DINA* (Colonia Dignidad – German model in Chile – a torture camp of DINA), but Schäfer's legal team blocked its publication, calling the paper defamatory and delaying its publication until 1996. Over the decades, other sporadic media reports also failed to bring sufficient attention to the commune or effect any real change. Officials excused their inaction, repeatedly pointing out that the colony was private property, and what went on was none of their business.

It was not until near the end of Pinochet's reign that Chile and the rest of the world were made aware of what had gone on at Colonia Dignidad and other notorious sites. The 1996 release of the dense 1,128-page *Report of the Chilean National Commission on Truth and Reconciliation* pointed the finger directly at Colonia Dignidad as a place where horrific things had happened, including interrogation and torture. Details from the Amnesty report are harrowing. Prisoners held at these secret installations were subjected to torturous interrogations by highly trained personnel. In one particularly horrific method, known as "the grill," prisoners were tied to a metal bedspring and an electric current was "applied to the most sensitive parts of the body."

Some victims were suspended by the knees or wrists for extended periods. The guards were said to have added their own weight by clinging to the hanging prisoners, putting a tremendous strain on their bodies. The suspended prisoners were often subjected to beatings, electrical shock and other painful humiliations.

During a form of torture referred to as "the submarine," the victim's head was forced into a tub of dirty water and held there until the person nearly asphyxiated before being taken out at the last moment, gasping for breath. The whole ordeal was repeated numerous times. "The dry submarine" involved placing a plastic bag over a person's head, again cutting off the supply of oxygen to the brain until close to the point of asphyxiation. The bag was then removed to allow the person to breathe before the process was started again.

Victims were beaten with various blunt instruments, including feet and fists. They were slashed or gouged with sharp-edged implements. Some were simply shot. Prisoners were tortured physically, psychologically and sexually, and some died from their injuries. Of those who survived, many had incurred horrendous wounds that left them permanently scarred.

In 1988, early escapee Wolfgang Mueller, who had changed his last name to Kneese after arriving back in Germany, founded an organization in Bonn called Emergency and Interest Group for the Injured of Colonia Dignidad. It was a non-profit charity focused on assisting children who had been abused in religious sects and raising public awareness to prevent further abuse.

Paul Schäfer continued abusing children back in Chile without consequence for the next few years, but the law eventually caught up with him. In 1996 he was accused of child abuse by 26 children who had grown up at the colony. Germany and France then sought the cult leader on charges of child sexual abuse.

Rather than face capture, upon hearing of the charges, Schäfer escaped from the colony. He was tried in absentia in both countries and found guilty in 2004. A year later, authorities found him hiding in Buenos Aires, Argentina, and brought him back to Chile; he was placed in a maximum-security prison until his trial. That same year, excavations on the grounds of the colony turned up the bodies of people who had been murdered at the site. Investigators also uncovered a massive cache of World War II German-made weaponry, including machine guns and hand grenades.

Schäfer was convicted in 2006 and sentenced to 33 years in prison for his multiple counts of child rape. The court also ordered him to pay his victims compensation of more than US$1.5 million. Paul Schäfer died in prison when his heart gave out in 2010. He was 92.

The Chilean state took over the colony after Schäfer went on the run. The government has since renamed it Villa Baviera to erase its past and has made the colony into a tourist destination.

Chapter 17

THE RIPPER CREW

S erial killers are typically lone wolves. There have been rare instances over time of what the experts refer to as folie à deux, when two people with a shared psychotic disorder combine forces in their efforts to murder one or more people. Examples of folie à deux would be the Canadian Ken and Barbie Killers, Paul Bernardo and Karla Homolka; California torture killers Leonard Lake and Charles Ng; and L.A.'s Hillside Stranglers, Angelo Buono and Kenneth Bianchi. There have been occurrences of folie à trois, but folie à quatre, serial killings with four perpetrators, is exceedingly rare. But in the early 1980s, there was a group of four honest-to-goodness bad guys killing people in and around Chicago, Illinois.

On June 1, 1981, as a maid was cleaning rooms at a seedy, low-cost motel called the Brer Rabbit, she noticed a sickening smell that appeared to be coming from the overgrown lot next door. She reported the stench to the motel's manager, who thought it might be a dead deer at first. When he investigated the source of the odour, he knew it was much worse than a deer. Among the trash and tall grass lay a decomposing human body, a semi-nude woman surrounded by flies and covered with maggots.

Police were familiar with the Brer Rabbit Motel. It was a place for folks to flop and shoot up or to rent a room with one of the many local sex workers, or both. The woman's death could have been a simple overdose or a robbery gone wrong.

The body was that of a black woman. She wore a sweater, but the bones of her ribs were exposed. Someone had handcuffed her hands behind her back. Her panties were down around her sock-clad ankles. An inspection of her socks revealed what was presumed to be her latest earnings, a wad of crumpled bills. It was clear that robbery was not the motive for her slaying; instead, it looked like a sexual homicide. The coroner told investigators that the body had been there at least three days and that both her breasts had been removed.

Thanks to dental records and fingerprints, the victim was identified as Linda Sutton, a 26-year-old sex worker and a mother of two young children. Linda had gone missing sometime on May 23. Nobody around the stroll where Linda typically worked had seen anything, so the police did not have a lot to go on and the case went cold.

Almost a year after police first discovered Linda Sutton's body, on the morning of May 15, 1982, Lorraine Borowski failed to show up for her job as an assistant at an Elmhurst, Illinois, real estate office. She was to open up the office that day, but when her co-workers arrived, they found Lorraine's shoes and some of her belongings near the still locked door. Lorraine was nowhere to be found. The pretty 21-year-old had vanished, snatched right out of her shoes.

In October, someone discovered Lorraine's mostly decomposed body on the grounds of a cemetery a 20-minute drive from the Brer Rabbit Motel. Lorraine had been there a while. Her body had deteriorated too much to determine her cause of death with any certainty. However, investigators determined that the woman's skull showed marks from what appeared to be a hatchet.

On May 29, 1982, two weeks after Lorraine had gone missing, 30-year-old Shui Mak disappeared while walking home after a fight with her brother in his car. The siblings had worked a shift at their parents' Chinese restaurant in Streamwood. On the ride home, Shui told her brother that she was in love with a white man, which she knew would be frowned upon by her traditional Chinese family. She had stormed away in a huff and her brother drove off. It was the last time she was seen alive. Her mutilated body turned up in late August, buried in a shallow grave at a construction site. Her left breast was missing.

On June 13, a group of men in a red van snatched a sex worker named Angel York off the street. They handcuffed her and took turns brutally raping her. One of the men produced a knife and told her to cut her left breast. When she hesitated, the man took the knife and slashed at her, becoming more and more sexually aroused with each stroke. Afterwards, for some unknown reason, Angel was dumped along a roadside, still alive. Despite her description of both the van and her attackers, police were unable to turn up any solid leads.

Two and a half months later, on August 28, a naked body, with her hands tied behind her back with a shoelace, was found under the Fullerton Avenue bridge, which ran over the Chicago River's North Branch. Her killer had amputated her left breast before strangling her with her bra. The police identified the girl as an 18-year-old sex worker, Sandra Delaware. She had been dead for only six hours.

In early September, a 30-year-old marketing executive, Rose Beck Davis, was abducted off the street. On September 8, a sanitation worker discovered her body stuffed under the back stairwell of 1250 North Lakeshore Drive in Chicago. Rose's face was severely mangled, a black sock was cinched tightly around her neck, and the rest of her clothes were in disarray. She had small punctures on her abdomen, consistent with wounds from an ice pick, and deep, vicious cuts to both breasts. The blood pooled around her body indicated she had been assaulted where she lay.

As the number of victims grew, the series of killings was now being called the Chicago Ripper murders in the press, and the public was beginning to worry who would be next. The pressure was finally on the police to do more to solve the brutal crimes.

But the Chicago police were stumped, so they called the FBI for assistance. None other than famed profiler Robert Ressler of the FBI Behavioral Science Unit created the profile of the potential killer of Rose Beck Davis. Ressler speculated that Rose's killer might be unsure of his sexuality and might even be bisexual. Ressler also noted that the man might be effeminate in affectation.

A break finally came in the case, but not before another woman suffered a brutal attack. On October 6, 1982, someone walking near train tracks found a 20-year-old sex worker, Beverly Washington, amid a garbage dumpsite. She was bleeding from vicious wounds, naked and barely conscious. Her attacker had severed one of her breasts, but she was alive. Paramedics rushed Beverly to the hospital, and her condition stabilized.

When Beverly regained consciousness, she was able to describe her attacker to investigators. She said the driver of the red van was a Caucasian man of around 25 years old, wearing boots and a flannel shirt. His brown hair was greasy, and he had a moustache. The man seemed nervous and offered her more money than she had negotiated. He ordered Beverly into the back seat, where he produced a gun, made her undress and cuffed her. She was forced to perform oral sex on the man. He then produced a handful of pills and told Beverly to take them or he would hurt her. She took the pills, which quickly made her feel drowsy to the point of passing out. Before she fell unconscious, Beverly recalled the man holding a cord over her, and she feared she would never wake up again.

Beverly also gave some specifics about the van that might prove helpful. She said the vehicle was a Dodge with tinted windows, a homemade wooden divider between the front and rear seats, and a roach clip with blue and white feathers hanging from the rear-view mirror. The description of the van and its potential occupant was given to officers patrolling the streets.

On October 20, 1982, cops pulled over a dark-windowed red Dodge van. Internally, the van had all the elements Beverly had described, but the man driving, Eddie Spreitzer, did not fit the description of Beverly's attacker. The van's registration, however, indicated it belonged to a man named Robin Gecht. Eddie said that Robin was his boss.

Police visited Gecht's residence, and when Robin emerged from the house, they noted that the man fit Beverly's description right down to his boots and shirt. Robin was cocky and unconcerned when initially questioned, acting like he didn't have a care in the world. He was taken by police to the station for further questioning. Beverly later picked him out of a photo lineup as her attacker. Gecht was also quickly made the prime suspect in Angel York's brutal assault.

Investigators soon discovered that Robin Gecht, a 28-year-old unemployed carpentry contractor, had an interesting past. As a teenager, he had gone to live with his grandparents after being accused of sexually assaulting his younger sister. But the most intriguing piece of information about Robin Gecht was his association with another notorious Chicago serial killer, John Wayne Gacy. The courts had sentenced Gacy to death two years before, on March 13, 1980, for murdering 33 young men and boys, some of whom had worked for Gacy in his construction business. Gacy had always tried to deflect responsibility for the murders, accusing other men who had worked for him of the crimes. Robin Gecht happened to be one of them.

A month after his initial arrest, Gacy had mentioned Robin Gecht to police. Gacy claimed Robin was bisexual, a detail that fit with Ressler's profile of the man killing and mutilating women in Chicago. Ressler had also profiled the Gacy murders and had suggested that more than one killer might have been involved in some of those killings.

Robin Gecht denied any involvement in the Gacy murders, and prosecutors and police believed Gacy was raising the possibility of other participants as a way to try to escape the death penalty. Yet it soon became clear that John Wayne Gacy did, in fact, know some uncomfortable truths about Robin Gecht.

When questioned by police, Gecht coolly denied having anything to do with the assaults on York and Washington and claimed he did not know about the other murders. Angel had described a group of men involved in her assault, so police knew Gecht had not acted alone. And while Gecht had not revealed anything to police, investigators could tell that Eddie Spreitzer was not as unflappable.

With no real evidence, cops released Gecht after questioning him and decided to focus on Eddie. Although initially he was not very talkative, they suspected he would give in eventually. Over the course of a few police interviews, Eddie Spreitzer slowly began to spill the beans. He gave police only little bits of information at first, but eventually police were able to pry the entire story from him.

When police first questioned Eddie, he told them he had been living at the Brer Rabbit Motel and working at the nearby Winchell's Donut House. He met Robin Gecht when he came into the donut shop late one night. Eddie said that same night, they went out in Robin's van and picked up a black sex worker. It was May 23, the day Linda Sutton had disappeared. Eddie claimed the woman got out of the van after he and Gecht had an altercation with "some pimps" and they never saw her again after that.

But police knew Eddie's story about Linda Sutton did not add up, so they brought him in for another interview on November 5, and that's when the floodgates opened. As Eddie spoke with Chicago detective Thomas Flynn and Cook County assistant state's attorney Richard Beuke, he confessed to his involvement in Linda Sutton's murder and the abduction and assault on Beverly Washington. Over the next few interviews, police believed they had all the information they needed to make a few more arrests.

During that second interview, Eddie gave a different version of events about the night they picked up Linda Sutton. He said Robin's plan was to have Eddie hide in the back of the van and remain out of sight while Gecht picked up a sex worker. When Eddie heard two taps on the side of the van, he was to get out and help Robin drag the victim into the back, where they would then have their way with her in private. That night, while he was waiting in the van, Eddie heard Robin chatting with a woman he described as having a black female voice. The woman entered the front seat, unaware that another man was in the rear of the vehicle. Robin offered the woman pills, which she took. They drove for what Eddie estimated was 30 minutes and then stopped.

Eddie heard two taps on the van and exited the rear of the vehicle. Gecht was already outside the front passenger door holding a pair of handcuffs and a knife. Linda Sutton was sitting in the front passenger seat. Gecht forced her out of the van, handcuffed her wrists and then pushed her into some bushes a short distance from the vehicle. There the two men sexually assaulted, killed and then mutilated Linda, taking her breasts as trophies.

In a second admission, which he later recanted, Eddie said that a friend, Andrew Kokoraleis, was also present at the murder.

Further investigation revealed that Robin Gecht, 28, Eddie Spreitzer, 21, Andrew Kokoraleis, 21, and Andrew's 23-year-old brother, Thomas, all lived at the Brer Rabbit Motel that spring, in adjoining rooms. The manager of the Brer Rabbit, when questioned, said the men were weirdos. They held loud parties and appeared to be involved in some kind of cult. He said he thought they may even be devil worshippers.

Police then visited Thomas Kokoraleis at his home and, after some initial questioning, brought him downtown to the police station to question him. Thomas initially denied any involvement and agreed to a polygraph exam. After he failed the polygraph miserably, Thomas began talking too.

He told police that Gecht had a "Satanic chapel" in his room, and it was there that all four had been involved in gang-raping and torturing women, and mutilating them with ice picks and knives. The last act was sacrificing the lives of these women to Satan. Thomas claimed that after removing a breast, all of the men would cannibalize a piece of it, in a sick performance of communion. Gecht would then toss the body part into a large box where he kept other similar trophies.

In the meantime, Eddie Spreitzer was in another interview room providing even more details. He claimed the men had picked up and murdered more women than just the one he'd previously confessed to. Eddie admitted he had been present when Gecht had killed and brutalized Lorraine Borowski and then dumped her in an undeveloped area of Clarendon Hills Cemetery. He confessed to having participated in the murder and mutilation of Shui Mak. He also admitted they had raped, killed and mutilated Sandra Delaware in August, dumping her in the Chicago River. Eddie said that he, Andrew Kokoraleis and Robin Gecht had raped, murdered and mutilated Rose Beck Davis as well.

In a surprise admission, Eddie also revealed he had been driving Robin Gecht's van on October 6, 1982, when Gecht told him to slow down. According to Eddie, Gecht shot two men standing on a corner, killing Rafael Tirado, 28, and wounding Alberto Rosario, 21, using a rifle and a .38 pistol. They had brutalized Beverly Washington later on the same day.

All four men were arrested and held on $1 million bonds. Andrew and Thomas Kokoraleis and Edward Spreitzer all confessed to the murders and their participation in a Satanic cult run by Robin Gecht. Gecht continued to deny his involvement in the crimes after his arrest, claiming he barely knew the other men.

During the series of trials, the Kokoraleis brothers and Spreitzer recanted their statements about the existence of the cult. They said they had been untruthful and the police had coerced their confessions.

In the end, Andrew Kokoraleis was convicted of murder and sentenced to death. He died by lethal injection in 1999, the last prisoner in Illinois to have his execution carried out. The Supreme Court of Illinois abolished the death penalty in that state in 2011.

Thomas Kokoraleis was convicted of murder and sentenced to 70 years to life as a reward for his initial confession. He was released from prison in 2019 thanks to a sparkling prison record after serving only half his sentence. In a television interview with a local ABC affiliate, Thomas vehemently denied any knowledge of the murders and was adamant there never was a cult.

Edward Spreitzer received a death sentence, but it was commuted to life in prison in 2003 by Governor George H. Ryan.

Robin Gecht, the crew's supposed leader, was convicted of the rape and attempted murder of Beverly Washington, but none of the other murders. He received a sentence of 120 years in prison for that crime. He remains in prison and continues to maintain his innocence.

Chapter 18

LOS NARCOSATÁNICOS

For many young adults, the college experience is the first time they can let loose and do what they like without parental supervision. There are no parents breathing down their necks, telling them what they can and can't do. They can go to class or not go. Sleep in if they have been up doing keg stands until 4:00 a.m. Get hammered the night before an important exam, "forget" to study and stumble home two hours before the exam's start. It's all their call. Some people overdo it and flunk out. But those relatively benign consequences of college life were not what 21-year-old University of Texas pre-med student Mark James Kilroy faced at the hands of a group known as Los Narcosatánicos the night he went out to party with his college buddies over the border in Mexico.

Brownsville, Texas, is a city of around 180,000 people. It sits on the southernmost tip of the western gulf coast of the Friendship State. The city's founding occurred during the Mexican–American War, which raged between 1846 and 1848. According to the city's website, Brownsville was an essential city to the South during the

Civil War. They called it "the back door to the Confederacy," as it kept the rebel trade routes open. Because of its proximity to Mexico, Confederate goods, like cotton, could easily be taken over the border and shipped from Mexican ports that were not under Union blockade.

Brownsville has a semi-tropical climate with mild winters and hot, humid summers, making it the perfect spring break destination for partiers since the 1930s. College students flock to the city looking to blow off the steam of two hard-fought semesters and clear their heads before the push to final exams for the year. The younger students, not yet 21 and old enough to drink, can cross over a bridge into Matamoros, Mexico, where the drinking age is only 16, and party with their older classmates legally.

The city of Matamoros in the Mexican state of Tamaulipas is officially called Heroica Matamoros. The city's metro population of almost 1.4 million people dwarfs Brownsville, just across the winding Rio Grande. Matamoros is the fourth-largest Mexican city on the U.S.-Mexico border. International trade, especially with the United States, is its lifeblood because the city is home to parts factories for numerous automobile companies. As well as legitimate trade, the city is also known to be the current home of the CDG, Cártel del Golfo, or, in English, the Gulf Cartel, a violent criminal organization and drug smuggling syndicate with ties to many nations, including the United States.

A 2019 report by the U.S. Department of State's Overseas Security Advisory Council advises Americans to stay out of Tamaulipas because it is a hotbed for crime. Tourists are at serious risk of becoming victims of violent crime in Matamoros, including murder, armed robbery, carjacking, kidnapping, extortion and sexual assault. Gang activity, including gun battles and blockades, is widespread. Armed criminal groups are known to target public and private passenger buses and cars travelling through Tamaulipas, often taking passengers hostage and demanding ransom payments. Mexican federal and state security forces have limited capability to respond to violence in many parts of the state.

There were no such warnings in 1989, when Mark Kilroy and his pals crossed the bridge into Matamoros, even though there should have been. Businesses in the city liked the injection of cash they received from the kids every spring. Issuing warnings would rock the boat and scare people off. Unknown to the party animals, Matamoros had clocked a staggering 60 unsolved homicides in the first 10 weeks of the year. However, awareness of that fact would most likely not have stemmed the tide of young American adults looking to whoop it up in the country.

Mark Kilroy and his three friends had been planning their spring break trip over the phone for months. Bradley Moore, a Texas A&M sophomore in electrical engineering, left his home in Bryan, Texas, in his Mustang around noon on March 10, 1989, making his way west 160 kilometres (100 miles) to Austin, where he picked up Mark. From there, it was a 320-kilometre (200 mile) drive to their hometown, Santa Fe, where they connected with another pair of long-time friends, their high school buddies Brent Martin and Bill Huddleston. They were in Brent's Cutlass and followed Bradley's Mustang. After Santa Fe, it was a 640-kilometre (400 mile) drive south to their destination, South Padre Island, a resort community just outside Brownsville, right on the coast.

The two cars drove through the night, not wanting to lose a day of spring break to something as silly as sleep. After the long drive, the young Texans arrived at the Sheraton hotel and checked in. They scarfed down some food and cleaned off the dust of the trip with a shower, and then it was off to the beach to ogle girls and, hopefully, get lucky.

On the evening of March 13, 1989, the group decided to go across the border. The four young men parked Brent's car in

Brownsville, excitedly walked the international bridge across the storied Rio Grande and found themselves in Mexico within minutes. They were looking forward to what they thought would be a night of drinking cheap margaritas and hitting on drunk American female coeds in the crowded Matamoros saloons, which were bursting at the seams with wild young gringos all there for the same reasons.

At around 2:00 a.m., as the fun was winding down, the four decided to make their way back across the bridge to Brownsville. Bradley and Brent walked ahead. Mark and Bill walked together behind them. Bill went to take a leak behind a tree while Mark waited for him near the road, but when Bill returned, Mark was gone. Thinking his pal had gone ahead to catch up with the other two, Bill ran to catch up to them. But Mark was not with Brent and Bradley either. The trio searched for Mark for the next two and a half hours but could not find him.

The three then considered that Mark might have taken another route, bypassing them, and had made it across the border on his own. They returned to Brent's car, but Mark was not there either. After waiting a while, the young men decided to return to their hotel. Maybe Mark had made it back there. On arriving at the Sheraton, it was clear Mark had not returned. The room was exactly how they had left it.

The three friends got a few hours of sleep, and when there was still no sign of Mark by the time they got up, they called the police. The authorities had heard this story before. Students "vanished" in Matamoros all the time, only to turn up bleary-eyed and hungover hours later, having passed out in an alleyway or under a tree.

But Mark did not return, and the search for him ramped up on both sides of the border. The case drew more attention than other disappearances in Matamoros earlier that year. Since the disappearance of an American tourist was terrible for business, Matamoros police initially denied it had happened on their side of the border. Eventually, they relented when Mark's uncle, a U.S. Customs official in California, became involved and threw his weight behind the search for his nephew. American officials accompanied by Mexican authorities interviewed people on the Mexican side of the border, while the sheriff's department in Brownsville scoured the U.S. side for clues.

Mark Kilroy's parents were active in searching for their son, travelling to the area and personally handing out 20,000 pamphlets with Mark's identifying information on them. Mark's worried parents made sure they had the ears of Attorney General Jim Mattox, Texas governor William Clements, and U.S. Senator Lloyd Bentsen to give weight to their search efforts and apply more pressure on the reluctant Mexican officials.

The popular true crime TV show *America's Most Wanted* featured Mark's disappearance on a March 26 broadcast segment, less than two weeks after he vanished. There were tips by phone and mail, but nothing concrete. His parents offered a reward of $15,000 for help finding their son. When the Kilroys returned home the next week, donations raised by the Santa Fe community kept the search going.

Matamoros police had roughly interrogated 127 known criminals in the area. Police indicated that Mark might have met with foul play, but not many specifics were uncovered during the initial investigation. There were no solid leads, only rumours about what might have happened to the pre-med student.

A break in the case came on April 1, 1989. A man driving a dusty, beat-up pickup truck had driven right past a police checkpoint. Police caught a glimpse of the man as he sped by without giving them a look. It was 20-year-old Serafin Hernandez Garcia. Garcia was well known to the cops as a local drug lord's nephew and had just crossed the U.S.-Mexico border. The *federales* tailed him, unseen, in an unmarked vehicle, and Garcia led them to a remote, rundown ranch 32 kilometres (20 miles) west of Matamoros.

The officers hung back and watched Serafin. He went in and out of a couple of buildings on the ranch, which seemed otherwise deserted. The man hopped back into his truck after only a few minutes. Once he had driven out of sight, the police went onto the property, looking around at what they could see out in the open. They found evidence leading them to believe there may have been a marijuana smuggling operation there. But there were some more disturbing finds as well. The police discovered what appeared to be an occult statue made of cement. It had a sinister-looking pointed head that was pear-like. Seashells formed its eyes, mouth and nose.

The officers left the ranch and took their findings to their superiors. It was decided to go back with a search warrant so they could investigate thoroughly and make some arrests. Cops suspected that marijuana and possibly other forms of narcotics were being stored at the ranch for smuggling across the international border. When they went back on April 9, they found evidence confirming the drug smuggling suspicions and revealing that more malevolent events had gone on there.

As police stormed the ranch, they apprehended Serafin Hernandez Garcia and his compatriot, David Serna Valdez, another well-known drug dealer. Investigators searched the ranch buildings, inside and out, and began finding drugs and more evidence of smuggling. They found 30 kilos (66 pounds) of marijuana in one of the buildings. That alone was enough to send Garcia and Valdez away for a long time, but the pair were defiant.

The behaviour of both prisoners unsettled the arresting officers. They acted like they did not have a care in the world. They told police they would be out soon, that they were "protected" and untouchable. Garcia's explanation was disturbing. He said his boss, Adolfo de Jesús Constanzo, el Padrino (the Godfather), was a powerful occult priest and an influential cult leader. Serafin said that el Padrino had used human sacrifice to protect himself and his followers and bring success in their drug smuggling efforts and other areas of their lives. Constanzo even claimed the rituals would make his followers immune to bullets.

In his teens, Adolfo Constanzo, 26, an American of Cuban background born in Miami, Florida, became an apprentice to a Miami sorcerer. The sorcerer introduced him to a religion called Palo Mayombe, a secretive ancient religion brought to Cuba by Congolese slaves. The practice is known for its dark rituals, sometimes involving animal and human remains, often obtained through grave robbing. The young cultist made a business of casting spells, using animal sacrifice, for drug dealers looking for protection. It was in Miami that he became involved in the lucrative drug trade, eventually aligning himself with big players on both sides of the U.S.-Mexico border, which eventually led him to Matamoros.

In jail, Serafin admitted that Constanzo had ordered him and three others to find and kidnap a young gringo and bring him back to the ranch for sacrifice. Constanzo said he needed help from the evil gods to safely move the 360 kilograms (800 pounds) of marijuana they had stolen from a rival group.

The group went into Matamoros on March 13 with their grim task in mind. They chose Mark Kilroy at random when they saw him standing by the road alone, where he was waiting for Bill Huddleston to finishing relieving himself. They pulled over their king cab pickup truck and dragged Kilroy inside. Mark escaped at one point, but the men ran him down and recaptured him. They bound and blindfolded him, then used back alleys to get out of Matamoros to the ranch.

Mark was held there until the next day, when el Padrino returned, pleased to find his men had done as he had asked. The cult, consisting of at least 14 members led by Adolfo Constanzo, stripped

Mark Kilroy naked and dragged him into the shed to the shrine where they worshipped Kadiempembe, the Palo Mayombe version of Satan. Mark was brutalized for hours there. Constanzo led the attack, beating, torturing, mutilating and sodomizing the young man over and over. Mark's suffering ended when Constanzo cleaved his skull with a machete, offering the pre-med student's brain as a sacrifice in his cauldron, called a *nganga*.

Mark Kilroy's death had not been the group's first human sacrifice. There had been others over the years, mostly transient Mexican nationals, but this was the first time they had taken an American. Constanzo believed that American brains were more potent in a sacrifice. He had been surprised when such a racket had arisen after Kilroy's disappearance. The spell had not worked as intended.

The *federales* asked Serafin where Constanzo was now. They had not picked him up in the raid. Garcia said that Constanzo and his girlfriend, co-cult leader and high priestess Sara Maria Aldrete Villareal, aka el Madrina (the Godmother), had somehow been made aware that the raid was about to happen and took off before it went down. Serafin believed no one would ever discover the pair because they were "untouchable." As a result, he did not think it was essential to cover up evidence, so he agreed to show investigators where he and the others had buried the bodies.

The devout Catholic *federales* searching the ranch confirmed Serafin's claims. They crossed themselves for protection on finding what they believed to be a shrine to the devil in a shed on the property. The shed smelled awful and was adorned with melted candles, and on the floor and outside, they found other items used in dark rituals, including bottles and cauldrons filled with unidentified substances.

It was clear to them that *brujos* (witches) had been practising black magic there. If that indeed was the case, this place was evil and possibly haunted by malevolent spirits. The police investigators refused to search any further until the higher-ups brought in a priest to rid the ranch of the sinister energy that might put their souls at risk.

The police *commandante* called on an Indigenous shaman specializing in cleansing places of evil, called a *curandero,* and he performed rituals to banish the demonic forces infesting the buildings. The terrified Mexican investigators returned to the site only after the *curandero* proclaimed the scene safe. Serafin, in cuffs, led investigators from spot to spot, pointing out gruesome evidence and giddily regaling them with stories about what had taken place there. He did not show a hint of remorse.

On April 11, Serafin showed the investigators, sick from the stench, the high priest's *nganga* and told them this was where Mark Kilroy's brain now lived. The stinking cauldron was full of sticks, bones and rotting flesh. The murder weapon, Constanzo's bloody machete, lay on the floor nearby, again highlighting the murderers' arrogance. They believed they were protected and had no cause to hide the evidence of their crimes.

Serafin then led them to a nearby corral, where several mounds of loose dirt resembled graves, some more freshly dug than others. The prisoner pointed to the pile of earth that appeared to be the most recent and told them that was where Mark Kilroy's remains lay. The exhumations began right away. Over the next six days, the butchered remains of 15 victims, including Mark Kilroy, were unearthed in two spots. There had been 12 victims in the corral alone.

The hunt for Constanzo, Sara Aldrete and the rest of the dangerous cult was now in full swing. On the same day that the police were exhuming the first bodies, Constanzo and a few other cult members had escaped the country. He had simply gone back across the United States border. He could be anywhere by now.

Three weeks later, in Mexico City, police were canvassing a neighbourhood investigating an unrelated crime, a child's disappearance.

Constanzo saw the lawmen outside the window of the apartment he was holed up in and believed they were there for him. He began firing at the officers with a machine gun, injuring one of them.

Almost 200 police surrounded the apartment block and exchanged sporadic gunfire for nearly an hour with the suspects barricaded inside. The gunfire finally stopped. Constanzo had convinced one of his followers to shoot him dead to avoid prison. After their leader died, the rest of the members, including Sara Maria Aldrete, surrendered.

Fourteen cult members were charged with and convicted of murder and various other crimes. They received sentences ranging from 30 to 60 years. None seem ashamed of their involvement in the horrific crimes, and some have denied participation in the murders. In a 2003 interview Sara Aldrete, serving her own 60-year sentence, told a Spanish-language newspaper, "I believe in God. I am calm because, before the law of God and the law of man, I have neither killed nor committed an act against anyone [and] I'm [not] going to bend over or ask for forgiveness for these things." The Kilroy family and the U.S. government have plans to prosecute Aldrete in the United States if she ever gains her freedom from a Mexican prison, but that doesn't look very likely.

In the years since this sensational case, students have continued to cross the border and party in Mexico.

Chapter 19

CHILDREN OF THUNDER

Glenn Taylor Helzer, a self-described prophet, had an idea. He wanted to take over the Mormon church by overthrowing the current leadership. But first, Helzer needed to make some quick cash to help with his goal. In summer 2000, employing his younger brother, Justin, and a handful of other minions to assist him, the group, who called themselves the Children of Thunder, went on a crime spree in Contra Costa County, California, that ultimately left five people dead, including the daughter of a well-known musician.

Decades earlier, Gerry Helzer, an insurance salesman, was excited when he found out that his wife, Carma Helzer, was expecting a baby. They were both devout Mormons, belonging to the Church of Jesus Christ of Latter-day Saints (LDS), and raising a healthy, happy family was something they aspired to. Their first child, Glenn Taylor Helzer, was born on July 26, 1970. The little boy, whom everyone referred to by his middle name, Taylor, quickly became the star of the family. They moved around a lot, finally putting down roots in a small town in California called Pacheco, which is about 48 kilometres (30 miles) outside San Francisco.

Gerry and Carma doted on their son even after his brother, Justin, was born, followed by his sister. People described them as friendly, normal kids.

Taylor was smart and charismatic early on. The local church leaders noted that his uncanny understanding and penchant for memorizing scripture of the Book of Mormon would see him rise to do great things for the church one day. Carma Helzer believed her son was a prophet.

Taylor was the family's golden boy. He was tall, athletic and good-looking as a teen. He loved the attention from his parents and had a huge ego and sense of entitlement. Julia Scheeres wrote in a TruTV.com article that Taylor often reminded his younger brother, "I'm No. 1, and you're No. 2."

Like many teens, however, Taylor was not without his problems. He once became suicidally depressed. Feeling himself an irredeemable sinner after an act of masturbation, Taylor attempted to kill himself. His worried parents sent him to a psychiatrist.

Still only 14 years old, Taylor began showing further signs of psychosis and other psychological problems. The teen believed he was a spiritual conduit and was receiving messages from higher beings. Taylor's mother, ignoring her son's possible mental health problems, told him he possessed the gift of revelation. Taylor said he was unsure about the source of the spiritual communication but admitted that, many times, the voices said evil things.

A few years later, Taylor had his eye on a mission, as every good young Mormon does. The website for the Church of Jesus Christ of Latter-day Saints says a mission is "a period of volunteer service, usually ranging from six to 24 months, when Church members devote themselves part-time or full-time to proselytizing, humanitarian assistance or other service," often in another country. Taylor decided to travel to Brazil, where he would carry the church's message and preach from the Book of Mormon as told to him by what he now called "Spirit," an internal voice that communicated with him regularly, leading him in his daily affairs.

When not ministering to the Brazilian masses, Taylor would pore over the Book of Mormon, looking for understanding and guidance from Spirit, which he wrote about at length in his journals. Others involved with Taylor at the time began to notice drastic changes in him. His mood began to darken, and he soured on the Brazilians, whom he believed would claim Christ with him, then go right back to their "unclean ways" when he was not around.

Latter-day Saints believe the world is currently in the final days before Christ's return, when he will rid the Earth of sin. Taylor prayed for this to happen soon and slowly began to believe it was up to him to help bring this prophecy about. He also developed a resentment toward the church's leadership in Utah, and his beliefs began to take on a more twisted and apocalyptic tone. If anyone disagreed with him, he would become agitated and criticize them as unsalvageable sinners who were not worth his efforts.

When Taylor came home from Brazil, he rekindled a relationship with a young woman named Ann. Although she was not a Mormon, Taylor was in love with her, and the two were married in 1993 and had a daughter soon after. After the birth of their daughter, thanks to Ann's uncle, Taylor got a job as a financial advisor trainee at Morgan Stanley Dean Witter. There, he began putting his charisma to use, and his portfolio quickly ballooned to more than 200 clients. Over the next few years, though, Taylor's typically smart appearance started to decline. His pressed white shirts and ties and clean slacks turned into rumpled T-shirts and jeans. He took up smoking and began spending late nights at local nightclubs, where he drank until closing time. He also started missing work and client meetings without any prior notification.

According to Robert Scott's book *Unholy Sacrifice*, by 1996, Taylor was drinking heavily, and a year later, he was smoking marijuana and had taken other drugs like cocaine, mushrooms and ecstasy. He would not come home for weeks, and Ann began to get tired of his behaviour. She was even scared to leave him alone with his daughter, because his behaviour had become so unpredictable and irresponsible.

Eventually, Taylor left Ann and moved back in with his parents and his brother, Justin. After a short time in the family home, the brothers cleared out and moved into their own place. Even though Taylor and Ann were separated, their relationship continued, and she became pregnant again, giving birth to their second daughter in March 1998. Despite the new child, Taylor kept drinking, taking drugs and carousing with other women.

Taylor's family and members of the LDS church finally decided to reach out to him, offering help, but he declined their offers. He had become disenchanted with the leadership of the church because he felt the current elders were steering the church in the wrong direction. Taylor told his friends he was disturbed by how far from the original mission the LDS church had strayed, and that he felt betrayed by the church he had given so much to. Taylor declared he was finished with the old church and was starting his own religion. He wanted to study and conduct his life with Spirit leading him, so he left the stock brokerage firm, feigned a bipolar disorder and began receiving support cheques from the government.

Taylor's absence from his job was supposed to be temporary, but in March 1999, when his psychologist believed he should be ready to return to work, Taylor intentionally went off his meds. He convinced a girlfriend to call the doctor and arrange an emergency appointment. Taylor faked his way into a psychiatric facility for a short stay and staved off his return to work so he could continue planning his new religion and plotting revenge against the LDS leadership. He claimed that Spirit had told him he was a prophet with important work to do.

Despite his strong feelings against the church, Taylor and Justin were still going to the occasional church function, perhaps to attract followers to their beliefs and keep their enemies close. The brothers would show up dressed strangely in all black with long coats. The Helzer brothers stuck out like a sore thumb at these gatherings, where the clean-cut and devout Mormons looked sideways at them. At one of these events, a murder mystery dinner, the brothers met 26-year-old Dawn Godman.

Dawn was a bit of an oddball and an outcast herself. She started dating Justin but then became infatuated with Taylor. Soon she moved into the house the brothers shared. Taylor began ministering to Dawn, and their little cult began to take shape.

Taylor developed a bizarre and twisted belief system, one that was built on his desire to fulfill the prophecies he claimed he received from Spirit. At the centre of his new religion was his theory that good and evil were flawed and primitive ideas created by man, not God. So for Taylor, there ceased to be a concept of right and wrong.

Taylor preached to the followers of his little cult, Dawn and Justin, often while he was stoned. He believed that anything he needed to do to achieve what he wanted was right and just, including extortion, blackmail, drug sales, prostitution and even murder. In his mind, all these activities were righteous.

The small group decided to call themselves the Children of Thunder. Taylor also wanted to start a new self-help group he referred to alternately as Impact America and Transform America. His fantastical plan was that the self-help group would ultimately defeat Satan and prove Taylor's place as a prophet of God, and it would do so by laying bare the LDS church's hypocritical beliefs. Taylor's plan was to kill the 15 leaders of the Mormon church using Brazilian orphans he would adopt and then train as assassins.

But Taylor would need lots of money to execute his plan. So Spirit gave Taylor another idea. In his work at the stock brokerage firm, he had developed a long client list. Some of them were sitting on massive portfolios. His idea was to extort money from ex-clients and then kill them to cover up the crimes. Taylor made a list of his first five potential victims.

In late July 2000, Spirit told Taylor the time was right. Taylor told Dawn of the divine plan and that he needed her help to carry out God's wishes. He asked if she was willing to kill someone for the greater good. By this time, Dawn, who was utterly enthralled with the elder Helzer brother, told him she was honoured to be considered for the task and agreed to participate, without reservation.

In truth, Taylor was not remotely interested in Dawn because he had another woman on the side. Selina Bishop and Taylor Helzer had met at a rave in the spring of 2000. She was smitten with the tall, dark, charismatic stranger who called himself Jordan. Twenty-two-year-old Selina was the daughter of famous blues guitarist Elvin Bishop, who sang the 70s hit song "Fooled Around and Fell in Love."

Selina believed she had a new boyfriend, but Taylor only wanted her for one thing—the bank accounts he had convinced her to open for him. Taylor wanted to use those accounts to launder the money he was going to extort from his victims, and after that, he'd do away with Selina too. She was disposable.

Selina bragged about "Jordan" to her family and friends. She said her new beau was about to come into a massive inheritance. Unknown to Selina, at the same time she was singing his praises, Taylor was out buying the large sports bags that he would stuff her body into after her murder.

Taylor had done his best to avoid meeting any of Selina's family and friends, making up excuses to prevent any encounters that would later lead to his identification. Selina's mom, Jennifer

Villarin, knowing "Jordan" would be at her daughter's place one afternoon, faked a reason to come over and meet him. She had no idea that this meeting would seal her own fate and that of her boyfriend, 54-year-old James Gamble.

Meanwhile, Taylor had chosen his first victims. Ivan Stineman, 85, and his wife, Annette, 78, a retired couple, trusted and liked Taylor Helzer. They considered him a family friend. He had helped them with their retirement by managing their substantial stock portfolio at the local branch of Morgan Stanley Dean Witter. They opened the door without a thought when the good-looking Helzer brothers, dressed in their Sunday best, came calling on July 30, 2000. Dawn Godman, driving a pickup truck, waited patiently for the brothers to finish their grim business.

Once the door was closed, Taylor and Justin quickly subdued the older couple, pointing a gun that Justin had purchased the week prior, and bound them with handcuffs and shackles they had bought from a local pornography shop. They loaded the terrified Stinemans into the back of their own van, and Dawn followed the vehicle back to the residence she shared with the brothers, where they would have more privacy.

The trio threatened Annette and demanded she call the brokerage office to liquidate their assets. Then they forced the pair to write out two cheques to Selina Bishop, totalling $100,000, the amount of Taylor's fake inheritance. After the Stinemans complied with the requests, Taylor drugged them with a massive dose of Rohypnol, which is more commonly known as the date rape drug called roofies.

When the pair did not die from the overdose of the date rape drug, Justin bashed Ivan's head on the bathroom floor until he died, while Taylor slit Annette's throat with a hunting knife. Taylor, who claimed he had better things to do, asked his brother to dismember the corpses with power tools. Justin then used a hammer and chisel to destroy the couple's teeth to thwart their identification through dental records.

As Justin went about his business, Taylor retired to his bedroom, where he meditated and communed with Spirit, asking the entity to guide his next move. After Justin finished his work, the group held a small ceremony around the corpses, thanking them for their service to the cause.

Dawn was sent to the bank to deposit the cheques wearing a disguise, including a gold cowboy hat and lime green pantsuit. She also arrived in a wheelchair to garner sympathy. The plan was for her to say she was doing a favour for the Bishop family, as Selina was having emergency surgery. The lie worked and the money was deposited into the bank account.

Now that the money was where Taylor could access it, Selina's services were no longer required. Taylor invited her over and, in his bedroom, offered her a massage. When she flipped over onto her stomach, he pulled out a hammer and bludgeoned her to death. After the murder, Taylor called Dawn Godman into the room. At that point, according to Robert Scott's *Unholy Sacrifice*, Taylor said cryptically, "Spirit says you get to know this isn't a dream," before starting to dismember Selina's body.

To further stump identification efforts, the body parts of the Stinemans and Selina Bishop were mixed together and placed into the duffel bags. The killers weighted down the duffel bags and tossed them into the Sacramento–San Joaquin River Delta using a boat that Dawn had rented.

The day after killing Selina, Taylor had to take care of loose ends. Selina's mother had seen him, and he knew she could identify him. So Taylor and Justin went to Jennifer Villarin's house and shot her and her boyfriend, James Gamble, with Justin's gun. Neighbours heard the shots and called police, but the brothers escaped before the cops arrived.

By that time, the Stinemans had also been reported missing, but it didn't take long to find out what had happened to them. The bags containing the bodies had floated to the surface of the river and began washing up on shore. A man on a Jet Ski discovered one of the bags and called the police. Police quickly connected the dots between the shabbily executed crimes. Glenn Taylor Helzer, 30, Justin Helzer, 28, and Dawn Godman, 26, were tied to the crimes and arrested.

Investigators found a note in the Stineman residence written by Ivan mentioning a meeting with Taylor Helzer. Police also interviewed friends of Selina Bishop who were with her on the night she met the man who had called himself Jordan. Each of Selina's friends identified Helzer as the man in a photo lineup.

Cops also discovered that Taylor owned a 1998 Saturn sedan, and Justin owned a white Nissan pickup. The Saturn was seen near Jennifer Villarin's home on the day of her murder, and witnesses identified the pickup as the one seen in the Stinemans' neighbourhood on the day they vanished. Fingerprints belonging to Justin and Dawn were in the Stinemans' van, which they had later abandoned. Witnesses were able to identify Dawn as the woman in the wheelchair at the bank. Her outfit and odd demeanour were unforgettable.

Dawn struck a deal with prosecutors to save herself from the death penalty. In exchange for her agreement to testify against the Helzer brothers, she was given 25 years to life for the murders and an additional 12 years and eight months on other charges.

It took four years for the case to get to trial. In court, Dawn testified against Justin, who, despite pleading insanity, was found guilty and sentenced to die. He died by suicide, hanging himself in his cell on April 14, 2013. Taylor pleaded guilty on all charges, hoping to save himself from the death penalty, but received a death sentence anyway. He remains on San Quentin's death row, awaiting his execution.

California has not executed anyone since 2006, and there are currently 700 inmates on the state's death row, many ahead of Helzer. He will likely die in jail before his execution is even scheduled.

PART FOUR
Notable Disasters

The disaster stories that follow include some of
the deadliest and most tragic in history.

Chapter 20

THE GREAT INFLUENZA PANDEMIC OF 1918

I nfectious diseases with terror-inducing names like typhus, cholera, polio, yellow fever, smallpox, leprosy, ebola, AIDS, bubonic plague and tuberculosis have killed hundreds of millions over the course of history. The etymology of the word *pandemic* has its roots in Greek: *pan* translates roughly to *all*, while *demos* is the Greek word for *people*.

Some of the world's deadliest pandemics have jaw-dropping numbers. One of the most famous, the Black Death (bubonic plague), ravaged Europe in the mid-1300s. It was spread by disease-ridden fleas on rats, which travelled happily from port to port aboard cargo and passenger ships and killed as many as 200 million people worldwide. At the time, that was almost half of the world's population.

Europeans also brought a plethora of diseases with them when they crossed the Atlantic and landed on the shores of the New World after 1492. At that time, the Indigenous peoples in the Americas had no immunity to diseases common to the Europeans. The worst of these was smallpox, a now eradicated and particularly terrible and painful virus. Smallpox decimated North America's Indigenous communities in the early 1500s, killing more than 50 million people, an estimated 90 percent of the population.

The worst pandemic in modern history, however, began in early 1918. Over the next two years, a virulent strain of influenza known as H1N1 killed more people than had died in World War I, which was slowly grinding to a halt in Europe as the pandemic began. The virus spread rapidly, infecting hundreds of millions of people and killing tens of millions more worldwide.

The word *influenza*, often shortened to *flu*, has its roots in the Italian language and was a word coined by astrologists in the 16th century. They believed the stars influenced some illnesses, because they seemed to appear only at certain times of the year. These scientists had recognized the annual patterns of influenza, which we now know is seasonal. It was another two centuries, after more virus research in the late 1800s, before scientists learned that some viral infections are more prevalent during cooler weather, which is why fall and winter are cold and flu season.

According to the World Health Organization (WHO), seasonal flu is an acute respiratory infection caused by influenza viruses that circulate in all parts of the world. Flu symptoms include a sudden onset of fever, cough (usually dry), headache, muscle and joint pain, severe malaise (feeling unwell), sore throat and a runny nose. The cough can be severe and can last two or more weeks. Most people recover from fever and other symptoms within a week without requiring medical attention. But influenza can also cause severe illness or death, especially in people at high risk, often in people with compromised immune systems or those over 65.

But the flu pandemic of 1918 was not your average seasonal flu. Although the elderly and infirm were vulnerable, they were not the most likely to perish from the virus; it was younger people who seemed at most risk from the disease. Of the fatal cases during the first year of the pandemic, nearly half were people between 20 and 40 years old.

Depending on where you lived at the time, the virus had different names. Although it was commonly called "the Spanish Flu," many experts do not believe the pandemic had its origins in Spain. Spain appeared to have enormous infection rates, but they were no worse than in many other countries. As a neutral non-combatant in the Great War, there was no censorship of Spain's news organizations, so the reports about the flu deaths from that country were particularly prevalent in the media, which led to the perception that it was a "Spanish flu."

Spaniards, however, referred to the illness as "the French Flu," believing that particular strain of influenza had originated in France, their neighbour to the north. The Brazilians called it "the German Flu," but to the Senegalese, it was "the Brazilian Flu." In Poland, they called it "the Bolshevik Disease," with Polish nationals believing the nasty bug originated in Russia. But in truth, no one was sure which country was the real source of the virus. Even today, it's still not clear where the virus originated.

The first officially recorded case of what would become one of the deadliest pandemics in modern history was that of Private Albert Martin Gitchell, a U.S. Army mess cook at Camp Funston in Fort Riley, Kansas. On the morning of March 4, 1918, Gitchell took himself to the base infirmary complaining of fever, body aches, a sore throat, fatigue and a headache. Base medics determined he had a temperature of 40°C (104°F). Believing he had a simple winter flu, doctors admitted Gitchell to the hospital and placed him in a ward reserved for contagious infections. Although some believe the illness had been circulating for months, many still labelled unlucky Private Gitchell as "patient zero" in the global outbreak.

By noon, another 100 soldiers had also become sick. The camp's medical wards filled with the sounds of racking coughs as the infected soldiers attempted to expel the stubborn mucus that quickly filled their lungs. Days later, more than 500 critically ill soldiers packed the hospital at Camp Funston. The flu appeared to cause a severe form of pneumonia that quickly killed otherwise healthy, physically fit young men. The lips and faces of many of the infected turned blue from cyanosis, a lack of oxygenation, as they struggled with the virus. Some flu victims died within a day of contracting the illness.

After the initial wave of influenza ended at Fort Riley, 46 of those first afflicted had died. Private Gitchell narrowly survived his bout with the infection and went on to live a long life, passing away in 1968 at the age of 78.

In the weeks that followed, outbreaks began occurring at other midwestern military installations. From there, it spread to camps to the southeast in Florida, South Carolina, Georgia, Virginia and Alabama. It also headed west, infecting soldiers on bases in California. These camps were enormous, each housing between 25,000 and 55,000 recently drafted recruits. It's believed that the flu spread when massive amounts of people were mobilized and moved around the planet to participate in the Great War.

March was also the month that battalions of U.S. doughboys were shipped out to fight in Europe. More than 80,000 U.S. soldiers boarded troopships that were cramped and poorly ventilated. As they headed off to Europe, the virus travelled with them. Many who believed they were merely seasick fell violently ill on the Atlantic crossing. In April, 100,000 American troops, some sick with the flu, made their way to Europe to fight. Upon arrival in Europe, the soldiers spread the sickness to fellow soldiers trapped in close quarters with them in damp, rat- and lice-infested trenches. Away from the fighting, the soldiers quickly gave the deadly virus to tens of thousands of unsuspecting locals.

Joshua Bryan Lee, a soldier in the U.S. Army's 135th Infantry, 34th Division, found himself stationed in France for 14 months after enlisting in 1917. To pass the time and fight off crushing bore-dom between battles, the young private wrote poems and a journal in a notebook he carried with him. He referred to his writings, later published in a booklet with other soldiers' musings, as the "jottings of a doughboy." Lee, who would later go on to a long, successful career in politics as a member of the national Democratic Party, wrote a poem he titled "The Flu," eloquently capturing his experi-ence during the pandemic. Its first stanza follows:

It stalked into camp
When the day was damp
And chilly and cold.
It crept by the guards
And murdered my pards
With a hand that was clammy
And bony and bold;
And its breath was icy
And mouldy and dank;
And it was so speedy
And gloatingly greedy
That it took away men
From each company rank.

By the end of May, the French Armed Forces were evacuating almost 2,000 influenza-infected soldiers per day from the front to the mobile hospitals set up to the rear. Other Allied forces reported similar numbers.

However, the flu did not take sides in the war. In their muck-filled trenches across no man's land, the German soldiers also became ill from the sickened Allies. They, in turn, spread the virus behind their lines. Between May and July, almost 1,000,000 German soldiers fell ill. In the first half of July, the 6th German

Army, dug in near Alsace, reported a whopping 10,000 cases of flu every day.

The American troops flooded into Europe at a rate of 250,000 a month. After a few key losses and a stark lack of supplies, the German soldiers began to feel discouraged. Now, with the brutal illness ravaging their ranks, they were utterly demoralized. At that point, the Germans had no fight left in them.

On November 11, 1918, in a railcar at Le Francport, near Compiègne, the Germans capitulated and signed the armistice ending hostilities with the Allied nations. World War I was over, but the pandemic had almost two more years to run its course.

Within weeks of the first infections in the United States in March of 1918, nearly every country in all corners of the globe reported cases of this horrible influenza. It spread throughout Asia in April and was present in Africa and most of South America by May. The flu even made it into the isolated prison island, Alcatraz, in San Francisco Bay, by way of guards who returned to the mainland each day after their shifts. According to an article on *Doctor's Review*, by the end of the pandemic, only one major region on the planet had not reported an outbreak: an isolated island called Marajo, located in Brazil's Amazon River Delta.

In September, the second and more deadly wave of the flu ripped across the planet, causing 90 percent of the pandemic's overall fatalities. In the United States, the flu emerged in a Boston Naval installation and at Camp Devens, an Army training camp outside that city, where it infected more than 14,000 and killed 757 by the end of the month.

Authorities discouraged large gatherings and implored people to stay home to help prevent the spread of the virus. Despite the warnings, the flu quickly spread up and down the eastern seaboard and made its way west again. Throughout October, more than 195,000 Americans died of the flu virus.

The war had taken many doctors and nurses overseas, but now the flu sidelined or killed many of those left, leaving medical centres woefully understaffed. Hospitals were overwhelmed, and medical authorities told patients with the flu to stay at home and isolate themselves. Multiple jurisdictions put out calls for volunteers because there were too many sick people for the hospitals to treat. Most civilians, however, fearing for their own lives, did not take up the call.

As the virus raged, children in the English-speaking world recited a grim rhyme by an unknown author as they jumped rope together:

I had a little bird,
Its name was Enza.
I opened the window And in flew Enza!

Throughout the pandemic, the average life expectancy in the United States plummeted by more than 12 years. Many of the country's large, crowded cities did not fare well. In Boston, 100 of every 1,000 residents died. In Washington, D.C., the death rate was 109 for every 1,000, while neighbouring Baltimore saw 148 deaths per 1,000 residents. Philadelphia fared the worst, as 158 of every 1,000 residents died from flu. By the end of the pandemic, about 675,000 Americans had died of the virus.

More than 50,000 Canadians died of flu during the pandemic, in addition to the 60,000 who lost their lives in the war. Many of the dead were the primary wage earners in their families. Thousands of Canadian children found themselves orphaned after both parents succumbed to the virus, and the impact of the pandemic on the country's economy was immense. In response to the flu epidemic, Canada created the federal Department of Health in 1919.

In Japan 390,000 died, in Britain 250,000 perished and in France 400,000 succumbed to the illness, while in Russia the virus killed an estimated 450,000 people. The death rate in India was, by a large margin, the highest, killing 5 percent of the population, at least 12 million Indian citizens.

Undertakers were overwhelmed by the sudden demand to bury bodies. In Monica Schoch-Spana's 2000 study titled "Implications of Pandemic Influenza for Bioterrorism Response" in the journal *Clinical Infectious Diseases*, she described the situation that funeral workers faced. At the height of the pandemic, the bodies were coming so quickly that gravediggers and undertakers were over-whelmed. Because of shortages of workers, coffins and grave plots, families had to keep their deceased loved ones at home, unburied, far longer than was typical. Morgues were overflowing with bodies, sometimes 10 times more than was ordinary. Woodworkers toiled day and night to keep up with the demand for caskets.

The virus did not discriminate; the powerful, wealthy and famous were not immune. Every demographic that the flu hit suffered fatalities. Famed Canadian physician and co-founder of Johns Hopkins Hospital William Osler died after exposure to the virus. Recently re-elected Brazilian president Francisco de Paula Rodrigues Alves died on January 16, 1919, days before he was to resume office. Frederick Trump, the grandfather of 45th U.S. pres-ident Donald Trump, died on May 30, 1918, during the first wave of the illness.

There were notable survivors, many of whom went on to do great things. Among them were budding cartoonist Walt Disney, Canadian-born star of silent film Mary Pickford and future U.S. president Franklin D. Roosevelt, who would see that country through the bulk of the next world war. President Woodrow Wil-son was said to have been sick from the virus and nearly collapsed during the signing of the Treaty of Versailles in 1919. He survived the flu but died five years later after ill health prevented him from running for a third term.

What made this influenza so different from the average flu? Because the virus was new, or "novel," as scientists now refer to an infection they have never seen before, there was no immunity. Everyone on the planet was susceptible, whether they were healthy or not, which accounts for the virility and high mortality rate of the 1918 flu. Doctors at the time also had no access to antiviral drugs or the vaccines we have today.

Once enough people had become sick from the four waves of deadly influenza, the world's population began developing immunity. Finally, in 1920, the pandemic sputtered to a stop. Since then, there have been other influenza pandemics, although none have been so devastating.

Right now, a hundred years later, the world is in the midst of a new pandemic. After its discovery in December 2019 in Hubei province in China, the highly infectious novel coronavirus (2019-nCoV, or COVID-19) spread rapidly, with the number of cases doubling every week. China, not wanting to damage its economy, waited too long to react to the virus, and the disease escaped over the border. In March 2020, the World Health Organization declared a global pandemic.

The tourism industry suffered a financial drought like none other before as countries, fearing COVID-19 infections, closed their borders to foreign visitors. First travel was closed from countries with high infection rates, then to all travellers. Many countries and provinces instituted states of emergency, giving special powers to health officials, who were now guiding the government and public through the pandemic. North American doctors feared that the further spread of the virus, which quickly overwhelmed hospitals in places like Italy and Spain, would put enormous pressure on underfunded medical systems. Officials told people to stay home. Businesses temporarily closed, and millions of non-essential workers lost their jobs, requiring countries to provide financial aid to their now suddenly unemployed citizens.

As of mid-July 2021, COVID-19 has infected more than 190 million people in 220 countries and territories worldwide. It has killed more than 4 million people, and, thankfully, more than 175 million people have recovered. Vaccines have arrived and are being administered, yet the infection numbers are still on the rise as new variants of the disease take hold.

Perhaps the most significant impact of the pandemic has been psychological. After months of enduring the endless pressures of fear, confusion, social isolation and financial difficulties due to high unemployment rates, some of the darker aspects of humanity are on the rise. Things like racist rhetoric and violence have increased, as have domestic violence and suicidal depression.

The pandemic of 1918 happened more than a century ago, but it did teach us a few things we are applying today to help stem the spread of COVID-19. Many of us are paying attention to health officials, washing our hands, wearing masks, staying away from large gatherings and trying not to touch our faces too much. Since the pandemic continues at the writing of this book, it's impossible to say when the deadly COVID virus will finally begin to dissipate.

Chapter 21

THE ERUPTION OF MOUNT ST. HELENS

On May 18, 1980, Mount St. Helens, a volcano in Washington State about 155 kilometres (95 miles) south of Seattle and 90 kilometres (55 miles) north of Portland, Oregon, spectacularly blew its top. The blast killed more than 50 people in the area, including children. American news organizations documented the aftermath of the explosion in heartbreaking detail. One particular wire service photograph taken from the air above the devastation showed the ash-covered body of a young boy, spread-eagle and face up in the back of an ash-covered pickup truck that had been wrecked by the blast. The images are haunting.

Inside the Gifford Pinchot National Forest, Mount St. Helens belongs to the large group of volcanoes making up the international Pacific Ring of Fire. St. Helens is one of 20 major volcanoes along the Cascade Volcanic Arc, which stretches over 1,100 kilometres (680 miles) from British Columbia south through Washington and Oregon and continuing into Northern California. The chain is a part of the Cascadia subduction zone, where three tectonic plates—Explorer, Juan de Fuca and Gorda—slide underneath the massive North American continental plate, creating friction that produces regular seismic activity in the region.

Mount St. Helens was named by Captain George Vancouver in 1792 to honour his friend, the British ambassador to the Court of Madrid, Alleyne FitzHerbert, whose title was Baron St. Helens. The Europeans did not recognize St. Helens as a volcano until 1835, even though the local Indigenous people knew better. They had named it long before Captain Vancouver, calling it Lawet-lat'la, which roughly translated means "the smoker" or "smoking mountain."

Dormant for more than 120 years, on March 16, 1980, Mount St. Helens rumbled back to life with a series of minor earthquakes. Over the next 11 days, a swarm of hundreds of earthquakes indicated to geologists at the United States Geological Survey (USGS) that an eruption was imminent. On March 27, the volcano erupted and a series of steam explosions threw ash as high as 60 to 75 metres (200 to 250 feet) into the air, blasting their way through the century of ice and snow built up on top of the mountain. An enormous crater appeared at the peak, growing to more than 400 metres (1,300 feet) across.

Since the 1700s, there have been six eruptions of Cascade-region volcanoes, making the area quite active in geological terms. With more than 10 million people living in major Pacific Northwest cities close to these rumbling behemoths, geologists had warned people about the possibility of a cataclysmic seismic upheaval in the region. However, geological time is hard to wrap one's mind around, so volcano warnings often go unheeded.

Mount St. Helens had not shown any significant activity since the 1800s, when there were a couple of decades of rumbling and small eruptions releasing ash and steam. Geologists knew there had been massive eruptions in the mountain's past, including one in 1482 that rivalled the 1980 blast. But that was a long time ago in human years. No one alive had ever seen the volcano active, and it didn't seem to pose a danger. There had been no significant volcanic eruptions in continental North America for decades. The big volcanic blasts always seemed to happen elsewhere, like Japan and New Zealand, but never so close to home.

This kind of "it won't ever happen to me" thinking seems to be one of the factors leading to the significant number of deaths after the Mount St. Helens blast. There were plenty of warnings given, but rather than leave the area and travel toward safety, some people did the opposite and decided to visit the mountain. Some were geologists and volcanologists, both amateur and professional. Many onlookers were drawn by the desire to witness what might be a once in a lifetime event; still others were just in the wrong place at the wrong time. Probably the saddest of all the unfortunate deaths that day were those residents of the region who refused to leave all they had behind, choosing instead to ride out the possible eruption like a captain wanting to go down with the ship.

For scientists observing the volcano, it soon became evident that a cataclysmic seismic event was imminent, but the scope of what might occur would not be known with any certainty until it happened. Acting on advice from geologists, in mid-April, the National Forest Service set up two safety hazard zones around the mountain. The red zone was the region scientists felt most likely to suffer catastrophic damage, including loss of life; this "no-go" zone encompassed the regions immediately to the north and east of the smoking crater. Only law enforcement and scientists involved in the study of the mountain had permission to be in that zone until the danger subsided.

The Washington Department of Emergency Services closed off the U.S. Forest Service roads in the vicinity, advising people that the area within a 24-kilometre (15 mile) radius of the volcano was unsafe. All people were to evacuate the area immediately. Around 300 loggers and support staff employed by Weyerhaeuser Company were among those told to leave, but the corporation threw its weight around, refusing to leave its land; there was a lot of money at stake. The company said they would take their investments to another state if they were forced to leave, so Washington worked out a deal that allowed them to stay.

An article from *American Scientist* at the time explained the restrictions in the area: "The blue zone extended to the southwest of the red zone; there, loggers and property owners could come and go during the daytime if they had permission. To the west and northwest of these zones sat prime Weyerhaeuser timberland. The Forest Service had no intention of restricting the lumber company's property and alienating the powerful employer."

The majority of residents within the red zone, which was presumed to be the area that would take the most damage, complied with the evacuation orders, as did those working there. One man, though, made a point of refusing to leave.

Harry R. Truman, 83, was no relation to his namesake, the famous U.S. president Harry S. Truman. For 54 years, Truman, a former bootlegger and veteran of World War I, lived with his many cats in a lodge he had built on his camping resort on the edge of Spirit Lake, which was inside the red zone. He had divorced one wife and outlived another and was well known locally as a colourful character with a salty tongue.

At the end of March 1980, omnipresent whiskey and Coke in his hand, Truman famously told a UPI reporter, "I ain't leaving. I've walked that mountain for 50 years. I know her. If it erupts with lava, it's not going to me at Spirit Lake. Those geologists might know something about the inside of the mountain, but I know her contours. If this place is gonna go, I want to go with it, 'cause if I lost it, it would kill me in a week anyway." Harry told other news reporters that he believed the whole thing was a big story cooked up by the authorities to make trouble for him. He thought it was all a ruse to pry him away from his property.

Harry became a national folk hero for his vocal refusals to leave his home. But rather than engaging in an unpopular public and potentially expensive legal battle with the old guy, authorities decided the best course of action was to officially warn Truman about the hazards he faced if he stayed and then leave him alone. Harry listened to what the officials had to say, and when they finished, he thanked them and walked back into his lodge with a friendly wave.

When the first eruptions started, they were hourly at first, slowing over the next month to daily eruptions. Children and adults all over the world sat glued to nightly news broadcasts from the mountain as the public waited anxiously to see what would happen. A few locals called the whole thing a farce, stating the volcano was an overpublicized joke. Then, on April 22, the eruptions and quakes abruptly stopped. To the untrained eye, the event appeared to be over. Some folks, wanting more fireworks, were disappointed that the mountain had not put on a better show. But volcanologists predicted that this time of calm was just the start of a more considerable period of activity. They were right.

On May 7, the needles on local seismometers sprang back to life, bouncing back and forth on their graph paper, drawing lines indicating a new swarm of small earthquakes centred under and around the volcano. In the next 10 days, more than 10,000 small earthquakes rocked the region. The mountain began to bulge outward more than 2 metres (6.5 feet) per day on its northern flank, as though about to give birth. By May 17, the north side of the mountain had ballooned outward by some 140 metres (460 feet). Cracks all over the mountain were growing by the minute. A few volcanologists predicted that a catastrophic eruption was about to occur at Mount St. Helens.

On Sunday, May 18, at 8:32 a.m., it happened, and it was far worse than had been predicted. It started with an earthquake measuring 5.1 on the Richter scale about 1.5 kilometres (1 mile) beneath the mountain. As the ground shook, the bulging north side of the mountain let go in a massive landslide, which, according to the USGS, was "the largest debris avalanche on Earth in recorded history." Seconds later, as the pressure of the magma built up inside the volcano, it finally let go and there was a massive lateral blast.

A 1990 report from the U.S. Geological Survey described the power of the eruption, indicating that debris from the blast accelerated from an initial speed of 355 kilometres per hour (220 miles per hour) to 1,080 kilometres per hour (670 miles per hour), nearly the speed of sound.

Chicago-born volcanologist David Johnston, a member of the USGS, had set up his instruments and watched the mountain from a camp called Coldwater II, in the blue zone close to the border of the red zone. Since he lost his life that day, it is unknown whether Johnston first felt or saw the eruption. All that can be proven is that he knew it was happening. The instant the landslide began, David yelled into his radio his famous last words: "Vancouver! Vancouver! This is it!"

Gerry Martin, a 64-year-old volunteer ham radio operator with the Radio Amateur Civil Emergency Service, watched from outside his motorhome on a ridge above Coldwater II, a few kilometres to the north, as the eruption began. He saw the debris field quickly overtake Johnston's position. His last words were "Gentlemen, the camper and car that's sitting over to the south of me is covered. It's going to hit me too."

The lateral blast levelled an area more than 20 kilometres (12 miles) north of Mount St. Helens and spanned east to west almost 30 kilometres (19 miles). Within 10 kilometres (6 miles) of the explosion, what used to be a majestic forest was decimated.

Beyond the initial blast zone, millions of once-proud evergreen trees lay like matchsticks, singed black and mostly stripped of their needles, their tops pointed away from the mighty wind that had blown them down. Even trees just beyond the blast area did not make out unscathed. The heat of the blast seared their bark and removed any green they had on them. A field of debris flung outward by the explosion covered more than 600 square kilometres (148,000 acres).

High above the volcano, at a safe vantage point, Keith Stoffel and his wife, Dorothy, both professional geologists, had been in the air for just over 40 minutes, flying in a small chartered aircraft taking photos, when the eruption began. Stoffel later described what he saw in a Department of Natural Resources circular, noting that they flew toward the summit at an elevation of around 3,400 metres (11,000 feet). First they witnessed landslides of ice and rock falling into the crater. As they circled for a better look, the entire north side of the mountain let go and began sliding toward Spirit Lake in one large mass. Then the explosion occurred.

The pilot of the plane, Bruce Judson of Executive Aircraft, had to act fast, throttling the light aircraft up to 320 kilometres per hour (200 miles per hour) to outrun the dark grey cloud of toxic gas and ash that began to bear down on them. They flew at top speed toward Mount Hood, looking back at St. Helens as the ash cloud obscured their view. They later landed safely at the Portland Airport. They were lucky.

Within the first 15 minutes of the explosion, the massive plume of ash blown into the atmosphere was more than 24 kilometres (15 miles) high. U.S. Geological Survey Fact Sheet 036-00 describes the scene:

> *Over the course of the day, prevailing winds blew 520 million tons of ash eastward across the United States and caused*

*complete darkness in Spokane, Washington, 400 km (250 mi)
from the volcano. Major ash falls occurred as far away as
central Montana, and ash fell visibly as far eastward as the
Great Plains of the Central United States, more than 1,500
km (930 mi) away. The ash cloud spread across the U.S. in
three days and circled the Earth in 15 days.*

In addition to explosions, lava, and falling rocks and debris, pyroclastic flow threatens the lives of all in its path during a volcanic eruption. The USGS defines pyroclastic flow as a "hot (typically >800°C), chaotic mixture of rock fragments, gas, and ash that travels rapidly (tens of metres per second) away from a volcanic vent or collapsing flow front." In the 1980 blast, the pyroclastic flow spread out for 8 kilometres (5 miles) from the mountain, creating an eerie pumice plane, which made the area look like the surface of the moon or Mars.

An article from Oregon State University's World Volcano website titled "What Were the Effects on People When Mt St Helens Erupted?" described the destruction.

*The Toutle River was flooded by melting snow and ice from
the mountain. About 12 million board feet of stockpiled lumber were swept in the river. Eight bridges were destroyed. 200
homes were destroyed or damaged. Debris dams were added
to help control sediment in the rivers. Thirty logging trucks,
22 transport vehicles, and 39 railcars were damaged or
destroyed along with 4.7 billion board feet of timber. Shipping
was stopped on the Columbia River and some vessels were
stranded. In eastern Washington, falling ash stranded 5,000
motorists. Ash had to be cleared from runways and highways.*

The most tragic tally of the day was the human cost. As many as

57 people died in the eruption. Only three, including Harry Truman, were within the red zone when the eruption occurred. Many of the bodies, including Harry's, were never found because they were buried deep underneath many metres of debris.

An article from *People* magazine interviewed a woman named Barbara Karr, a 37-year-old Seattle schoolteacher, about the death of her son on that day. It was the body of her 11-year-old son, Andy, in the back of the wrecked pickup truck that appeared in the famous photo. Barbara also lost her husband, Day, 37, and her younger son, Michael, 9, in the blast. The boys and their dad were on a father–son weekend and had been camping in the area.

Forty years after the eruption, the crater at Mount St. Helens is still smoking. Small sprigs of green have begun poking through the debris and pumice field, bringing new life to the desolate landscape. At least until the next eruption.

Chapter 22

THE SPACE SHUTTLE
CHALLENGER EXPLOSION

S ince people first noticed the twinkling stars overhead, they have dreamed of exploring and travelling to space. On April 12, 1961, the USSR launched *Vostok 1*, piloted by cosmonaut Yuri Gagarin, the first human ever in space. Astronauts set foot on the moon eight years later, and rocket scientists have landed several remotely piloted rovers on faraway planets over the decades.

Yet human space flight remains a complicated and dangerous endeavour. Since Gagarin's flight, there have been 19 space flight–related fatalities. In five separate incidents, 15 American astronauts and four Russian cosmonauts have perished. Many others have been killed in training-related incidents or massive explosions due to the accidental ignition of highly volatile rocket fuel while still on the ground. One of the most catastrophic, and public, failures happened on January 28, 1986, when the space shuttle *Challenger* exploded just over a minute after lifting off, killing all seven aboard.

The *Challenger* was a go-to shuttle for NASA, and it flew on 85 percent of the shuttle missions. The *Challenger* was also a storied craft, carrying the first Canadian (Mark Garneau), the first Dutch-man (Wubbo Ockels), the first American woman (Sally Ride) and the first African-American (Guion Bluford Jr.) into space.

The doomed shuttle mission in 1986 was no routine launch. The crew of seven astronauts consisted of five men and two women. One of them was a special passenger, the first participant of Ronald Reagan's Teacher in Space Project (TISP), which aimed to spur student interest in mathematics, science and space explo-ration to inspire future astronauts. When the Reagan government announced TISP in 1984, more than 11,000 applications flooded NASA's mailrooms. When the applications were evaluated, two teachers, both women, stood out from all the rest.

The first candidate was Christa McAuliffe, a 37-year-old high school teacher from Concord, New Hampshire, who taught econom-ics, American history, law and a social history course she had devel-oped called "The American Woman." Christa was born in Boston, Massachusetts, on September 2, 1948, and was the oldest of five children. Along with her husband, Steven, Christa was a proud and loving parent of two children, Scott, nine, and Caroline, six.

The second woman chosen was Barbara R. Morgan. Born and raised in Fresno, California, Barbara obtained a BA in human biol-ogy at Stanford before earning her teaching credentials. She taught second, third and fourth grades at McCall-Donnelly Elementary School in Donnelly, Idaho.

The two educators trained alongside grizzled USAF pilots and other experienced astronauts. Ultimately, it was Christa who was chosen to be the designated payload specialist for the ill-fated flight. Morgan would stay behind, acting as Christa's backup for the mission, in case McAuliffe had to pull out at the last moment for one reason or another.

Over the week-long mission, as the *Challenger* was to have orbited the Earth 96 times, McAuliffe was going to teach the first-ever classes from space during two live telecasts. She would also record four other science-based lessons. Many school classrooms worldwide made plans to watch the historic broadcasts.

The first of Christa's lessons from space was titled "The Ultimate Field Trip" and would include a tour of the elaborate flight deck and an introduction to the commander and pilot. She was then to move on to the mid-deck to describe how humans survive in space, highlighting the specialized equipment required to do everyday tasks in microgravity. Her second lesson was a humanities-based lecture involving the other astronauts, using models to highlight the 82-year journey from when the Wright Brothers first flew to the current day, including showing viewers the model of a proposed space station.

Christa became a media darling in the lead-up to the launch. She began making the rounds on television talk shows and appeared on all three major U.S. networks' morning shows. Six months before the launch, McAuliffe had a seat in one of the most famous chairs on television, next to Johnny Carson for a segment on *The Tonight Show*.

Alongside McAuliffe on the mission were a number of veteran astronauts who were crewing the *Challenger* for a second time:

- **Commander:** Lieutenant-Colonel Francis R. (Dick) Scobee, USAF. During his stint as an Air Force test pilot, Scobee flew more than 45 types of aircraft and logged more than 6,500 hours of flight time.
- **Mission specialist 1:** Hawaiian-born engineer Ellison Shoji Onizuka, who was the first person of Japanese heritage to make it into space.
- **Mission specialist 2:** American electrical engineer, software engineer, biomedical engineer and pilot Judith A. Resnik, PhD, who also had the distinction of being the first Jewish woman of any nation to have been to space.

- **Mission specialist 3:** Physicist Ronald E. McNair,
  only the second African-American to fly in space. On
  his first mission in 1984, McNair was the operator of
  the Canadarm, the remote-controlled mechanical arm,
  also known as the shuttle remote manipulator system
  (SRMS), that was used to move cargo, like satellites, into
  and out of the shuttle's cargo bay.

McAuliffe was listed as payload specialist 1, alongside two other
first-time space travellers:

- **Pilot:** Captain Michael J. Smith, a naval aviator and experienced test pilot. He had logged 4,300 hours of flight
  time while flying 28 different aircraft types in his role as a
  United States Navy test pilot.
- **Payload specialist 2:** Engineer Gregory B. Jarvis, who
  was scheduled to conduct experiments about the effects
  of weightlessness on fluids for Hughes Aircraft.

NASA set the official time and date for the launch at 3:43 p.m.
EST on January 22, 1986. The *Challenger* was going to be the first
shuttle to lift off from the Kennedy Space Center Launch Complex
at Cape Canaveral, Florida. Everything had to line up perfectly
to facilitate the launch, and the mission was plagued with delays.
Because of some unforeseen problems arising from a previous
mission weeks earlier involving space shuttle *Columbia*, liftoff was
postponed from its original date of January 22 to the 23rd. The
date of the launch was then delayed further to January 24 and then
again to January 25.

Having the perfect climate is essential for a shuttle launch, and
weather at the launch site is a significant factor in determining
whether or not to proceed. However, the weather at other spots

around the world is also important, especially at launch abort locations, which are emergency shuttle landing spots chosen all over the globe, depending on the craft's geographical location at the time of an incident. The weather was inclement in Dakar, Senegal, one of the default transoceanic abort landing (TAL) sites. So NASA officials rescheduled the *Challenger* launch to January 27, at 9:37 a.m. EST, and they moved the TAL site to Casablanca. A technical delay with a stubborn ground servicing equipment hatch refusing to close, along with a rise in crosswinds, delayed the liftoff again to January 28, at 9:37 a.m. EST.

The weather was unseasonably cold that week, and on the evening before the launch, NASA had a conference call to discuss the weather conditions. Engineers from Morton Thiokol, the Utah company responsible for the $800 million construction of the shuttle's solid booster rockets, were concerned that the temperature that morning, close to −1°C (30°F), was too cold for the giant rubber O-rings that held sections of the boosters together. There was no data indicating that the O-rings could create a seal between the sections of the booster at anything colder than 12°C (54°F). The engineers feared that if the O-rings failed to make the seal, the shuttle would not make it off the launch pad, exploding where it stood.

NASA's deputy director for science and engineering, George Hardy, was livid at this disclosure. Every delay of a shuttle launch costs a lot of money and work hours. Hardy was not up for any more launch delays that did not have data to back up the engineers' claims, reported Howard Berkes in a 2012 article.

"I am appalled," Hardy said on the call. "I am appalled by your recommendation."

Another shuttle program manager, Lawrence Mulloy, didn't hide his disdain. "My God, Thiokol," he said. "When do you want me to launch—next April?"

The decision was made to go forward despite the warnings. NASA was not going to scrub the launch again.

Co-workers told Bob Ebeling, one of the engineers not on the call, about the decision to push ahead with the launch. He had expressed his concerns about O-rings and temperature as early as 1985 in a memo to his boss titled "Help!" He signed off on the project with a caveat, calling the O-rings issue "a red flag." He was so disturbed by what he was told that before bed on January 27 he said to his wife, Darlene, "It's going to blow up," Ebeling recalled in 2016.

There was one more two-hour delay when issues were discovered with the fire detection system aboard the *Challenger*. After that delay, the clock started ticking again, this time moving the launch to 11:38 a.m. EST.

As with every launch, spectators, including the astronauts' families and friends, were on site to watch the shuttle take off. That morning they had to bundle up a little more than usual. The temperature on January 28 was the lowest ever for a shuttle launch. The coldest launch of any space shuttle before the *Challenger* had been at 12°C (54°F), but on January 28, it was below freezing at −2.2°C to −1.7°C (28.0°F to 28.9°F). Again, despite the warning of engineers, NASA decided to forge ahead. The *Challenger* was readied for flight.

The *Challenger's* liftoff appeared normal at first. Everything seemed to be going as planned until 73 seconds after takeoff. After Commander Scobee repeated the command from ground control ("Go with throttle up"), the space shuttle *Challenger* exploded into a large orange, white and grey fireball. Thanks to the television coverage and NASA's long-range cameras that had been following the *Challenger's* ascent, millions witnessed the tragic events unfold in real time. Two plumes of smoke from the solid booster rockets created a Y shape and then snaked away from the fireball, which sped off uncontrolled in a separate direction. Other smaller smoke trails were visible as debris from the blast began to rain down from the sky into the ocean below.

The radio chatter went silent for a moment after mission control realized what had happened. A NASA public affairs officer giving the play-by-play to television viewers, a record of which can be found on Spaceflight Now, said: "Flight controllers here are looking very carefully at the situation. Obviously, a major malfunction. We have no downlink."

Then he said what everyone watching already knew: "We have a report from the flight dynamics officer that the vehicle has exploded. The flight director confirms that. We are looking at checking with the recovery forces to see what can be done at this point."

When the catastrophe happened, the *Challenger* was travelling at a speed of Mach 1.92, almost twice the speed of sound, at an altitude of 46,000 feet. There was no way anyone on board could have survived.

The flight recorder in the crew compartment was recovered later from the bottom of the Atlantic. The last words on the tape at the moment of the explosion were from the *Challenger*'s pilot, Captain Michael J. Smith, who said simply, "Uh-oh."

President Ronald Reagan was due to give his State of the Union address that same evening, but the White House decided the president should instead make a brief statement remembering the seven astronauts who had lost their lives. Reagan began by expressing his condolences to the astronauts' families, friends and co-workers. He then addressed the millions of schoolchildren who had been watching that day: "I know it is hard to understand, but sometimes painful things like this happen. It's all part of the process of exploration and discovery. It's all part of taking a chance and expanding [our] horizons. The future doesn't belong to the fainthearted; it belongs to the brave. The *Challenger* crew was pulling us into the future, and we'll continue to follow them." The president then closed with one of the most memorable lines from any speech during his tenure in the Oval Office: "The crew of the space shuttle *Challenger* honoured us by the manner in which they lived their lives. We will never forget them, nor the last time we saw them, this morning, as they prepared for their journey and waved goodbye and 'slipped the surly bonds of earth' to 'touch the face of God.'"

The recovery operations began immediately and the investigation into the tragedy began. Investigators meticulously put the shuttle back together as recovery crews plucked pieces of the destroyed spacecraft from the ocean floor.

The crew compartment was discovered on March 7, and the find was announced publicly two days later. Divers from the USS *Preserver* found the astronauts' pulverized bodies still strapped into their seats. Since they had been in the water for over a month, their bodies had deteriorated significantly.

The remains of the two women were the first taken out—Judith Resnik and then Christa McAuliffe. During the recovery operation, Gregory B. Jarvis's body floated out of the crew compartment and away with the current. Veteran astronaut Robert Crippen refused to give up looking for Jarvis and rented a fishing boat, acting as a one-person recovery crew. Thankfully, on April 15, near the end of the salvage operations, Jarvis's body was discovered by Navy divers on the ocean floor. It was carefully recovered and brought back aboard a waiting naval vessel before being returned to the Jarvis family for burial.

The subsequent investigation revealed that the accident was not survivable. After continuing upward briefly, the *Challenger*'s crew cabin had crashed into the Atlantic Ocean at over 320 kilometres per hour (200 miles per hour) with a force of over 200 Gs, which is two hundred times normal gravity.

The autopsies performed on the astronauts did not provide any solid answers about how they died. The bodies had deteriorated so severely after their time in the water that an exact cause of death was impossible to determine. Investigators suspected the crew might have lost consciousness from a lack of oxygen when the crew compartment suddenly depressurized during the explosion. Because of the massive forces the astronauts endured during the explosion, they most likely died instantly.

All the crew members were buried by their families, with many dignitaries, other astronauts and NASA officials at each funeral. In 2004 President George W. Bush posthumously awarded all seven astronauts with the highest honour he could, the Congressional Space Medal of Honor. Congress had authorized the award in 1969 to honor "any astronaut who in the performance of his or her duties has distinguished himself or herself by exceptionally meritorious efforts and contributions to the welfare of the Nation and mankind." To date there have been 28 recipients. Many schools and other government buildings were named after the *Challenger* astronauts as well.

After a 38-month hiatus to investigate the incident and implement new safety protocols, the shuttle program began flying again. The second TISP candidate, teacher Barbara R. Morgan, finally got her chance to go to space, spending 12 days, 17 hours and 53 minutes orbiting the planet. Upon her return to Earth, Barbara was congratulated by NASA mission control in a memorable quote: "You've given a new meaning to higher education."

Bob Ebeling, the former rocket engineer at Morton Thiokol who had been so vocal about his concerns about the O-rings failing in cold weather, was haunted by the *Challenger* disaster for the rest of his life. In 2016, 89-year-old Ebeling participated in an NPR interview, where he called himself a "loser" and stated that he should have tried harder to make people listen.

As well as other words of encouragement, including from his former boss at Morton Thiokol, a statement was released from NASA administrator Charles F. Bolden Jr., who had heard about Ebeling's ongoing feelings of guilt. The note read: "We honor [the *Challenger* astronauts] not through bearing the burden of their loss, but by constantly reminding each other to remain vigilant, and to listen to those like Mr. Ebeling who have the courage to speak up so that our astronauts can safely carry out their missions."

Ebeling's daughter later told the *Washington Post* that her father, sitting in his wheelchair, had clapped when he read those words. He died only months later, we hope feeling vindicated.

Chapter 23

THE GRENFELL TOWER FIRE

In the early hours of Wednesday, June 14, 2017, in the Grenfell Tower block of flats in North Kensington, West London, Behailu Kebede had just fallen asleep on his mattress in his sitting room when a loud beeping noise woke him up. Not sure what the sound was, Behailu got up to investigate. The sound was coming from the kitchen, and when he opened the kitchen door to look inside, he saw thick white smoke coming from behind the fridge. Behailu ran back into the sitting room, grabbed his phone and dialled 999 while he awakened his two flatmates, Elsa Afeworki and Almaz Kinfu, by banging on their doors and yelling about the fire.

Kebede's 999 phone call connected with an operator four minutes later, at 12:54 a.m.

> **OPERATOR:** *Fire brigade.*
> **CALLER:** *Yeah, hello, hi. It's a fire in flat 16, Grenfell Tower.*
> **OPERATOR:** *Sorry, a fire where?*

CALLER: *Flat 16, Grenfell Tower. In the fridge.*

OPERATOR: *Right, hang on.*

CALLER: *Flat 16, Grenfell Tower.*

OPERATOR: *Flat 16. And what's the postcode?*

CALLER: *W11 1TG.*

OPERATOR: *W11, 1 T for Tango?*

CALLER: *Yeah, but coming quick, please.*

OPERATOR: *Yeah, would you just—I have to get the address, okay. Glen—*

CALLER: *Flat 16, Grenfell Tower, W11 1TG.*

OPERATOR: *The fire brigade are on their way. Are you outside?*

CALLER: *Yes, yes. I'm outside.*

OPERATOR: *Yeah, well the fire engines are on their way, just tell me how many floors you've got there?*

CALLER: *It's the fourth floor.*

OPERATOR: *Right, okay.*

CALLER: *Quick, quick, quick.*

OPERATOR: *They're on their way already.*

CALLER: *It's burning.*

OPERATOR: *Yes, I know it's burning, but they are on their way. You've only just called. As long you're okay, yeah?*

CALLER: *Okay.*

The Ethiopian-born caller and the operator struggled to understand each other because of the caller's panic and a language barrier. Confusing things further, Behailu Kebede switched back and forth between languages on the call. He spoke English with the operator and then shouted orders to leave in Amharic to his panicked roommates.

Behailu was not outside the tower, despite what he said to the operator. He was still in the fourth-floor hallway with his roommates. After the 999 call, the trio from flat 16 began banging on doors to alert other residents to the fire. Behailu, who had been in his undershorts at the time, went back to his flat to put on pants to cover himself. As he left his flat to head downstairs and outside to meet the fire brigade, Behailu switched off the main electricity switch at the fuse box in the hallway. His logic was that if the fire was electrical, this might help the situation.

Five minutes after the 999 call, the fire brigade's first trucks arrived at Grenfell Tower, a 24-storey residential tower block in the area of the city known as North Kensington. The firefighters looked up at the tower and could see the fire's possible location thanks to a bright orange glow in a fourth-floor window. There was no smoke visible at this point.

Other residents in the tower called 999 after being awakened by the smell of burning, the commotion and the sound of smoke alarms. Operators told concerned callers to "stay put," which was departmental and building policy if a fire appeared contained within one suite, and at that point it was. As in most buildings of this size, there was no centrally activated fire alarm system, only alarms on individual floors and within the flats. Many residents may not have known there was a fire in the building at all.

In flat 205, on the 23rd floor, Farhad Neda detected an electrical smell. He investigated and later explained he had thought the smell was coming from the vents in the elevator lobby. In his witness statement for the inquiry into the tragedy, Neda said, "So it began off quite light and it started getting stronger and stronger. But what I clearly remember is that it was definitely coming from the vents."

Outside, Behailu Kebede ran up to fire crews just after they arrived, confirming that the fire was in his flat—number 16, on the eastern side of the fourth floor. Behailu told them the fire was in the fridge and that he and his flatmates were safely outside.

Firefighters connected the hoses and pumpers to the hydrant nearest the tower and then connected more hoses to the building's exterior intakes, which fed water to the floor the fire was on, prepping for what they hoped would be a simple kitchen blaze. Firefighters wanted to not only extinguish the fire but also contain it, to minimize damage and the possible loss of life. In a fire like this, containment procedures include a covering jet—which is water sprayed on the building's exterior to prevent further spread. However, fire hoses require time to charge to pressure before use, and firefighters are painfully aware of those precious seconds ticking away as they wait. And in this fire, it was mere seconds that made the difference.

As their comrades did their jobs outside, a cohort of firefighters attempted to enter the building and made their way to Behailu's suite to fight the blaze. The firefighters did not have an entry fob for the building and were let into the tower at 1:01 a.m. by Maria de Fatima Alves, who was already outside. As she let the fire crew into the building, Fatima told them her family was still inside flat 105 on the 13th floor and asked whether they should come outside. Operators told Fatima that everyone should stay where they were. Fatima tried to call her family, still upstairs, using the intercom, but she did not get through.

Inside there were more minor delays. It took extra time to get the elevator to the ground because the firefighters' express drop key malfunctioned, requiring them to call the elevator as any resident would. As the water from the pumper trucks outside filled the building's pipes and built the pressure required to fight the fire, the firefighters connected hoses on the third floor, walking them up to the fourth floor through the stairwell.

Behailu, who wanted to document the goings-on, pointed his mobile phone up at his flat window and began recording video. At first, stills from Behailu's video show only the flickering orange flames contained behind the window. Starting at 1:05:43, a still image shows a small flame outside the building around the window frame. Investigators later determined that this might be the exact moment the fire made its way outside the flat and set fire to the building's eastern facade.

At this point, the covering jet of water had not yet started. The hose was still not charged, and the leadership told the firefighters outside to hold off because of the possibility of blowing back scalding steam on the firefighters about to make entry into flat 16.

Firefighters did not get into flat 16 until 1:14. By 1:15, the covering jet was finally soaking the building's eastern facade. But unknown to the firefighters, the fire was already spreading up the building through the flammable polyethylene core of aluminum cladding on the building's exterior. It was too late, and no one present could have predicted the scope of tragedy to follow.

The firefighters inside flat 16 worked to extinguish the blaze over the next five minutes. They soon became alarmed when their thermal imaging camera showed flaming bits of the building falling past the window from above at 1:21. It was at this moment they realized the fire had gotten away from them.

Other residents began calling 999. Naomi Li, from flat 195 on the 22nd floor, called at 1:21. She said there was no smoke in her flat, but she could smell and see what she thought was faint wood smoke in the hall. The 999 operator told Naomi that the fire brigade was on site and that she should return to her flat. Naomi did as she was told.

At 1:24, Damiana Louis, who lived in flat 96 on the 12th floor, eight floors directly above flat 16, called 999. She said there was a fire in her kitchen, and she was unable to breathe. A minute later, Denis Murphy called 999. Murphy lived in flat 111 on the 14th floor. He said he could smell smoke but could not see any in his flat, but as the call progressed, he saw smoke coming into his flat from the hallway.

Another 999 call quickly followed Murphy's. The caller, who was audibly upset, said he was scared. The caller gave flat 91 as his location, but investigators believe the caller was Abdeslam Sebbar, who lived in flat 81. Abdeslam was flustered and had given the wrong flat number.

The fire spread quickly up the eastern side of the building once outside the confines of flat 16. Starting at 1:22, large flaming panels of the building's aluminum cladding came loose from the tower and hurtled dangerously toward the ground, hampering the firefighting efforts below. Drawn by the commotion, mesmerized neighbours and tower residents made their way outside, ignoring the stay-put order enacted to prevent people from being impaled or badly burned by the falling pieces of the building. Firefighters told bystanders to back away for their safety, but many stood their ground, shooting photos and videos on their cellphones to share on social media.

The spread of the fire was rapid, as the second volume of the Grenfell Tower Inquiry's first report indicates: "Between 01.23 and 01.26 the rate of fire spread accelerated from approximately two storeys per minute to approximately four storeys per minute. At the start of this period the fire extended to the top of floor 15; after 60 seconds it had reached the top of floor 17; after 120 seconds it was at the top of floor 19; after 180 seconds it was in the middle of floor 23. By 01.26 the fire had spread 19 floors in approximately 14 minutes."

The fire brigade's leadership upgraded the blaze to a major incident at 1:26. It dispatched units from other firehouses to help fight the fire that was now well out of control. A minute later, the fire reached the tower's roof and spread horizontally toward its other facades.

Firefighter Desmond Murphy described what he saw in testimony given later to the Grenfell Tower Inquiry: "We saw flames move up the tower between the panelling and they lit up the building reminding me of neon lights being turned on in a vertical line between the panels, with bright white-hot glow of fire then spreading rapidly left and right."

By 1:30, the east side of the tower was a wall of flame. There was a lot of confusion inside the building. A few of the residents on higher floors saw flames in their kitchens because the flat layouts matched from floor to floor, and the burning external walls were giving way to the blaze. Some people decided to evacuate, using the single emergency stairwell at the centre of the tower on the east side. It was the only means of escape other than the elevator.

Before many of the potential evacuees could descend even a single storey, they were met by others on their way back, waving them off, telling them to return to their flats and to stay inside. This stay-put policy is common in many apartment towers in the United Kingdom and around the world. The logic is that the fire doors and internal concrete walls will contain the fire to a single flat, and firefighters will not have to deal with the possible pandemonium of an evacuation, which might hinder their efforts to extinguish the fire.

Instead of going back to their suites, the tenants knocked on the doors of neighbours along the side of the building that was not on fire. Residents on the highest floor tried to flee to the roof but found the doors locked. At 1:31, as the fire began to spread down the building's north side, only 110 out of 297 occupants had been able to get out.

Over the next few minutes, more fire trucks arrived. Two were from different firehouses. They came equipped with 30-metre (98 foot) ladders, but the fire had already burned far above their reach. There were now multiple fires on numerous floors inside Grenfell Tower. As flames entered suites on lower floors, some of those residents, not wanting to contravene the stay-put order, fled to the flats of neighbours on higher floors, endangering their lives further. Another lucky 58 residents escaped the tower using the stairwells by 1:50, ignoring the stay-put advice the 999 operators provided; some had to fight through black smoke, and more than a few almost succumbed before exiting the building.

According to the timeline in the executive summary of the Grenfell Tower Inquiry report at 2:00: "Flames travel across the north and east elevations of the tower and start to spread around the crown and diagonally across the face of the building, affecting flats in the south-east and north-west corners."

By 2:06, the additional fire engines dispatched began arriving at the scene, and London Fire Brigade declared the fire a "major incident." A police helicopter arrived on site to assist. Over the next three-quarters of an hour, the flames reached all sides of the building.

The fire brigade rescinded the stay-put order at 2:35, and from that point, 999 operators told the callers still in the tower to leave right away. But it was too late for many on the higher floors. As residents tried to escape, they were driven back upward by the increasing heat from the flames below and the thick, black, poisonous smoke that filled the escape stairwell. The real horror of the night continued as people tried to escape and firefighters attempted to rescue them while trying to fight the stubborn fire.

Residents who had fled the tower and neighbours from homes nearby recounted what they saw throughout the night. Frantic people stuck in the fire were screaming for help, leaning out their windows as far as they could to gulp in the fresh air. They banged pots and pans, waved towels and blankets, and used flashlights and the light from their cellphones in an attempt to draw attention to themselves and be rescued. In many cases, they were on floors far beyond the limited reach of the fire equipment below. The falling flaming debris made an external rescue, even from lower floors, a dangerous undertaking. Inside, firefighters wearing breathing apparatus struggled against intense heat. As the ferocity of the fire grew behind them, some people, desperate to escape the fire, leaped to their deaths.

The day after the fire a *Daily Mail* article reported on the horrors people had witnessed:

> One resident wept as he described how people "just threw their kids out, screaming 'save my children'." Another said his mother stepped over a dead body to escape the building.
> One man claimed he saw a child who was on fire leap from the 22nd floor, adding: "He walked to the window, and he jumped."

Resident Kadelia Woods, 20, told *The Sun* newspaper about one story of heroism when another resident ran to catch a four-year-old girl who was tossed out a window by her desperate mother. At around 2:00 a.m. a frantic woman was seen in a window holding a child whose head was wrapped in a towel. Smoke poured out the window as the fire raged behind her. A man below yelled for the woman to drop the child, that he would catch her. The woman initially refused, but the man was insistent that he could safely catch the little girl. Witnesses gasped as the desperate woman dropped her daughter, but the man caught the girl and took her to safety. It is unclear whether the mother survived the fire—moments later the entire floor was ablaze and the woman was no longer visible in the window.

On the 23rd floor at 2:15, one of the bedrooms in flat 205 was on fire. Four women from a lower floor had taken refuge with the family. Saber Neda, the family patriarch, told his family it was time to go. He implored them to go ahead and was last seen handing soaked towels to the other women in the flat.

At 2:37, Saber telephoned his nephew, telling him he was still in the flat and could not understand why no firefighters had come to the rescue. The nephew could hear female voices in the background. As reported in volume 3 of the inquiry report, Saber Neda called his brother-in-law at 2:40 and left a voice mail: "Goodbye. We are now leaving this world, goodbye. I hope I haven't disappointed you. Goodbye to all."

Just minutes after he left the voice mail, firefighters found Saber Neda's body in the children's playground on the tower's west side. He had jumped.

Saber's family made it to safety, helped down the stairwell into the fresh air outside by a firefighter. It was not until much later that they found out the fate of their beloved father and husband.

By 2:51, the fire had reached the western elevation of Grenfell Tower. At least 63 flats were ablaze, and more than 100 people were still inside the building. Twenty-eight of those remaining inside made it to safety. By 4:30, more than 100 flats were on fire, and there were flames on every floor of the building, inside and out.

At 8:07, the partially blind resident of flat 83, Elpidio Bonifacio, was the last person to be plucked out of the building alive. After being awakened by a phone call from his wife at 1:00 a.m., Elpidio wet towels, stuffed them against the door to prevent smoke from entering his flat, packed his suitcase and waited for rescue, following orders to stay put. A policeman who had seen Elpidio waving a towel at his window directed fire crews to his location.

The fire was not fully extinguished until 1:14 the next morning, after burning for more than 24 hours. British prime minister Theresa May visited the site and promised a full investigation into the events.

The tragedy at Grenfell Tower was the deadliest fire in the United Kingdom since 1988 and the worst residential fire since World War II. A total of 72 residents perished that night. The youngest was six-month-old Leena Belkadi, who died in her mother's arms from smoke inhalation as they were trying to escape.

Sure enough, investigators later discovered that the blaze started behind the fridge in flat 16 from an electrical malfunction. The fire may have been exacerbated early on by the presence of other flammable materials, including a hot plate, improperly stored between the larger appliance and the wall behind. A portion of the building's recent £8.6 million refurbishment had been completed only a month before the fire. Contractors had installed cheap aluminum cladding with a highly flammable polyethylene core outside the tower to cut costs. It was this material that allowed the flames to spread around the structure so quickly.

In the years before the fire, Grenfell residents had complained loudly about fire hazards and safety concerns in the building, but their calls for improvement fell on deaf ears.

To this point, the investigation into the fire has cost more than £40 million. Several years on, delayed by the COVID-19 pandemic, officials are still writing the second part of the report into their findings. Possible criminal charges, including manslaughter and other offences, may be levelled against multiple parties sometime in 2021. The London Fire Brigade's stay-put policy has also brought that organization under heavy scrutiny.

The U.K. government stepped up to help victims, promising them £28 million in compensation. The government is adamant that this kind of tragedy should not happen a second time and have asked local authorities to do what they can to ensure tenants' safety throughout the country. The deadly cladding, a popular low-cost option, is being replaced with flame-retardant material on other buildings in the United Kingdom. The costs of making this change have ballooned to more than £200 million; however, this is a small price to pay given the potential lives saved.

Chapter 24

THE BOXING DAY TSUNAMI

Translated from Japanese, the word *tsunami* consists of two characters, one atop the other. The top character, "tsu," represents the word *harbour*, and below is "nami," the figure for the word *wave*. In reality, a tsunami is not a single wave but a series of them, and the initial wave may not be as destructive as those that follow. Intervals between each wave may be as short as a few minutes to as long as an hour. Thus, many times, people are falsely led to believe the worst is over only to be swept away by a later, more powerful wave.

Tsunamis are a common danger after deep-sea earthquakes. Many of the 15 nations around the Pacific Ring of Fire, including Canada, the United States, Japan, Indonesia, Guatemala, Russia, Papua New Guinea, New Zealand, the Philippines, Chile and Peru, have sophisticated tsunami warning systems in place. In 2004, however, there was no such system in the region around the Indian Ocean. Millions of people in 14 countries had no idea they were about to learn about a tsunami's power first-hand.

The third most powerful earthquake ever recorded happened just before 8:00 a.m. local time, on December 26, 2004, Boxing Day. The shaking originated near the island of Simeulue, off the west coast of Sumatra. The megathrust earthquake, registering between 9.1 and 9.3 on the Richter scale, took place some 30 kilometres (19 miles) under the floor of the northern Indian Ocean, where the major Indian tectonic plate, moving northeast at a rate of 5 centimetres (2 inches) per year, subducts under the Burma microplate, a part of the larger Sunda plate.

The earth shook for more than eight harrowing minutes, with the quake moving northward across the ocean floor at a speed of 2.5 kilometres per second (1.6 miles per second), travelling more than 1,200 kilometres (750 miles) before it stopped. The Indian plate sprung upward and westward as much as 20 metres (66 feet), displacing trillions of tons of rock and releasing energy equivalent to 1,500 times that of the nuclear bomb dropped on Hiroshima.

Near the epicentre of the quake, Sumatrans were hit with the worst initial effects. The ground shook for thousands of kilometres. People more than 4,000 kilometres (2,500 miles) northwest, in India, Sri Lanka and the Maldives, felt the earth moving, as did people 5,000 kilometres (2,100 miles) north, as far as Thailand, Myanmar and Bangladesh, and also in the most eastern parts of Indonesia, to the south of the epicentre. Seismic instruments all over the planet picked up on the massive earthquake. The shaking was so severe that it triggered other, smaller quakes as far away as Alaska, on the opposite side of the globe.

Charles Ammon, associate professor of geosciences at Penn State University, told CNN, "Globally, this earthquake was large enough to basically vibrate the whole planet as much as half an inch, or a centimetre. Everywhere we had instruments, we could see motions."

The quake's duration was also unusually long, and to that point, it was the longest ever measured. Ammon explained: "Normally, a small earthquake might last less than a second; a moderate-sized earthquake might last a few seconds. This earthquake lasted between 500 and 600 seconds."

Although destructive enough on its own, the quake itself was a harbinger of a more deadly threat that, in some cases, came ashore as many as seven hours afterwards. With a gigantic hiccup, the ocean floor shot up as much as 6 metres (20 feet) during the enormous seismic event, instantly displacing 30 cubic kilometres (7 cubic miles) of water. A tsunami, deceptively appearing as a mere bump in the deep ocean water, radiated outward across the Indian Ocean at speeds equivalent to a jet plane, between 700 and 800 kilometres per hour (430 and 500 miles per hour). It slowed and grew in height as it reached the shallows of the shorelines it was about to devastate.

Indonesia was hit the hardest of any nation because of its proximity to the gigantic shaker. Within a few minutes after the ground stopped moving, a tsunami hit the Indonesian island of Simeulue, only 40 kilometres (25 miles) from where the quake originated. Indonesian radio stations took to the airwaves, announcing the deaths of at least nine villagers in seaside communities that were suddenly inundated by a rush of seawater from waves measuring 15 to 30 metres (49 to 98 feet) high.

By 8:30 a.m. that morning, Sumatra had been devastated by the powerful tsunami. Local officials in Aceh province reported waves as high as 35 metres (115 feet) bullying their way inland, flattening buildings and carrying away everything in sight, residents included. Entire villages on the western side of Sumatra, dozens of them, were gone, smashed to matchsticks by the waves. The waves pounded thousands of kilometres of coastline, destroying infrastructure and lives. The rushing water carried debris and bodies inland between 500 metres (1,600 feet) and 2 kilometres (1.2 miles) and travelled as far as 6 kilometres (3.7 miles) inland up rivers and other waterways. Rebound waves also hammered the eastern coast of Sumatra, wreaking similar havoc there. As the water later subsided, the region looked nothing like it had only the day before.

Ten years after the tsunami, Marthunis, who was 17 years old on the day it occurred, gave a hair-raising account of the tsunami to Kate Lamb of the *Guardian* newspaper. At the time, he lived with his family in Alue Naga, a traditional fishing village a 15-minute drive over bumpy, narrow roads outside Banda Aceh city in Aceh province on the northern tip of Sumatra, some 300 kilometres (190 miles) away from the quake's epicentre.

That morning, as Marthunis kicked a soccer ball around with some friends, they felt the massive earthquake. Running home, he heard a loud hissing noise that he said sounded like a jet airplane's engines. His family piled into their minivan to get to higher ground, but they found the dirt roads clogged with vehicles full of other families who had the same idea. Earthquake damage and debris in the streets also blocked potential escape routes.

But it was already too late. Only 30 minutes after the quake, the first of the waves came and would continue to batter the area for hours before subsiding.

Marthunis explained what happened next: "When I looked at the sea, I saw something I had never seen before, and I was terrified. The black wave hit our minivan, turning us over several times before I blacked out."

When Marthunis came to, he was floating amid debris in the dirty water just offshore. He had no idea where the rest of his family were or how long he had been unconscious. Grabbing a school chair floating nearby, Marthunis used it to help himself as he swam for shore, dazed. He was disoriented and nothing looked familiar to him. The powerful tsunami had washed his village away, along with any familiar landmarks. There were human bodies and debris everywhere.

Marthunis found a waterlogged mattress and dragged it underneath the shade of a battered mangrove tree. Parched and hungry, he scavenged for bottles of water and packages of noodles to feed himself as he awaited rescue. Even with rationing, his meagre provisions lasted him only five days. Somehow, he managed to survive on the beach for 20 days before he was discovered by a body recovery team and taken to hospital in Fakinah. He found his father in the hospital and learned that his mother and sister had perished in the tsunami.

At 9:30 a.m., the waves hit the beaches of southern Thailand. Happy, relaxed tourists from around the world on long-planned Christmas vacations packed the resorts that morning. Videos captured at the time reveal the surprise of travellers and locals as the water along the coast rapidly receded out into the sea, creating an abnormally low tide. Fishing and pleasure boats sat high and dry at the spots where they typically floated at wharves or other mooring places. Comments on the videos made by locals highlight the rarity of the event, with many saying they had never seen anything like it. Several tourists walked out onto the now exposed ocean floor to get a better look, hoping to see where the water had gone.

People on the higher floors of the hotels saw the wave first. There was a roiling white wall of water rushing toward the beach. They started screaming at the people on the beaches and those who were milling around on the ground below. Thai tour guides and resort employees began yelling for people to leave the beach and get to higher ground. As locals ran past them, some tourists, not realizing the danger they faced, walked toward the incoming wave, taking photos and shooting videos.

In one video, shot from a hotel balcony, a vacationer in nothing but a red bathing suit walks toward the wave as the videographer and her companion yell for the man to run. As the water approaches, rather than flee, the man turns his back to the enormous wave, possibly hoping to ride it out, but he quickly disappears as it swallows him whole, carrying him off. He does not reappear, and his fate is unknown.

In similar scenes all across the coast, there was pandemonium in the resort courtyards, beaches and streets as wave after wave came ashore, flooding the carefully manicured landscape, carrying debris as it went. The waves swept people right off their feet. Many found themselves on dry land in one moment and swimming for their lives the next, as the filthy brown water carried them helplessly away. Those witnessing the event from hotel balconies, helpless to do anything else, screamed in horror. Their yells were drowned out by the ocean water's roar as it flowed into the lower two floors of the hotels, effortlessly smashing through sliding glass doors and windows and flooding suites, shops and restaurants there. Some hotel guests, still sleeping in their rooms, were trapped and drowned right there in their suites.

When the first wave began to retreat, it engulfed people who had been unable to escape and carried them back toward the ocean. The lucky ones managed to grab onto a tree or structure as they passed, saving their lives. Many others, injured and dazed, were swept out to sea, where they drowned. Recovery crews found scores of people far out in the ocean, floating among the debris, which covered large portions of the Indian Ocean like an oil slick.

Lisa Anckarman was on vacation in a beachside bungalow with her family on the morning the tsunami hit the Thai resort island of Koh Lanta. The 15-year-old had previously found fame after competing in season seven of *Sweden's Next Top Model*. Lisa had a video camera handy that day and recorded her experience. She later posted it to her popular YouTube channel, intercut with more video, after her return to Thailand in 2018.

In the 2018 video, back at the scene for the first time in 14 years, Lisa recalls her five-year-old sister, Sofi, waking her that morning. Sofi wanted to show Lisa kittens the family had found outside on the veranda of the bungalow. Lisa threw on a flowery blue dress, grabbed the family camera and headed out into the sunshine. She raised the camera and hit record as her pregnant mother, Anna, her dad, Magnus, and her younger brother, Olle, watched Sofi feed and pet the kittens.

The tide then went out quickly, and many people on the beach began pointing out into the ocean. An angry, foaming wave, approximately 4 metres (13 feet) tall, could be seen cresting rapidly toward the shore. Vacationers began scampering back toward dry land as the wave approached, but it was moving too quickly and ran some of them down. Not knowing the severity of what was about to happen, some stood in place, amused and mildly shocked by what they were watching. But the water kept coming in, rushing farther inland with more force than any normal wave, picking up beach chairs and people's belongings as it went.

Only moments later a deafening roar arose from the sea. Lisa turned her camera toward the sound and captured a massive wall of brown and white water racing toward her and her family. It took only a few seconds for the danger to register with the people on the beach, but when it did, everyone began running for higher ground. Lisa's father ran off with her brother. Without a thought, Lisa's body was in motion. She could see her mother running around the hotel's pool as she too sprinted for higher ground: a mountain in the middle of the island surrounded by jungle.

"I don't know if I wanted to know how far from land the wave was, or if my subconscious took over, but for a brief second, I look over my shoulder," she said. "And there, on the beach, I see something. Something that I will never forget. My terrified 5-year-old sister left on the beach. Alone."

Lisa watched her sister being jostled by strangers frantically searching for their loved ones. Sofi looked around, frightened that she did not see anyone familiar. Lisa turned and ran back toward danger, her love for her sister outweighing the abject terror in her gut. She scooped Sofi into her arms and ran faster than she knew she could, the thunderous sound of the killer wave nipping at her heels.

She recalled thinking that every step felt as though it were slow motion. She thought, "Is this how we die? Am I even running?"

Lisa ran past the hotel, still carrying Sofi, across the road and onto a patch of grass. She saw her mother ahead, making her way up the path leading to the top of the hill. Lisa's pace began to slow down; her legs were leaden, and Sofi was too heavy, but the screams behind them as the wave hit the hotel drove her forward.

When she felt she could not carry her sister another step, Lisa said to the little girl, "I'm gonna put you down now, and then you're gonna run faster than you've ever [run] before, Sofi!"

Hand in hand, the sisters ran up the hill, navigating the thorn bushes and other tourists also fleeing. Their mom would turn now and then and encourage the girls to go faster. After an arduous climb, they made it to a clearing at the top of the hill. One of Lisa's first thoughts was, "Did we survive?"

Lisa's father and Olle were there too. The whole family had made it. But many did not. Some people missing loved ones screamed their names repeatedly, calling out, hoping for answers that never came; others simply screamed. The scene was surreal, and one that would haunt Lisa's thoughts for years after.

As rumours about a wave 100 metres (330 feet) high rippled through the group, Lisa considered climbing one of the tall palm trees and wondered if it was high enough to escape. That wave never came. After hours on the hill, Lisa and her family walked down the slope and returned to the hotel.

"Inside the hotel, we saw bloody floors, palm trees in the reception area, odd baby shoes and flip-flops in the hallways. Everything covered in mud," Lisa said.

Their rented bungalow was now just walls. The guts of it, along with all their possessions, had been washed away. Lisa realized that if little Sofi had not awakened her that morning, she would have died there. Amazingly, she had been able to hang on to her camera through the whole thing and had a record of what she'd been through.

Also hit hard was the island nation of Sri Lanka, 1,800 kilometres (1,100 miles) northwest of the quake's epicentre near Simeulue island. The waves there began two and a half hours after the earthquake. Even though it was far away, waves reported in Sri Lanka were as high as 6 metres (20 feet).

A Sri Lankan doctor named Vinya Ariyaratne recalled his experience with the tsunami to Bradley Campbell of Public Radio International. "The houses were completely destroyed—the ones that were closest to the beach," he says. "There were many bodies lying around. People were traumatized. They had gathered in temples, churches and public places. We were also traumatized by what we saw."

"It affected maybe 200 metres [650 feet] onto land. But everything beyond that point was normal. So, people could actually go and help," he says. "There was what we call a wave of compassion to counter the waves of destruction. People collected whatever they could collect and went and shared with the people who were affected. That was really a key part that helped to try and make things normal."

The tsunami continued for hours after the earthquake. It hit Somalia, 5,000 kilometres (3,100 miles) away, eight hours after the quake, with waves as high as 5 metres (16 feet). Twelve hours after the earthquake, 8,000 kilometres (5,000 miles) from the quake's epicentre, 2-metre (6.5 foot) waves reached Rooi-Els, South Africa, and an hour later, 9,080 kilometres (5,600 miles) from Simeulue island at Showa Station in Antarctica, the tsunami measured 1 metre (just over 3 feet).

The death toll was estimated to be nearly 230,000 people across the 14 countries affected by the tsunami. More than 165,000 people died in Indonesia, more than 35,000 in Sri Lanka, over 16,000 in India, and more than 8,000 in Thailand. In eastern Africa, thousands of kilometres away, more than 300 people died. At least 125,000 people were injured, more than 40,000 were missing, and the tsunami displaced almost 1,750,000 people from their homes.

The economic impact on the coastal villages hit the hardest was also immense. The fishery was the primary source of employment in many of the settlements wiped off the map by the tsunami. The waves destroyed tens of thousands of fishing vessels and washed away much of the infrastructure supporting the industry, including shops that sold those fish to locals in some of the region's most impoverished communities. In Sri Lanka alone, more than 51,000 boats were sunk or smashed to tinder, and at least 250,000 people lost jobs related to the fishery.

The rest of the world watched events unfold in real time thanks to live television news feeds and Internet updates. Afterwards, many people stepped up to help. I felt particularly proud of Canada's response, as private citizens alone gave C$230 million for tsunami relief, while Canadian businesses gave another C$36 million. Those numbers were matched nearly dollar for dollar by the government of Canada, with provinces kicking in with more. Over the next few months, citizens from 55 countries around the world donated more than US$9 billion, while the World Bank donated another US$1 billion.

Although the tragedy of the tsunami was thousands of miles away, it still managed to reach into my life as well. I received an email from a photographer friend of mine only days after the tsunami, saying that a couple I knew was missing. John and Jackie Knill, both 54, owned a beautiful home and property in North Vancouver, B.C. The Knills had been kind enough to allow us to use their swimming pool for a photo shoot five months earlier, in July of 2004, when I was producing a bathing suit calendar. I recall them as kind, happy people and the proud parents of three grown boys. John was a musical composer, and he ran a recording studio in North Vancouver.

John and Jackie were vacationing on the beach in Khao Lak, Thailand, over the Christmas break. They loved Thailand and considered it their second home. While it was Boxing Day in Thailand, it was still Christmas Day in Canada, owing to the 14-hour time difference. Jackie and John called their kids to wish them a merry Christmas before picking up their camera and going out to the beach for a morning walk. That was the last time anyone heard from them.

On December 31, 2004, recovery crews discovered John Knill's body. Searchers found Jackie's body on January 13, 2005. Their bodies were shipped home for a memorial service.

The story of John and Jackie Knill did not end there, though. A missionary who was part of the relief effort found the Knills' waterlogged digital camera amid the debris on the beach near Khao Lak. The camera was unusable, but the memory card inside was intact and included earlier photos of the couple's holiday. One snap shows bathing suit–clad Jackie and John smiling among palm trees. The final eight pictures on the card were photos of the tsunami as it rushed toward the couple. An angry white and brown wave fills the frame in the last image.

In 2005 the Intergovernmental Oceanographic Commission formally established a framework for a global early-warning system for tsunamis and other ocean-related hazards. They also created the Indian Ocean Tsunami Information Centre (IOTIC), head-quartered in Jakarta, Indonesia. The IOTIC's goals are to study and educate people in the region about the dangers of tsunamis and prepare them for future events like the one on Boxing Day 2004.

Chapter 25

THE CHILEAN MINING ACCIDENT

In prehistoric times, humans discovered that the gods had buried glittering treasures beneath the earth; we began digging for them and have been at it ever since. Accidents in mining have been taking place as long as people have been going underground. Even with modern safety technology and an excellent understanding of geology and physics, mining remains a dangerous, and sometimes deadly, trade.

Each time a miner dons their safety equipment and heads underground for another shift, they know it could be their last. Mining is an inherently dangerous occupation. So much so that between 2005 and 2019, there were at least 1,888 mining-related casualties reported in 26 countries.

One of the most memorable mining accidents in this century happened in northern Chile in 2010, at the San José copper and gold mine, which had been operating under numerous management groups since 1889. The mine is located in the Atacama region of Chile, 45 kilometres (28 miles) west of Copiapó, the region's central mining city. In 1957, a Hungarian immigrant named Jorge Kemeny Letay founded Compañía Minera San Esteban (the San Esteban Mining Company), or CMSE, a fairly lucrative operation and the only one owned by the company. More than 300 workers extract 600 tons of ore annually. Sales from the workings top US$20 million per year.

At 2:00 p.m. on the afternoon of Thursday, August 5, 2010, the ground around the mining operation began to rumble. An enormous piece of granite more than 135 metres (445 feet) high by 100 metres (330 feet) wide and 30 metres (98 feet) thick, weighing some 700 tons, let go inside the mountain and smashed down through the maze of tunnels, causing a catastrophic collapse. The rock came to rest at about 500 metres (1,600 feet) below the surface.

One group above the rock was able to escape unharmed, but deep in the mine, more than 200 metres (650 feet) below the collapse, there were 33 miners—all men, ranging in age between 19 and 63. It was not clear whether they had survived the cave-in, and as rescuers came up against the massive rock blocking their way down to their comrades, many were not hopeful.

For the next two days, the rescue team made numerous fruitless attempts to get around or through the rock in their way. On August 7, a second collapse occurred, blocking the ventilation shaft, which was the only link between the deepest parts of the mine and the surface.

The world's attention was on the story almost from the beginning. Two days after the cave-in, Chilean president Sebastian Piñera cut short a visit with the president of Colombia to fly immediately to Copiapó and personally attend the site. Worried families of the missing miners set up a tent city just outside the entrance to the mine. They called it Camp Esperanza (Hope). The miners' families were pleased to see the president taking the matter seriously.

Piñera promised them he would spare no expense in rescuing their loved ones. He appealed to Peru, Canada, Australia and the United States for their expertise and resources to help them locate and rescue any miners who may have survived the collapse.

The rescue team, now consisting of 130 people, brought in drilling equipment and began sinking 16-centimetre (6 inch) exploratory boreholes into the ground to find the 33 miners. On August 9, rescue teams lowered a listening device into the first borehole, hoping to hear some signs of life. There were none.

By August 11, there were 200 people at Camp Esperanza. Families and friends erected flags in the camp for the missing men. Pictures of each miner adorned a shrine at the foot of each of the flags. Family members would huddle around the flags, praying to the Virgin Mary for the safe return of the trapped workers.

As the story began unfolding in the international media, major press outlets from all over the globe flocked to the site. They filed stories via satellite, often interviewing frantic and weeping family members, who sometimes criticized the rescuers, already under immense pressure to find some signs of life.

The rescuers continued drilling boreholes using a narrow perforation drill, but it was slow going. There were hundreds of metres of rock to bore through, and the inaccurate mine shaft maps steered them off course several times, wasting precious minutes. The work carried on day and night for more than two painful weeks. With little to report on, the story began to fade from the news.

On August 20, drillers sunk a borehole into the section where they assumed the men might have been at the time of the collapse. There was only silence. Many family members and co-workers of the missing had lost hope, and some erected crosses on the property commemorating the workers that many now presumed dead. The buzz around the site was that this was no longer a rescue but a recovery operation.

Then, on August 22, a miracle happened. The eighth borehole dropped into a cavern at the 688-metre mark (2,257 feet). As the drill stopped spinning, rescuers heard a metallic tapping sound on the drill casing coming from far below. Someone was alive! Excited cheers went up from the men working the drill at the borehole. Word travelled quickly to families at Camp Esperanza, and they rushed en masse to the site. As the drill bit came out of the hole, rescuers found a note attached to it.

Written in bold red ink was a phrase that would later become the motto for the miners. It said *"Estamos bien en el refugio los 33"* ("All 33 of us are fine in the shelter"). In one famous photo distributed by the Associated Press, a grinning President Piñera—surrounded by reporters, relieved rescuers and weeping family members, and flanked by Chilean mining minister Laurence Golborne—holds the miners' note triumphantly aloft. "Today all of Chilé is crying with excitement and joy," he said. That was certainly true: as the wonderful news got out, Chileans celebrated in the streets, banging pots and pans and honking their car horns as though they had won the World Cup of soccer.

After the discovery, the engineers went right back to work, reinforcing the 15-centimetre-wide (6 inch) borehole and sending supplies down to the men, who had been underground and out of touch for more than 17 days. It took an hour for each of the 1.5-metre-long (5 foot) blue plastic capsules nicknamed *palomas* (doves) to reach the miners and another hour for them to ascend to the surface.

The first of these carried bottles of oxygen, rehydration tablets and high-energy glucose gel to help the starving and dehydrated men recover enough to have real food. In another note attached to one of the *palomas*, the men asked for food, toothbrushes, peaches and beer. Later, the capsules began carrying food, changes of clothing and more comfortable bedding to the trapped men.

Although many of the notes sent up from the workers indicated they were in good spirits, the men's psychological health was a concern. The trauma of more than two weeks in darkness, trapped in cramped quarters with their co-workers, had taken an enormous emotional and mental toll. Above ground, the engineers told the doctors it might be four months before they could extract the men from the mine. The outside estimate was that the men might be underground until Christmas.

Chilean authorities reached out to NASA for help. NASA had expertise in dealing with human beings living together in confined spaces for protracted periods. Using some of the information that was provided to them by the space agency and from submariners in the Chilean Navy, psychiatrists worked with the family members back on the surface to help build psychological profiles for each of the survivors. They sent questionnaires down to the men to determine the state of their mental fitness and to determine who would be the group's natural leader.

The rescue engineers sunk a second borehole, meant for communication, close to the first and carefully lowered a video camera down through the opening. When it emerged from the hole, 31-year-old miner Florencio Ávalos grabbed it and looked into the lens, giving the families and others on the surface the first glimpse of one of the trapped miners.

In a 40-minute video, then sent to the surface, the miners recalled the day of the collapse, how they survived and what they had endured. While one miner held the camera, another used the light from his mining helmet to illuminate the video's frame as it went from man to man, all of them sweaty, dirty, unshaven, a little thinner and shirtless. All of them waved and greeted their families.

Mario Sepulveda, the appointed spokesperson for the miners, gave a tour of the refuge where they had been living since the mine collapsed above them. The stories the men told of their survival were both fascinating and harrowing.

The initial cave-in knocked many of the miners right off their feet. Their lights were useless for hours afterwards because of the dust kicked up by the collapse. Eventually, they made their way to an emergency space of only 50 metres square (540 square feet), which was their first underground home. Poor air quality forced them to move into the tunnels along with their meagre provisions.

After correctly realizing that rescue might be weeks away, the miners carefully rationed the small amount of food they had. Every 48 hours, each man had only two spoonfuls of tuna or mackerel, half a glass of milk and half a cookie. They had discovered a duct providing potable water and used a chemical toilet found in the refuge as well as latrine trenches they dug away from their living area.

The men had almost given up after hearing nothing from the surface for the first 15 days. On day 16 and 17, the sound of drilling became closer, bolstering their spirits, and they prepared their famous note.

In the days after the miraculous discovery of the men, the rescue team provided a fibre-optic uplink for the miners to chat with doctors and their families waiting for them 700 metres (2,300 feet) above. Doctors sent down a biometric belt so they could give each of the miners a thorough virtual checkup. They also received a power line to run lights and other electronics.

To keep their spirits up, the surface team provided the men with newspapers, Bibles and even rosaries blessed by Pope Benedict himself. Using a small projector sent to them and pointing it toward a darkened mine wall as a screen, the men watched a live feed of Chile's friendly soccer match against Ukraine. They also passed the time playing cards, dominoes and other games.

The engineers planning to extract the miners had a daunting task ahead of them. To cover all their bases, the mine rescue engineers came up with three possible locations to bring the miners safely out of the mine via rescue cages. The rescue engineers would run three crews from three different rescue teams, all working at the same time, each using different equipment, to bore through rock and find the best location to bring the men to the surface. The tubular steel contraptions to be used for the rescue, dubbed Fénix (Phoenix), were 2 to 2.5 metres (6.5 to 8 feet) long and only between 55 and 60 centimetres (22 and 24 inches) in diameter. Doctors put the men on a diet of no more than 2,200 calories per day to ensure they were slim enough to fit inside the rigs.

Plan A began first, on August 31, and used a Strata 950 drill provided by a South African mining company. It had a 702-metre (2,303 foot) target depth at 90 degrees.

Plan B, utilizing a Schramm T-130XD drill from an American company, started boring into the ground on September 5, with a 638-metre (2,093 foot) target depth at 82 degrees.

Plan C, using a Canadian-made RIG-421 oil drilling rig, went into action on September 9. It had a 597-metre (1,959 foot) target depth at 85 degrees.

It was plan B that reached the miners first. On the evening of Tuesday, October 12, Operación San Lorenzo began, so named for St. Lawrence, the patron saint of miners. More than a billion people worldwide tuned in to watch the rescue.

The engineers lowered the first of two rescuers, Manuel Gonzalez, down to the men in the Fénix 2 capsule. He and another five rescuers, who went down in later drops, prepped the men for their ascent to freedom. The first miner rescued was Florencio Ávalos, who emerged from the mine at 12:51 a.m. on October 13. Ten hours later, 54-year-old Luis Urzúa was the last of the 33 to come out of the mine. Once all the miners had been extracted, the rescuers who remained in the mine chamber displayed a banner reading "Misión cumplida Chile" ("Mission accomplished Chile") before they too were brought up to safety.

On the morning of August 5, 2010, the San José mine was just a dusty, nondescript hole in the ground in the remote, mountainous Chilean desert. Over the next 69 days, it became one of the most talked-about places on the planet. Millions of people around the world followed the story, hoping to learn the fates of the miners while praying for a positive outcome.

During the two months that the men spent underground, milestones came and went. Miner Claudio Acuña celebrated his 44th birthday on September 6, while on September 14, 29-year-old Ariel Ticona's wife gave birth to their daughter; they named her Hope. She was a day shy of a month old when her father finally breathed fresh air again.

Although a few of the 33 trapped miners had had other occupations before working at the San José mine, working underground was the highest-paying job that some of these men could acquire. Others had no aspirations for any other trade; the mining life was the only one they had ever known. Many of them came from mining families, and their fathers, uncles, brothers and cousins all worked, or had worked, in the mines.

There have been movies made and books written about the 33 men who spent 69 days underground. Since their rescue, although they were celebrities for a short time, many of the former miners continue to struggle to make ends meet; some went back to mining. Most suffer from severe post-traumatic stress and debilitating nightmares from the disaster. Many do not interact with those they had been trapped with in the mine, because seeing them brings up painful memories. There have also been divisions over money, as many felt they were not compensated fairly for what they had to endure. Still others do not like the attention some of the men, like Mario Sepulveda, have enjoyed after their ordeal.

After his rescue, when asked by reporters how he stayed sane in the mine, Mario Sepulveda said in an October 17 news article, "The only thought that kept going through my head was that I didn't want to die before my children had an education. It sounds like a crazy thought, but that is so important to me." He hinted that he wanted to go back to mining to mentor younger miners new to the trade. Sepulveda also pointed out that the mental health care he and his colleagues received from the Chilean government was sorely lacking.

The August 2010 incident was not the first black mark on the mine's safety record. Miners at San José had complained endlessly about the unsafe conditions they worked in daily. The mine had a long history of workplace safety violations, and the Chilean regulatory agency, National Geology and Mining Service, fined CMSE 42 times between 2004 and 2010, according to an August 26 article in *The Telegraph*. In 2004, miner Pedro Gonzalez died after a minor cave-in. In 2006, truck driver Fernando Contreras lost his life in an accident. Two CMSE owners, Marcelo Kemeny and Alejandro Bohn, were held and charged with involuntary manslaughter in Contreras's death, but the charges were not pursued after Kemeny and Bohn agreed to pay Contreras's family US$170,000, as reported by Pascale Bonnefoy in an article on the mine's poor safety standards. In 2007 the mine closed for almost a year after the accidental death of a geologist working there, and in July 2010, another miner, Gino Cortes, lost his leg in an incident.

After a three-year investigation into the collapse, investigators decided there was not enough evidence to determine the cause of the collapse. The San José mine has remained closed since the accident, and the rescue tunnel has been sealed.

ACKNOWLEDGEMENTS

I want to thank my parents, Dr. Edward O. and Marion Browne, for adopting me all those years ago on a Hallowe'en night. They saw me through a lot of dark times in my teens and early adulthood. I know they were frustrated and frightened that I might not make it, but here we are. You are both fine examples of humanity and compassion.

Thank you so much to my birth mother, Dianne, for making the hardest decision a mother has to make. You have become one of my biggest cheerleaders.

To my grandmother, Vera Hall, thank you for introducing me to the world of true crime. Your legendary kindness, your selfless years of service to others and your smile continue to inspire me, even though you've been gone for many years.

To my sister, Rachel, I love you. I am so glad the rocky times between us are long past.

Of course, I want to thank my wife, Carol, for being in my corner and encouraging me to move forward even when I did not want to.

I would have been at sea without you and your consistent support throughout the years, before and during the writing of this book.

To the thousands of loyal *Dark Poutine* listeners and members of the Yumber Yard, you are all good eggs. There is not a bad apple among you. Thank you so much for supporting the show and the writing of this book. A few of you have become dear friends.

Thanks to Janice Zawerbny, the HarperCollins editor who took a chance on me, an untested writer, and prompted me to start this rewarding process.

Thanks so much to the rest of my family and friends for sticking by me and just being there when I need you.

I have so many people I can count on, especially the network of those who shall remain anonymous who have taught me a better way to live "one day at a time."

SOURCES

PART 1: MURDER WITH A TWIST

Chapter 1: Girl Gone

Barron County Sheriff's Department. "Missing Person: Jayme Closs." Facebook, 15 November 2018. www.facebook.com/barroncountysheriff/photos/a.316866791663362/2453918717958148/?type=3&theater.

FBI Milwaukee (@FBIMilwaukee). "The Jayme Closs 'Tree of Hope' on display in the lobby of the Barron County Justice Center reminds the public we still need your tips to help #FindJayme." Twitter, 28 November 2018.

FBI. "Missing Person: Jayme Closs" [poster]: https://dci832c741skk.cloudfront.net/assets/files/6829/jayme-closs.pdf.

State of Wisconsin v. Jake T Patterson. Case 2019CF000020 (Barron County Circuit Court, 14 January 2019). https://gray-arc-content.s3.amazonaws.com/WBAY/jayme%20closs%20complaint.pdf.

Barron County Sheriff's Department. Evidence log. Case 1831604. 2018.

Barron County Sheriff's Department. Police report. BNSO 1831604 Primary, Closs/Patterson. 2018.

Barron County Sheriff's Department. Police report. BNSO 1831604 Extra, Closs/Patterson. 2018.

Barron County Sheriff's Department. Transcription of Barron County SO 911 call.mp4. 2018.

Barron County Sheriff's Department. Transcription of Erik Sedani squad video.mp4. 2018.

Barron County Sheriff's Department. Transcription of James Pressley squad video 1.mp4. 2018.

Barron County Sheriff's Department. Transcription of James Pressley squad video 2.mp4. 2018.

Barron County Sheriff's Department. Transcription of James Pressley squad video 3.mp4. 2018.

Barron County Sheriff's Department. Transcription of Jon Fick squad video 1.mp4. 2018.

Barron County Sheriff's Department. Transcription of Jon Fick squad video 2.mp4. 2018.

Barron County Sheriff's Department. Transcription of Erik Sedani body camera video 1 audio only.wav. 2018.

Barron County Sheriff's Department. Transcription of Erik Sedani body camera video 2 audio only.wav. 2018.

Barron County Sheriff's Department. Transcription of James Pressley body camera video 1 audio only.wav. 2018.

Barron County Sheriff's Department. Transcription of James Pressley body camera video 2 audio only.wav. 2018.

Barron County Sheriff's Department. Transcription of Jon Fick body camera video 1 audio only.wav. 2018.

Barron County Sheriff's Department. Transcription of Jon Fick body camera video 2 audio only.wav. 2018.

Barron County Sheriff's Department. Transcription of Jon Fick body camera video 3 audio only.wav. 2018.

Barron County Sheriff's Department. Transcription of Jon Fick body camera video 4 audio only.wav. 2018.

Barron County Sheriff's Department. Transcription of Jon Fick body camera video 5 audio only.wav. 2018.

Douglas County Sheriff's Office. Report for case 19DC00130. 2018.

Douglas County Sheriff's Office. Transcription of Douglas County SO 911 call.mp4. 2018.

Douglas County Sheriff's Office. Transcription of 140202_001-Patterson transport w919.mp4. 2018.

Wisconsin Department of Justice. Division of Criminal Investigation. Case Master Report 18-7648.

Wisconsin Department of Justice. Department of Transport footage. 18-7648. 37. 2018-10-15_01-00-00_(13) I-94 at US 63.mp4 and 2018-10-15_01-00-00_09 US 53 at County X+47+Business 29.mp4. 2018.

Wisconsin Department of Justice. Interview of Kyle Jaenke-Annis. 18-7648.238.0-2018-10-27 03-22-00-117.mp4 and 0-2018-10-27 04-47-11-920.mp4. 2018.

Associated Press. "Statement of Jayme Closs at Sentencing for Abductor." 24 May 2019. https://apnews.com/article/ 35ea3b5b1b49488fa8ba5584c2acfebc.

Chapter 2: Spell Murder for Me

Buhk, Tobin T. *Skeletons in the Closet: Stories from the County Morgue.* Buffalo, NY: Prometheus Books, 2008.

Davis, Carol Anne. *Women Who Kill: Profiles of Female Serial Killers.* London: Allison and Busby, 2001.

Froeling, Karen T., ed. *Criminology Research Focus.* New York: Nova Science Publishers, 2007.

Schlesinger, Louis B. *Serial Offenders: Current Thought, Recent Findings.* Boca Raton, FL: CRC Press, 2000.

Michigan Department of Corrections. Offender Tracking Information System (OTIS). Catherine May Wood, offender profile. http://mdocweb.state.mi.us/OTIS2/otis2profile.aspx?mdocNumber= 204315.

Michigan Department of Corrections. Offender Tracking Information System (OTIS). Gwendolyn Gail Graham, offender profile: http://mdocweb.state.mi.us/OTIS2/otis2profile.aspx?mdocNumber= 206096.

Cauffiel, Lowell. *Forever and Five Days: The Chilling True Story of Love, Betrayal, and Serial Murder in Grand Rapids, Michigan.* Holland, OH: Dreamscape Media, 2016, 691.

Cauffiel. *Forever and Five Days*, 632.

Howard Stern Show news archive. MarksFriggin.com. 24–28 June 2019. www.marksfriggin.com/news19/6-24.htm.

Cauffiel. *Forever and Five Days*, 625.

Ramsland, Katherine. *Inside the Minds of Serial Killers: Why They Kill.* Westport, CT: Praeger, 2006.

The Serial Killers. "Cathy Wood and Gwen Graham: The Lethal Lovers, Part One." IMDb, 1995. www.imdb.com/title/tt1478219.

The Serial Killers. "Cathy Wood and Gwen Graham: The Lethal Lovers, Part Two." IMDb, 1995. www.imdb.com/title/tt1478221.

Bartlette, DeLani R. "Gwen Graham and Cathy Wood." Medium, 18 February 2019. https://delanirbartlette.medium.com/gwen-graham-and-cathy-wood-ac774d3c7750.

Chapter 3: The Boozing Barber

Court of Appeal for British Columbia. R. v. Jordan, 1991 CanLII 203 (BC CA). 26 November 1991. https://canlii.ca/t/1d8km.

Court of Appeal for British Columbia. R. v. Jordan, 1991 CanLII 526 (BC CA). 1 October 1991. https://canlii.ca/t/1d8rt.

Court of Appeal for British Columbia. R. v. Jordan, 2002 BCCA 330 (CanLII). 21 May 2002. https://canlii.ca/t/5k7h.

Court of Appeal for British Columbia. R. v. Jordan, 2002 BCCA 595 (CanLII). 21 October 2002. https://canlii.ca/t/58lv.

Court of Appeal for British Columbia. R. v. Jordan, 2003 BCCA 64 (CanLII). 28 January 2003. https://canlii.ca/t/5dnp.

Court of Appeal for British Columbia. R. v. Jordan, 2004 BCCA 70 (CanLII). 6 February 2004. https://canlii.ca/t/1gh2x.

Court of Appeal for British Columbia. R. v. Jordan, Excerpt Reasons for Sentence, 2005 BCPC 68 (CanLII). 3 February 2005. https://canlii.ca/t/1jx22.

Sheehy, Elizabeth A., ed. *Sexual Assault in Canada: Law, Legal Practice and Women's Activism*. Ottawa: University of Ottawa Press, 2012, CanLIIDocs 335. www.canlii.org/en/commentary/doc/2012CanLIIDocs335?zoupio-debug#!fragment/zoupio-_Tocpdf_bk_2/(hash:(chunk:(anchorText: zoupio-_Tocpdf_bk_2),notesQuery:'',scrollChunk:!n,searchQuery:'" GILBERT%20PAUL%20JORDAN"',searchSortBy:RELEVANCE, tab:search)).

National Inquiry into Missing and Murdered Indigenous Women and Girls. www.mmiwg-ffada.ca.

National Institute on Alcohol Abuse and Alcoholism. *Understanding the Dangers of Alcohol Overdose*. www.niaaa.nih.gov/publications/brochures-and-fact-sheets/understanding-dangers-of-alcohol-overdose.

Machiskinic, Nadine. "Unresolved: Case Closed or Murder?" Missing & Murdered: The Unsolved Cases of Indigenous Women and Girls, CBC News. www.cbc.ca/missingandmurdered.

Beatty, Jim. "The Demon Barber." *Vancouver Sun*, A4, 4 November 2000.

"Death by Alcohol." *Vancouver Sun* Special Report, A11, 22 October 1988.

Culbert, Lori. "Woman Recounts Escape from Alcohol Killer." *The Province*, A7, 30 March 2001.

Edge, Marc, and Keith Fraser. "Booze Killer's Term Reduced by Six Years." *The Province*, A5, 27 November 1991.

Chapter 4: The Elementary School Murderer

Sereny, Gitta. *Cries Unheard: The Story of Mary Bell*. London: Macmillan, 1998.

"Mary Bell: The Ten-Year-Old Murderer Who Terrorized Newcastle in 1968." All That's Interesting, 16 March 2018. https://allthatsinteresting.com/mary-bell.

Fan, Ryan. "The 11-Year-Old Serial Killer." CrimeBeat. Medium, 22 July 2020. https://medium.com/crimebeat/the-11-year-old-serial-killer-6c64a552ffe8.

Monacelli, Antonia. "Murderous Children: 11-Year-Old Serial Killer Mary Bell." Owlcation, 11 January 2018. https://owlcation.com/social-sciences/Murderous-Children-Mary-Bell.

White, Abbey. "15 Killer Children Who Will Change the Way You See Kids." The Lineup, 8 February 2019. https://the-line-up.com/killer-children.

Sereny, Gitta. The Case of Mary Bell. Vintage Digital, New Ed edition, 2013, 127.

Roser, Max, and Hannah Ritchie. "Homicides." Our World in Data. https://ourworldindata.org/homicides.

"The Hounding of Mary Bell." The Economist, 2 May 1998. www.economist.com/britain/1998/04/30/the-hounding-of-mary-bell.

Irvine, Chris. "Child Killer Mary Bell Becomes a Grandmother at 51." The Telegraph, 9 January 2009. www.telegraph.co.uk/news/uknews/4178772/Child-killer-Mary-Bell-becomes-a-grandmother-at-51.html.

Chapter 5: Bad Apples

Baniszewski v. State. Supreme Court of Indiana Decisions, 1970. Justia. https://law.justia.com/cases/indiana/supreme-court/1970/256-ind-1-1.html.

Monroe, Heather. "The Disturbing Death of Sylvia Likens." Medium, 20 October 2019. https://medium.com/@hlemonroe/the-disturbing-death-of-sylvia-likens-ba64ec62d345.

Stall, Sam. "Looking Back on Indiana's Most Infamous Crime 50, Years Later." Indianapolis Monthly, 21 October 2015. www.indianapolismonthly.com/longform/likens-looking-back-indianas-infamous-crime-50-years-later.

"Where Are They Now? Updates on the Perpetrators." In Memory of Sylvia Marie Likens, 6 November 2013. http://fortheloveofsylvia.blogspot.com/2013/11/where-are-they-now-updates-on.html.

Snipes, Lucas Wesley. "15 Chilling Facts About 'The Torture Mother,' Gertrude Baniszewski." TheRichest, 2 July 2017. www.therichest.com/shocking/15-chilling-facts-about-the-torture-mother-gertrude-baniszewski.

Ng, Christina. "Teacher's Aide Fired for Revelation of Role in Grisly 1965 Killing." ABC News, 24 October 2012. https://abcnews.go.com/US/iowa-teachers-aide-fired-role-grisly-1965-killing/story?id=17555655.

Oliver, Mark. "Sylvia Likens, the Teenager Murdered by Her Caretaker and Neighbors." All That's Interesting, 22 January 2019. https://allthatsinteresting.com/sylvia-likens-gertrude-baniszewski.

"Trials: Avenging Sylvia." *TIME*, 27 May 1966. http://content.time.com/time/magazine/article/0,9171,835635,00.html.

"Sylvia Likens: The Girl Next Door." InfoBarrel, 4 July 2011. www.infobarrel.com/Sylvia_Likens_The_Girl_Next_Door.

Dean, John. *House of Evil: The Indiana Torture Slaying*. New York: St. Martin's Press, 2008, 63.

Dean. *House of Evil*, 82.

Dean. *House of Evil*, 26.

Chapter 6: Sing a Song of Murder

Record of trial of Leonski, Edward J. Supplement A (Exhibits). https://recordsearch.naa.gov.au/SearchNRetrieve/Interface/DetailsReports/ItemDetail.aspx?Barcode=101038&isAv=N.

A472: W7493: Part 5: Court Martial of Edward J. Leonski (NAA catalog entry).

A816: 1/301/542: Private E.J. Leonski (NAA catalog entry).

Trials of American Servicemen for Crimes under Aust. Law Case of Pte E J Leonski. MP508/1: 4/702/943.

Leonski Case. Representations to Commander in Chief, Southwest Pacific Area. October 1942. A5954: 287/6.

"Matches for *Edward Leonski* from 1940 to 1949." *The Age*, Melbourne, Australia. Newspapers.com. www.newspapers.comsearch/#query=Edward+Leonski&t=3673&dr_year=1940-1949.

"The Brown-out Strangler." Ergo. http://ergo.slv.vic.gov.au/explore-history/rebels-outlaws/city-criminals/brown-out-strangler.

Shaw, Ian W. *Murder at Dusk: How US Soldier and Smiling Psychopath Eddie Leonski Terrorised Wartime Melbourne*. Sydney: Hachette Australia, 2018.

Chapman, Ivan. *Private Eddie Leonski: The Brownout Strangler*. Sydney: Hale & Iremonger, 1982.

"US Soldier Eddie Leonski's Murder Spree—in Wartime Australia (1942)." *Art and Architecture, mainly*, 11 January 2014. https://melbourneblogger.blogspot.com/2014/01/us-soldier-eddie-leonskis-murder-spree.html.

Chapter 7: Antifreeze and a Cold Heart

Chambers, Angela, and Jon Meyersohn. "Exhumed Body Reveals Stacey Castor's First Husband 'Didn't Just Die.'" ABC News, 20 April 2009. https://abcnews.go.com/2020/story?id=7394363&page=1.

Battiste, Nikki. "Exclusive: Mother and Daughter Face Off in Murder Mystery." ABC News, 20 April 2009. https://abcnews.go.com/2020/story?id=7389055&page=1.

Associated Press. "NY Mother Says Daughter Killed Father, Stepfather." *New York Post*, 30 January 2009. https://nypost.com/2009/01/30/ny-mother-says-daughter-killed-father-stepfather.

Suicide letter scan. ABC News. http://a.abcnews.go.com/images/2020/Suicide_Letter_scan0001_090422.pdf.

"No Obvious Cause of Death for Killer Stacey Castor; Lab Tests Could Take Months." Crime and Safety. syracuse.com, 22 March 2019. www.syracuse.com/crime/2016/06/no_obvious_cause_of_death_for_killer_stacey_castor_lab_tests_could_take_months.html.

"Stacey Castor on Lifetime: 5 Chilling Details from Syracuse's 2009 Antifreeze Murder Trial." Crime and Safety. syracuse.com, 31 January 2020. www.syracuse.com/crime/2020/01/stacey-castor-on-lifetime-5-chilling-details-from-syracuses-2009-antifreeze-murder-trial.html.

"Stacey Castor Murder Trial: Detective Testifies About Castor Interview." YouTube, 17 September 2018. https://youtu.be/LsIxgyS0KeI.

"Hear Stacey Castor's Frantic 911 Call to Police About Daughter Who Overdosed." ABC News. https://abcnews.go.com/2020/video/hear-stacey-castors-frantic-911-call-police-daughter-60891950.

Duff, Chelsea. "Who Is Stacey Castor: Get to Know the True Crime Story Behind Lifetime's New 'Poisoned Love' Movie." In Touch, 21 February 2020. www.intouchweekly.com/posts/stacey-castor-real-story-behind-lifetimes-new-nia-vardalos-movie.

Munro, Ian. "Death by Anti-freeze 'Perfect Murder.'" The Age, 13 October 2007. www.theage.com.au/world/death-by-anti-freeze-perfect-murder-20071013-ge61i3.html.

Kenyon, Jim. "David Castor's Family Struggles to Settle Estate." CNY Central, 2 February 2010. https://cnycentral.com/news/local/david-castors-family-struggles-to-settle-estate.

Nicolaou, Elena. "Hear Ashley Wallace of *Poisoned Love* Tell Her Story—in
Her Own Words." Oprah Daily, 24 February 2020. www.oprahmag.
com/entertainment/a30718474/ashley-wallace-stacey-castor-
daughter-now.

Centers for Disease Control and Prevention. WISQARS Leading Causes of
Death Reports, 1991–2019. https://webappa.cdc.gov/sasweb/ncipc/
leadcause.html.

"The State vs. Stacey Castor, the Black Widow." The State Vs., 15 October 2018.
https://thestatevs.wordpress.com/2018/10/05/the-state-vs-stacey-
castor-the-black-widow.

Yang, Allie, Keturah Gray, and Jon Meyersohn. "Timeline of 'Black Widow'
Stacey Castor's Shocking Crimes." ABC News, 6 February 2019.
https://abcnews.go.com/US/timeline-black-widow-stacey-castors-
shocking-crimes/story?id=60860538.

"Stacey Castor Found Guilty of Murdering Husband." WSYR.com, 24 April 2009.
https://web.archive.org/web/20090424083504/http://www.9wsyr.
com/news/local/story/Stacey-Castor-found-guilty-of-murdering-
husband/yUV7UZWKp0iSQr5BY8F0-w.cspx.

"Ethylene Glycol." Agency for Toxic Substances and Disease Registry. Toxic
Substances Portal. https://wwwn.cdc.gov/TSP/substances/
ToxSubstance.aspx?toxid=21.

PART 2: PERPETUAL PUZZLES

Chapter 8: The Oak Island Mystery

Macphie, Les. *Early Oak Island Documents*. May 2014. www.oakislandtours.ca/
uploads/5/0/8/8/50887171/b01_early_oak_island_docs_compiled_
by_les_m_may_2014.pdf.

Oak Island Treasure: The Home of Oak Island's Money Pit Mystery Since
2001. www.oakislandtreasure.co.uk.

Joltes, Richard. "History, Hoax, and Hype: The Oak Island Legend." Critical
Enquiry. www.criticalenquiry.org/oakisland.

The Oak Island Scrapbook. www.oakislandbook.com.

Robertson, Larry. "What 'The Curse of Oak Island' Teaches About Actually Finding Treasure." Inc.com, 24 January 2020. www.inc.com/larry-robertson/what-the-curse-of-oak-island-teaches-about-actually-finding-treasure.html.

Hahn, Tim. "Researcher Digs Deeper into Oak Island Mystery." AP News, 9 November 2019. https://apnews.com/ff6fdd8311f04c9d8a63101d8a76b498.

"Manuscripts of Francis Bacon." Oak Island Mystery. www.oakislandmystery.com/the-mystery/popular-theories/manuscripts-of-francis-bacon.

"Sir Francis Bacon." Oak Island Treasure. www.oakislandtreasure.co.uk/research-documents/theories/sir-francis-bacon.

McGrath, Jane. "How Oak Island Works." HowStuffWorks. https://people.howstuffworks.com/oak-island.htm.

Nickell, Joe. "The Secrets of Oak Island." Skeptical Inquirer. https://skepticalinquirer.org/2000/03/the-secrets-of-oak-island.

Oak Island Treasure Act. Bill No. 81, 2010. https://nslegislature.ca/legc/bills/61st_2nd/3rd_read/b081.htm.

The Curse of Oak Island. History Channel. www.history.com/shows/the-curse-of-oak-island.

"The Mystery Pit of Oak Island." Unmuseum. www.unmuseum.org/oakisl.htm.

Leary, Thomas P. *The Oak Island Enigma: A History and Inquiry into the Origin of the Money Pit.* Self-published, 1953.

Sullivan, Randall. *The Curse of Oak Island: The Story of the World's Longest Treasure Hunt.* New York: Atlantic Monthly Press, 2018, 369.

O'Connor, D'Arcy. *The Secret Treasure of Oak Island: The Amazing True Story of a Centuries-Old Treasure Hunt.* Lanham, MD: Lyons Press, 2004.

Chapter 9: Who Was the Persian Princess?

Stolze, Dolly. "A Mummy Hoax Might Be Wrapped Up in a Modern Murder." Atlas Obscura, 17 November 2014. www.atlasobscura.com/articles/a-mummy-hoax-might-be-wrapped-up-in-a-modern-murder.

Romey, Kristin M., and Mark Rose. "Special Report: Saga of the Persian Princess." *Archaeology* 54, no. 1 (January/February 2001). https://archive. archaeology.org/0101/etc/persia.html.

"Princess of Persia: 17 Years Ago, a Woman's Mummy Was Rescued from the Antiquities Black Market. 21 Years Ago She Actually Died." UnresolvedMysteries. Reddit. www.reddit.com/r/UnresolvedMysteries/ comments/6vckgw/princess_of_persia_17_years_ago_a_ womans_mummy.

Brodie, Neil. "Persian Mummy." Trafficking Culture, 21 August 2012. https://traffickingculture.org/encyclopedia/case-studies/ persian-mummy.

Transcript. *The Mystery of the Persian Mummy*. Science & Nature. BBC, 20 September 2001. www.bbc.co.uk/science/horizon/2001/ persianmummytrans.shtml.

The Mystery of the Persian Mummy. BBC Horizon. https://ok.ru/video/ 281956125413.

Khan, Aamer Ahmed. "Burial for Pakistan's Fake Mummy." BBC News, 5 August 2005. http://news.bbc.co.uk/2/hi/south_asia/4749861.stm.

"Authentic Egyptian Mummy Head." Lot #53196. Heritage Auctions. https://fineart.ha.com/itm/archeological-artifacts/ authentic-egyptian-mummy-head/a/6036-53196.s.

Koenig, Robert. "Modern Mummy Mystery." AAAS, 27 June 2001. www.sciencemag.org/news/2001/06/modern-mummy-mystery.

"The Persian Princess." Unresolved. YouTube, 22 June 2018. www.youtube. com/watch?v=hdUW0b_cWSE.

"Pakistan: 2,600 Year Old Mummy Found." AP Archive. YouTube, 21 July 2005. www.youtube.com/watch?v=0uBT7nE8KKk.

"Was the Persian Princess Mummy Actually a Murder Case?" The Infographics Show. YouTube, 25 April 2018. www.youtube.com/watch?v=it52tEVhrdY.

Noroozy, Heidi. "The Mystery of the Persian Mummy." *Novel Adventurers*, 24 January 2011. http://noveladventurers.blogspot.com/2011/01/ mystery-of-persian-mummy.html.

Cowasjee, Ardeshir. "Mummiya." dawn.com, 5 April 2021. www.dawn.com/ news/1072381.

Origin and meaning of *mummy*. Online Etymology Dictionary. www.etymonline.
com/word/mummy.

Chapter 10: The Love Me Tender Murders

Zabiegalski, Robin. "15 Things to Know About the Unsolved Murder of the
Grimes Sisters." TheTalko, 17 May 2017. www.thetalko.com/15-
things-we-know-about-the-unsolved-murders-of-the-grimes-sisters.

"The Grimes Sisters." The Theorem Factory, 31 May 2017. https://theorem-
fact.wordpress.com/2017/05/31/the-grimes-sisters.

Shaffer, Tamara. "Death and the Maidens." Chicago Reader, 20 March 1997.
www.chicagoreader.com/chicago/death-and-the-maidens/
Content?oid=892961.

Nix, Naomi. "Murders of 2 Sisters in 1956 Getting New Look." *Chicago Tribune*,
30 May 2013. www.chicagotribune.com/news/ct-xpm-2013-05-30-
ct-talk-grimes-cold-case-20130530-story.html.

"The Unsolved Murder of the Grimes Sisters." *20th Century Murder: A True
Crime Blog and Podcast*, 23 October 2019. https://20thcenturymurder.
home.blog/2019/10/23/the-unsolved-murder-of-the-grimes-sisters.

"The Grimes Sisters Murder and Ghost Car of German Church Road." Chicago's
Haunt Detective. www.hauntdetective.com/hauntings-legends-folklore/
chicago/southside/66-grimes-girls.

"The Grimes Sisters (Dec. 28, 1956)." Data. magicvalley.com, 15 September
2015. https://magicvalley.com/news/data/the-grimes-sisters-dec/
article_8753b1e1-7641-5d50-bc29-4a96dc440eac.html.

United Press. "Elvis Urges Missing Girls to Go Home." *The Times* (Hammond,
Indiana), 20 January 1957, 19. https://www.newspapers.com/clip/
3263776/the-times/.

Associated Press. "Police Check Confession of Girls' Killing." *The Rock Island
Argus* (Rock Island, Illinois), 29 December 1962, 1. https://www.
newspapers.com/clip/80016915/man-admits-to-killing-grimes-
sisters/.

"The Grimes Sisters." UnresolvedMysteries. Reddit. www.reddit.com/r/
UnresolvedMysteries/comments/4hp31f/the_grimes_sisters.

"Grimes Sisters' Murder: Ray Johnson Wants to Solve Unsolved Deaths of Barbara, Patricia Grimes." HuffPost, 31 May 2013. www.huffpost.com/entry/grimes-sisters-murder-ray-johnson-solve_n_3366069.

"Grimes Sisters Murder Case." Chicago Tribune, 1 December 2019. www.chicagotribune.com/news/chi-120119-flashback-grimes-sisters-pictures-photogallery.html.

"Cold Case File: Barbara and Patricia Grimes." Cook County Sheriff's Office. www.cookcountysheriff.org/case/819.

Edwards, Brad. "2 Investigators: The Unsolved 1956 Murder of the Grimes Sisters." CBS Chicago, 22 January 2018. https://chicago.cbslocal.com/2018/01/22/grimes-sisters-murder.

Trost, Rachael. "Chicago Grimes Sisters' Murders Hit 59 Years Without Answers." NBC News, 7 January 2016. www.nbcnews.com/feature/cold-case-spotlight/chicago-grimes-sisters-murders-hit-59-years-without-answers-n486401.

Gill, Moriah. "64 Years Later, the Grimes Sisters' Murder Remains Unsolved." Rare, 12 February 2020. https://rare.us/entertainment-and-culture/the-grimes-sisters.

Johnson, Ray. "Unsolved Chicago Grimes Sisters' Murder—New Witness Info and a New Reward Fundraiser." Chicago History Cop, 21 January 2020. www.chicagonow.com/chicago-history-cop/2020/01/unsolved-chicago-grimes-sisters-murder-new-witness-info-and-a-new-reward-fundraiser.

"The Grimes Sisters." Unsolved Mysteries. YouTube, 15 April 2016. www.youtube.com/watch?time_continue=18&v=avVZ8zuuxck&feature=emb_logo.

"Barbara and Patricia Grimes." Unsolved Mysteries Wiki. Fandom. https://unsolvedmysteries.fandom.com/wiki/Barbara_and_Patricia_Grimes.

Bovson, Mara. "Sixty Years Later, the Case of the Elvis Presley-Loving Grimes Sisters' Murders Remains Cold." New York Daily News, 24 December 2016. www.nydailynews.com/news/crime/elvis-presley-loving-grimes-sisters-found-dead-60-years-article-1.2922567.

Hoover, Marc. "Unsolved Murders of the Grimes Sisters." Clermont Sun, 1 November 2019. www.clermontsun.com/2019/11/01/marc-hoover-unsolved-murders-of-the-grimes-sisters.

Grossman, Ron. "Grimes Sisters' Deaths, Still Unsolved, Part of Series That Shook City in 1950s." *Chicago Tribune*, 22 January 2012. www.chicagotribune.com/ct-per-flash-grimes-0122-20120123-story.html.

Help Solve Chicago's Grimes Sisters' Murder [public group]. Facebook. www.facebook.com/groups/GrimesSisters.

Tona. "The Grimes Sisters, Innocence Lost." Medium, 20 April 2019. https://medium.com/@tonafambrough/the-grimes-sisters-innocence-lost-bb71dfb675cc.

de Sturler, Alice. "Case of the Month: Barbara and Patricia Grimes." Defrosting Cold Cases, 1 February 2016. https://defrostingcoldcases.com/case-of-the-month-barbara-and-patricia-grimes.

"Grimes Sister's Haunted Murder Location & Archer Ave Haunted Locations—Tour." Edward Shanahan. YouTube, 23 August 2011. www.youtube.com/watch?v=p28uqoS-Iv4.

"History Cop Grimes Murders of 1956." Raymond Johnson. YouTube, 21 January 2017. www.youtube.com/watch?v=BxKNXbBZlsM.

"2 Investigators: Revisiting the 1956 Murder of the Grimes Sisters." CBS Chicago. YouTube, 23 January 2018. www.youtube.com/watch?v=Kq-q6AsSEHI.

"Presley Urges Girls to Return Home." *Paducah Sun*. Newspapers.com, 20 January 1957. www.newspapers.com/image/428956870/?terms=elvis%20Presley%20grimes&match=1.

Chapter 11: Dark Water

Elisa Lam. Nouvelle/Nouveau. Tumblr. https://nouvelle-nouveau.tumblr.com.

Lam, Elisa. *Ether Fields*. http://etherfields.blogspot.com.

Elisa Lam (moulesmariniere). Instagram. www.instagram.com/moulesmariniere.

Elisa Lam (@lambetes). Twitter. https://twitter.com/lambetes.

"The Mysterious Death of Elisa Lam." The Post-Mortem Post, 11 January 2017. https://web.archive.org/web/20180410022852/http://www.thepostmortempost.com/2017/01/11/the-mysterious-death-of-elisa-lam.

"Elisa Lam Missing Person Updated Alert.02.11LAPD." Scribd. www.scribd.
    com/document/477942107/Elisa-Lam-Missing-Person-Updated-
    Alert-02-11.

County of Los Angeles. Elisa Lam Autopsy Report.
    https://17fsgr2ly346nty8b2l5hcie-wpengine.netdna-ssl.com/
    wp-content/uploads/2019/12/Elisa-Lam-Autopsy-Report.pdf.

Symptoms—Psychosis. NHS. www.nhs.uk/conditions/psychosis/symptoms.

"Surveillance Video of Cecil Hotel on the Night of Elisa Lam's Disappearance."
    YouTube, 14 February 2013. www.youtube.comwatch?v=3TjVBpyTeZM.

"Resolved: Elisa Lam." UnresolvedMysteries. Reddit. www.reddit.com/r/
    UnresolvedMysteries/comments/3amnrx/resolved_elisa_lam_long_
    link_heavy.

Chapter 12: The Unknown Man

Abbot, Derek. "The Taman Shud Case Coronial Inquest." www.eleceng.adelaide.
    edu.au/personal/dabbott/wiki/index.php/The_Taman_Shud_
    Case_Coronial_Inquest.

Abbot. "Taman Shud Case," Page 18.

Abbot. "Taman Shud Case," Page 13.

Abbot. "Taman Shud Case," Page 2.

Abbot, Derek. "Primary Source Material on the Taman Shud Case." www.
    eleceng.adelaide.edu.au/personal/dabbott/wiki/index.php/
    Primary_source_material_on_the_Taman_Shud_Case.

Abbot, Derek. "List of Facts We Do Know About the Somerton Man." www.
    eleceng.adelaide.edu.au/personal/dabbott/wiki/index.php/
    List_of_facts_we_do_know_about_the_Somerton_Man.

Abbot, Derek. "Timeline of the Taman Shud Case." www.eleceng.adelaide.
    edu.au/personal/dabbott/wiki/index.php/Timeline_of_the_
    Taman_Shud_Case.

Abbot, Derek. "List of Facts on the Taman Shud Case That Are Often Misreported."
    www.eleceng.adelaide.edu.au/personal/dabbott/wiki/index.php/List_
    of_facts_on_the_Taman_Shud_Case_that_are_often_misreported.

Abbot, Derek. "List of People Connected to the Taman Shud Case." www.eleceng.
　　adelaide.edu.au/personal/dabbott/wiki/index.php/
　　List_of_people_connected_to_the_Taman_Shud_Case.

Abbot, Derek. "Cipher Cracking 2009." www.eleceng.adelaide.edu.au/per-
　　sonal/dabbott/wiki/index.php/Cipher_Cracking_2009.

Dash, Mike. "The Body on Somerton Beach." *Smithsonian Magazine*, 12 August 2011.
　　www.smithsonianmag.com/history/the-body-on-somerton-beach-
　　50795611.

"Somerton Man: The Corpse Found on an Australian Beach Still Unsolved."
　　All That's Interesting, 12 March 2019. https://allthatsinteresting.
　　com/tamam-shud-somerton-man.

"The Somerton Man's Rubaiyat." Anemptyglass Wikia. Fandom. https://
　　anemptyglass.fandom.com/wiki/The_Somerton_Man%27s_Rubaiyat.

Inquest into the Death of a Body Located at Somerton on 1.12.48.
　　GRG 1/27 File 71/1949, 17 and 21 June 1949 (PDF). State
　　Records of South Australia, Cleland. Thomas Erskine, 1949. www.
　　eleceng.adelaide.edu.au/personal/dabbott/tamanshud/
　　inquest1949ocr.pdf.

Inquest into the Death of a Body Located at Somerton on 1.12.48. GRG 1/27
　　File 53/1958, 14 March 1958 (PDF). State Records of South Australia,
　　Cleland. Thomas Erskine, 1958. www.eleceng.adelaide.edu.au/
　　personal/dabbott/tamanshud/inquest1958.pdf.

Khayyam, Omar. *The Rubaiyat of Omar Khayyam*. 1st and 5th ed. Translated by
　　Edward FitzGerald. Mineola, NY: Courier Dover Publications, 1990.

"Unknown Somerton Man" (Unknown–1948). Find a Grave Memorial. www.
　　findagrave.com/memorial/162837769/unknown-somerton_man.

"15 Conflicting Facts About the Tamam Shud Case." TheRichest, 2 February 2017.
　　www.therichest.com/shocking/15-conflicting-facts-about-the-
　　tamam-shud-case.

Grace, Lynton. "Has Part of the Mysterious Somerton Man Code Been Cracked?"
　　The Advertiser, 2 July 2014. www.adelaidenow.com.au/news/south-
　　australia/has-part-of-the-mysterious-somerton-man-code-been-
　　cracked/news-story/3951eef52092ee56916aeefbc1b7007b.

Vergano, Dan. "DNA Just Tied a Mystery Death in Australia to Thomas Jefferson."
　　BuzzFeedNews, 26 September 2016. www.buzzfeednews.com/
　　article/danvergano/who-is-the-somerton-man.

Stevens, Kylie, and Adam McCleery. "Notorious Murder Mystery Is One Step Closer to Being Solved as 'Somerton Man' to Be Exhumed." *Daily Mail Online*, 15 October 2019. www.dailymail.co.uk/news/article-7573831/Notorious-murder-mystery-one-step-closer-solved-Somerton-Man-exhumed.html.

"Genetic Evidence." Anemptyglass Wikia. Fandom. https://anemptyglass.fandom.com/wiki/Genetic_Evidence.

"The Funeral." Anemptyglass Wikia. Fandom. https://anemptyglass.fandom.com/wiki/The_Funeral.

Chapter 13: The Dyatlov Pass Incident

DyatlovPass.com. https://dyatlovpass.com.

"Diaries and Chronology of Events." DyatlovPass.com. https://dyatlovpass.com/diaries.

"Dyatlov Pass Case Files." DyatlovPass.com.

"Death." DyatlovPass.com. https://dyatlovpass.com/death.

"Medical Autopsy of the Bodies Discovered on Dyatlov Pass." Ermak Travel Guide. https://ermakvagus.com/Europe/Russia/Cholat-%20Syachil/dyatlov_pass_incident_autopsy.html.

"The Dyatlov Pass Accident." Curious World. Aquiziam. https://web.archive.org/web/20111227034827/http://www.aquiziam.com/dyatlov_pass_1.html.

Van Huygen, Meg. "31 Days of Hallowee: Day 21—the Dyatlov Pass Incident." *Atlas Obscura*, 21 October 2013. www.atlasobscura.com/articles/31-days-of-halloween-dyatlov-pass-incident.

"The Dyatlov Pass Mystery." BBC World Service. *The Documentary Podcast*, 14 July 2019. www.bbc.co.uk/programmes/p07grys7.

Andrews, Robin George. "Has Science Solved One of History's Greatest Adventure Mysteries?" *National Geographic*. 28 January 2021. https://web.archive.org/web/20210129101315/https://www.nationalgeographic.com/science/2021/01/has-science-solved-history-greatest-adventure-mystery-dyatlov.

Eichar, Donnie. *Dead Mountain: The Untold True Story of the Dyatlov Pass Incident*. San Francisco: Chronicle Books, 2013.

PART 3: THE MADNESS OF CROWDS

Chapter 14: Northern Rampage

Price, Mark. "Mystery Grows in 'Brutal' Murders of Charlotte, NC, Woman and Her Boyfriend in Canada." *Charlotte Observer*, 19 July 2019. www. charlotteobserver.com/news/local/article232881247.html.

"Chynna Noelle Deese, July 15th, 2019." Obituary. Alternatives Funeral & Cremation Services. www.myalternatives.ca/west-vancouver/ obituaries/2019-deese-chynna-noelle.

Proctor, Jason. "A Year After Northern B.C. Murders, Victim's Mother Finds Support in Canadian Trucker Who Also Lost Child." CBC News, 15 July 2020. www.cbc.ca/news/canada/british-columbia/ northern-bc-murders-chynna-deese-lucas-fowler-1.5648176.

Dao, Christa. "Leonard Dyck Remembered, Family of B.C. Murder Victim Remembers Leonard Dyck as 'Gentle Soul,' Family Man." Global-news.ca, 8 August 2019. https://globalnews.ca/news/5742622/ bc-murder-victim-leonard-dyck-remembered.

Fowler, Lucas. "Surveillance Tape of Murdered Couple Chynna Deese, Lucas Fowler." *Vancouver Sun*, 23 July 2019. www.youtube.com/watch?v= q24C9ZHD488.

Miljure, Ben. "Woman Saw Man in Heated Exchange with Slain Tourist Couple." CTV News, 21 July 2019. https://bc.ctvnews.ca/woman-saw-man-in-heated-exchange-with-slain-tourist-couple-1.4517580.

Azpiri, Jon. "Who Are Kam McLeod and Bryer Schmegelsky? What We Know About the Suspects in Northern B.C. Deaths." Globalnews.ca, 24 July 2019. https://globalnews.ca/news/5677485/kam-mcleod-bryer-schmegelsky-suspects-northern-bc-deaths.

Carrigg, David. "New Details Emerge in Slaying of UBC Lecturer by Port Alberni Teens." *Vancouver Sun*, 20 December 2019. https://vancouversun. com/news/local-news/new-details-emerge-in-slaying-of-ubc-botany-lecturer-by-port-alberni-teens.

Lamoureux, Mack. "BC Murder Suspects Died by Apparent Suicide: Autopsy Report." Vice News, 8 December 2019. www.vice.com/en/article/ ywaz9m/bc-murder-suspects-died-by-apparent-suicide-autopsy-report.

Boynton, Sean. "The Northern B.C. Murders Were 2019's Most Gripping Story. Here's How It All Unfolded." Global News, 27 December 2019. https://globalnews.ca/news/6331779/northern-bc-murders-how-it-unfolded.

Kotyk, Alyse. "New Documents Shed Light on McLeod, Schmegelsky Manhunt and 3 Northern B.C. Deaths." CTV News Vancouver, 20 December 2019. https://bc.ctvnews.ca/new-documents-shed-light-on-mcleod-schmegelsky-manhunt-and-3-northern-b-c-deaths-1.4738391.

Murphy, Jessica. "Lucas Fowler and Chynna Deese: The Forgotten Faces in Canadian 'Fugitives' Story." US & Canada. BBC News, 16 August 2019. www.bbc.com/news/world-us-canada-49349883.

Chapter 15: The UFO Cult

How and When "Heaven's Gate" (The Door to the Physical Kingdom Level Above Human) May Be Entered: An Anthology of Our Materials. Heaven's Gate. https://heavensgate.com/book/book.htm.

Hafford, Michael. "Heaven's Gate 20 Years Later: 10 Things You Didn't Know." Rolling Stone, 24 March 2017. www.rollingstone.com/culture/culture-news/heavens-gate-20-years-later-10-things-you-didnt-know-114563.

Heaven's Gate podcast. www.heavensgate.show.

"Heaven's Gate Timeline." World Religions and Spirituality Project. https://web.archive.org/web/20130302021044/http://www.has.vcu.edu/wrs/profiles/Heaven'sGate.htm.

"List of Class Members with Vehicular (Human Legal) Names." crlody, 22 October 2018. https://crlody.wordpress.com/2018/10/22/list-of-class-members-with-vehicular-human-legal-names.

Ramsland, Katherine. "Heaven's Gate." 5 March 2005. https://web.archive.org/web/20050305162149/http://www.crimelibrary.com/notorious_murders/mass/heavens_gate/1.html?sect=8.

"Heaven's Gate." Cult Education Institute. Group Information Archives. https://culteducation.com/group/968-heaven-s-gate.html.

"Hale Bopp Brings Closure to Heaven's Gate" (main page). Heaven's Gate. www.heavensgate.com.

"Heaven's Gate 'Away Team' Returns to Level Above Human in Distant
Space." Heaven's Gate, 22 March 1997. heavensgate.com/misc/
pressrel.htm.

"Rosetta's Final Sprint to the Comet." Max-Planck-Gesellschaft, 20 January
2014. www.mpg.de/research/comets-cultural-history.

Schwarz, Joel. "Humans Have Feared Comets, Other Celestial Phenomena
Through the Ages." University of Washington Office of News and
Information, 24 March 1997. www2.jpl.nasa.gov/comet/news59.
html.

Jaroff, Leon. "The Man Who Spread the Myth." *TIME*, 14 April 1997. https://
web.archive.org/web/20070403080653/http://www.time.com/
time/magazine/article/0,9171,986171-1,00.html.

The Chuck Shramek Home Page. https://web.archive.org/web/20060821192905/
http://www.techmonkeys.org/~tothwolf/mirrors/www.neosoft.
com_cshramek.

Brown, Courtney. "Remote Viewing the Hale-Bopp Anomaly." *Coast to Coast
AM* with Art Bell. Podcast on Spotify, 14 November 1996.

"On This Day: Bodies of Heaven's Gate Cult Members Discovered After
Mass Suicide." Finding Dulcinea, 26 March 2011. www.findingdulcinea.
com/news/on-this-day/March-April-08/On-this-Day--39-Heaven-s-
Gate-Cult-Members-Found-Dead-after-Mass-Suicide.html.

Miller, Mark. "Secrets of the Cult." *Newsweek*, 13 April 1997. www.newsweek.
com/secrets-cult-171744.

Chapter 16: Colonia Dignidad

United States Institute of Peace. *Report of the Chilean National Commission on Truth and Reconciliation*, 61. www.usip.org/sites/default/
files/resources/collections/truth_commissions/Chile90-Report/
Chile90-Report.pdf.

Finger, Evelyn. "Colonia Dignidad: Der Zeuge." Zeit Online, 10 March 2016.
https://web.archive.org/web/20180319162025/http://www.zeit.
de/2016/10/colonia-dignidad-interview-wolfgang-kneese.

"The Colony: Chile's Dark Past Uncovered." History. Al Jazeera, 15 December 2013.
www.aljazeera.com/programmes/aljazeeracorrespondent/2013/11/
colony-chile-dark-past-uncovered-2013114105429774517.html.

"Schäfer, Paul." Wikipedia. https://en.wikipedia.org/wiki/Paul_
Sch%C3%A4fer.

"Colonia Dignidad." Cult Education Institute. Group Information Archives.
https://culteducation.com/group/1140-colonia-dignidad.html.

"Colonia Dignidad." Wikipedia. https://en.wikipedia.org/wiki/
Colonia_Dignidad.

Branford, Becky. "Secrets of ex-Nazi's Chilean Fiefdom." Americas. BBC News,
11 March 2005. http://news.bbc.co.uk/2/hi/americas/4340591.stm.

Collins, John. "Colonia Dignidad and Jonestown." Alternative Considerations
of Jonestown & Peoples Temple. https://jonestown.sdsu.edu/
?page_id=67352.

Falconer, Bruce. "The Torture Colony." *The American Scholar*, 1 September
2018. https://theamericanscholar.org/the-torture-colony.

"Ratlines (World War II aftermath)." Wikipedia. https://en.wikipedia.org/
wiki/Ratlines_(World_War_II_aftermath).

Harvey, Ian. "The Nazi Ratlines: The System of Escape Routes for Nazis Fleeing Europe at the End of WWII." The Vintage News, 4 February 2017.
www.thevintagenews.com/2017/02/04/the-nazi-ratlines-the-system-
of-escape-routes-for-nazis-fleeing-europe-at-the-end-of-wwii.

Infield, Glenn B. *Secrets of the SS*. New York: Military Heritage Press, 1988.
https://archive.org/details/secretsofss0000infi.

Oppenheim, Marella. "Excavations at Chile Torture Site Offer New Hope for
Relatives of Disappeared." World news. *The Guardian*, 2 May 2018.
www.theguardian.com/world/2018/may/02/chile-disappeared-
excavations-colonia-dignidad.

"Muere en una prisión de Chile el nazi Paul Schaefer, fundador de Colonia
Dignidad." ABC Internacional, 25 April 2010. www.abc.es/internacional/
abci-muere-prision-chile-nazi-paul-schaefer-fundador-colonia-
dignidad-201004240300-14090919233_noticia.html.

"Paul Schaefer." TRIAL International. http://web.archive.org/web/20180420181146/
https://trialinternational.org/latest-post/paul-schaefer.

Brown, Emma. "Paul Schaefer, 89; Led Sect in Chile, Convicted of Abuse."
    Boston.com, 27 April 2010. http://archive.boston.com/bostonglobe/
    obituaries/articles/2010/04/27/paul_schaefer_89_led_sect_in_
    chile_convicted_of_abuse.

"Paul Schaefer: Demon of Two Nations." HubPages, 28 December 2018. https://
    hubpages.com/education/Paul-Schaefer-Demon-of-Two-Nations.

Krause, Charles A. "Colonia Dignidad: Nobody Comes, Nobody Goes Mystery
    Veils Colony in Chile." *Washington Post*, 11 February 1980. www.
    washingtonpost.com/archive/politics/1980/02/11/colonia-
    dignidad-nobody-comes-nobody-goes-mystery-veils-colony-in-
    chile/6fbfe01c-9cc2-424e-a225-daf41296cb92.

Der Colonia Dignidad Public History Blog. https://colonia-dignidad.com.

Kornbluh, Peter. *The Pinochet File: A Declassified Dossier on Atrocity and
    Accountability*, 2nd ed. New York: The New Press, 2016.

Brown, Stephen, and Oliver Ellrodt. "Insight: German Sect Victims Seek
    Escape from Chilean Nightmare Past." Reuters, 9 May 2012. www.
    reuters.com/article/us-germany-chile-sect/insight-german-sect-victims-
    seek-escape-from-chilean-nightmare-past-idUSBRE8480MN20120509.

Löhning, Ute. "Wieder und wieder davongekommen." Amnesty International,
    28 August 2019. www.amnesty.de/informieren/amnesty-journal/chile-
    wieder-und-wieder-davongekommen.

Colonia Dignidad. Daily Archives, 14 August 2019. https://colonia-dignidad.
    com/2019/08/14.

*ECCHR-Stellungnahme zu der Rolle von Hartmut W. Hopp1 innerhalb der Colonia
    Dignidad* [German]. European Center for Constitutional and Human
    Rights, October 2011. www.ecchr.eu/fileadmin/Pressemitteilungen_
    deutsch/Stellungnahme_Colonia_Dignidad_Hopp_-_2011-10-06.pdf.

Chapter 17: The Ripper Crew

People v. Kokoraleis. Supreme Court of Illinois decisions. Justia, 1989. https://law.
    justia.com/cases/illinois/supreme-court/1989/65229-7.html.

People v. Spreitzer. Supreme Court of Illinois decisions. Justia, 1988. https://law.
    justia.com/cases/illinois/supreme-court/1988/63423-7.html.

Kokoraleis v. Gilmore. FindLaw, 1997. https://caselaw.findlaw.com/us-7th-circuit/1257055.html.

Ramsland, Katherine. "The Chicago Rippers." Crime Library. https://web.archive.org/web/20081121215734/http://www.trutv.com/library/crime/serial_killers/partners/chicago_rippers/index.html.

Sargent, Irika. "The 'Ripper Crew' Terrorized Women in 1980s; One of the Members, Thomas Kokoraleis, Tells CBS 2 'I Am Not a Monster.'" CBS Chicago, 12 June 2019. https://chicago.cbslocal.com/2019/06/12/ripper-crew-victims-thomas-kokoraleis.

Ramsland, Katherine. *The Human Predator: A Historical Chronicle of Serial Murder and Forensic Investigation* [eBook]. New York: Berkley, 2007. www.amazon.ca/Human-Predator-Historical-Chronicle-Investigation-ebook/dp/B0095ZMRHA/ref=sr_1_1?dchild=1&keywords=The+Human+Predator%3A+A+Historical+Chronicle+of+Serial+Murder+and+Forensic+Investigation&qid=1592341093&sr=8-1).

Shewan, Dan. "Conviction of Things Not Seen: The Uniquely American Myth of Satanic Cults." *Pacific Standard*, 14 June 2017. https://psmag.com/social-justice/make-a-cross-with-your-fingers-its-the-satanic-panic.

"Spreitzer, Edward." Murderpedia. https://murderpedia.org/male.S/s/spreitzer-edward.htm.

"Gecht, Robin." Murderpedia. https://murderpedia.org/male.G/g/gecht-robin.htm.

"Kokoraleis, Andrew." Murderpedia. https://murderpedia.org/male.K/k1/kokoraleis-andrew.htm.

"In First On-Camera Interview, Thomas Kokoraleis Claims Innocence: 'Everybody Thinks I'm a Monster.'" CBS Chicago. YouTube, 14 June 2019. www.youtube.com/watch?v=O4hXIVRZ3Uw.

Gutowski, Christy. "The Ripper Crew Abducted and Murdered Women in the '80s. Now Thomas Kokoraleis, 58, Is Set to Go Free." *Chicago Tribune*, 29 March 2019. www.chicagotribune.com/news/ct-met-ripper-crew-thomas-kokoraleis-release-20190327-story.html.

Furio, Jennifer. "A Letter from Robin Gecht to Jennifer Furio." Excerpt from *The Serial Killer Letters: A Penetrating Look Inside the Minds of Murderers*. Philadelphia: The Charles Press, Publishers, 1998. https://charlespresspub.com/the-serial-killer-letters-robin-gecht.

"Robin Gecht - Chicago Ripper - 9X12 Original Artwork." Serial Killers Ink.
http://serialkillersink.net/skistore/robin-gecht-chicago-ripper-9x12-
original-artwork.html.

Chapter 18: Los Narcosatánicos

Garcia, Guy. "The Believers: Cult Murders in Mexico." *Rolling Stone*,
29 June 1989. www.rollingstone.com/culture/culture-features/
the-believers-cult-murders-in-mexico-53577.

Cartwright, Gary. "The Work of the Devil." *Texas Monthly*, June 1989.
www.texasmonthly.com/articles/the-work-of-the-devil.

Newton, Michael. "Adolfo Constanzo." Spring Break. Crime Library. https://
web.archive.org/web/20141019120814/http://www.crimelibrary.com/
serial_killers/weird/constanzo/1.html.

"Mexico 2019 Crime & Safety Report, Matamoros." Overseas Security Advisory
Council, 2 April 2019. www.osac.gov/Content/Report/
03b73ba8-0cd3-4772-bc97-15f4aebfc985.

Overseas Security Advisory Council. www.osac.gov.

Kennedy, Michael. "Mexico Massacre: Potent Mix of Ritual and Charisma."
Los Angeles Times, 16 May 1989. www.latimes.com/archives/la-xpm-
1989-05-16-fi-385-story.html.

García Araujo, Raúl. "Narcosatánica: 'Pido perdón a Dios'" [Spanish]. El
Universal, 9 September 2003. https://archivo.eluniversal.com.mx/
ciudad/53172.html.

Hudson, Elizabeth. "Apparent Victims of Satanic Ritual Found Slain."
Washington Post, 12 April 1989. www.washingtonpost.com/archive/
politics/1989/04/12/apparent-victims-of-satanic-ritual-found-slain/
599e1db8-0e37-49b4-91e6-b4c9831ec879.

"The Kilroy Tragedy." *Galveston Daily News*,13 April 1989, 9. www.newspapers.
com/image/13380109.

"Archivo muerto: 'Los Narcosatanicos' que sacrificaban gente en rituals"
[Spanish]. Excélsior TV. YouTube, 23 August 2015. www.youtube.
com/watch?v=-ZRwj9DMMQk.

"Leader in Cult Slayings Ordered Own Death, Two Companions Say."
New York Times, 8 May 1989. www.nytimes.com/1989/05/08/us/
leader-in-cult-slayings-ordered-own-death-two-companions-say.html.

Fox, James Alan, Jack Levin, and Emma E. Fridel. Extreme Killing: Understanding
Serial and Mass Murder, 4th ed. Thousand Oaks, CA: Sage, 2018.

Humes, Edward. Buried Secrets: A True Story of Serial Murder. New York:
Diversion Books, 2014.

Mark Kilroy Foundation. Santa Fe, Texas. www.markkilroyfoundation.org/
index.html.

Memory Mark Kilroy. YouTube. www.youtube.com/channel/
UCLOUvc07XYdkoKuek9PZL8A.

Lebedev, Evgeny. "Dawn of the Dead." GQ, 22 October 2014. Cult Education
Institute. www.culteducation.com/group/1135-santa-muerta-saint-
death/27938-dawn-of-the-dead.html.

"Matamoros Slaying Still Fuels Parents' Anti-Drug Effort." Dallas Morning
News, 11 April 1999. Cult Education Institute. https://culteducation.
com/group/1138-satanism/18284-matamoros-slaying-still-fuels-
parents-anti-drug-effort.html.

"Case 123: Mark Kilroy." Casefile: True Crime Podcast. https://casefilepodcast.
com/case-123-mark-kilroy.

Chapter 19: Children of Thunder

Scheeres, Julia. "Children of Thunder: The Helzer Brothers—Bags of Bodies."
TruTV. Crime Library. https://web.archive.org/web/20140403062340/
http://www.crimelibrary.com/notorious_murders/classics/helzer_
brothers/index.html.

Scheeres, Julia. "Children of Thunder: The Helzer Brothers—'Normal' Kids."
TruTV. Crime Library. https://web.archive.org/web/20090212113757/
http://www.trutv.com/library/crime/notorious_murders/classics/
helzer_brothers/2.html.

"Mission." The Church of Jesus Christ of Latter-day Saints. https://news-ca.
churchofjesuschrist.org/article/mission.

"Glenn Helzer." Wikipedia. https://en.wikipedia.org/wiki/Glenn_Helzer.

"Notorious Killer Who Murdered Five People in Bizarre Plot 'to Speed
      Christ's Return to Earth' Hangs Himself on Death Row." Daily Mail
      Online, 16 April 2013. www.dailymail.co.uk/news/article-2309952/
      Justin-Helzer-case-Notorious-killer-murdered-people-bizarre-plot-
      speed-Christs-return-Earth-hangs-death-row.html.

Scott, Robert. *Unholy Sacrifice*. New York: Pinnacle Books, 2014, 30.

Scott. *Unholy Sacrifice*,148.

Children of Thunder. Cult Education Institute. Group Information Archives.
      https://culteducation.com/group/869-children-of-thunder.html.

"Children of Thunder." *Occult Crimes*. IMDb, 2015. www.imdb.com/title/
      tt6980614/reference.

"Children of Thunder." Tumblr. https://childrenofthunder5.tumblr.com.

"Glen and Justin Helzer: Children of Thunder." The World of Serial Killers.
      http://aboutserialkillers.blogspot.com/2012/03/glen-and-justin-
      helzer-children-of.html.

Truesdell, Jeff. "Inside a 'Bizarre' Cult That Led to 5 Murders." PEOPLE.com,
      28 January 2019. https://people.com/crime/children-of-thunder-cult-
      5-murders-people-magazine-investigates.

"Glen Taylor Helzer: Children of Thunder." *True Crime with Aphrodite Jones*.
      IMDb, 2011. www.imdb.com/title/tt1933333/reference.

"Glenn Taylor, Justin Helzer & Dawn Godman: 'Children of Thunder.'" True
      Crime & Justice. www.karisable.com/crhelzer.htm.

"Children of Thunder," International Cultic Studies Association. https://web.
      archive.org/web/20170705115904/www.icsahome.com/groups/
      childrenofthunder.

"Glenn Taylor and Justin Helzer." Murderpedia. https://murderpedia.org/male.
      H/h/helzer-brothers-photos.htm .

Lee, Henry K. "Justin Helzer Hangs Himself in Prison." SFGate, 16 April 2013.
      www.sfgate.com/crime/article/Justin-Helzer-hangs-himself-in-prison-
      4436354.php.

Adwar, Corey. "Dramatic Reddit AMA Provides a Rare Glimpse into the
      Mind of a Death Row Inmate." Business Insider, 29 April 2014.
      www.businessinsider.com/nancy-mullane-interviewed-justin-
      helzer-on-death-row-2014-4.

Read, Simon. "Ex-Wife Wants Helzer Spared." *East Bay Times,* 17 August 2016. www.eastbaytimes.com/2004/12/14/ex-wife-wants-helzer-spared.

"Cult-Murder Extortion Brother Attempts Suicide." *Religion News Blog,* 23 January 2010. www.religionnewsblog.com/category/glenn-and-justin-helzer.

"Glenn Taylor and Justin Helzer aka The Children of Thunder." Crime Documentaries. YouTube. www.youtube.com/watch?v=YLzMBBq4EV0.

"Glenn Helzer: Quick Facts." People Pill. https://peoplepill.com/people/glenn-helzer.

"Justin Alan Helzer" (1972–2013). Find a Grave Memorial. www.findagrave.com/memorial/142308867/justin-alan-helzer.

Harris, Ron. "Blues Guitarist's Daughter Killed." ABC News, 7 January 2006. https://abcnews.go.com/US/story?id=96209&page=1.

Mullane, Nancy. "Full Interview with Justin Helzer." Life of the Law, 16 April 2013. www.lifeofthelaw.org/2013/04/interview-justin-helzner.

"Justin Alan Helzer—California." Crime & Capital Punishment. www.cncpunishment.com/forums/showthread.php?434-Justin-Alan-Helzer-California.

"Glenn Helzer 'Children of Thunder Cult' Handwritten Letter and Envelope *RARE*." Serial Killers Ink. http://serialkillersink.net/skistore/glenn-helzer-children-of-thunder-cult-handwritten-letter-and-envelope-rare.html.

Bulwa, Demian. "Contra Costa County / Playboy Model Says Killer Held Her Spellbound / She Lived by His 'Principles of Magic.'" SFGate, 14 May 2004. www.sfgate.com/bayarea/article/CONTRA-COSTA-COUNTY-Playboy-model-says-killer-2778700.php.

PART 4: NOTABLE DISASTERS

Chapter 20: The Great Influenza Pandemic of 1918

Rosenhek, Jackie. "The So-Called 'Spanish Flu.'" *Doctor's Review,* November 2005. www.doctorsreview.com/history/nov05-history.

Schoch-Spana, Monica. "Implications of Pandemic Influenza for Bioterrorism Response." *Clinical Infectious Diseases* 31, no. 6 (December 2000): 1409–13. https://doi.org/10.1086/317493.

The American Influenza Epidemic of 1918–1919. A Digital Encyclopedia. www.influenzaarchive.org.

Andrews, Evan. "Why Was It Called the 'Spanish Flu?'" History, 27 March 2020. www.history.com/news/why-was-it-called-the-spanish-flu.

"Influenza (Seasonal)." World Health Organization. www.who.int/news-room/fact-sheets/detail/influenza-(seasonal).

"World War One's Role in the Worst Ever Flu Pandemic." The Conversation, 5 August 2014. https://theconversation.com/world-war-ones-role-in-the-worst-ever-flu-pandemic-29849.

LePan, Nicholas. "Visualizing the History of Pandemics." Visual Capitalist, 14 March 2020. www.visualcapitalist.com/history-of-pandemics-deadliest.

"First Cases Reported in Deadly 1918 Flu Pandemic." This Day in History, March 04. www.history.com/this-day-in-history/first-cases-reported-in-deadly-influenza-epidemic.

"Reported Cases and Deaths by Country or Territory." www.worldometers.info/coronavirus/#countries.

Chapter 21: The Eruption of Mount St. Helens

Lewis, James G. "Explosive Truths." *American Scientist*, March–April 2017. www.americanscientist.org/article/explosive-truths.

"Shrouded volcano 'clears throat' with another loud bang." *Times-News* (Twin Falls, ID), 30 March 1980. www.newspapers.com/image/394691491.

"1980 Cataclysmic Eruption." United States Geological Survey. https://volcanoes.usgs.gov/volcanoes/st_helens/st_helens_geo_hist_99.html.

Tilling, Robert I., Lyn Topinka, and Donald A. Swanson. "Eruptions of Mount St. Helens: Past, Present, and Future." United States Geological Survey, 1990. https://web.archive.org/web/20111026174423/http://vulcan.wr.usgs.gov/Volcanoes/MSH/Publications/MSHPPF/MSH_past_present_future.html.

Korosec, Michael A., James G. Rigby, and Keith L. Stoffel. "The 1980 Eruption of Mount St. Helens, Washington." Department of Natural Resources Information Circular 71, June 1980. www.dnr.wa.gov/publications/ger_ic71_1980_erup_mtsthelens.pdf.

Peckyno, Robert. "What Were the Effects on People When Mt St Helens Erupted?" Volcano World, Orgeon State University, 13 May 2010. http://volcano.oregonstate.edu/faq/what-were-effects-people-when-mt-st-helens-erupted.

Hunter, Dana. "The Cataclysm: 'Vancouver! Vancouver! This Is It!'" *Scientific American*, 9 August 2012. https://blogs.scientificamerican.com/rosetta-stones/the-cataclysm-vancouver-vancouver-this-is-it.

Kean, Sam. "Harry Versus the Volcano." Science History Institute, 12 December 2018. www.sciencehistory.org/distillations/magazine/harry-versus-the-volcano.

Greenfield, Charlotte. "'She Is Speaking Out to Us': Māori Leader Says Volcano Eruption Was a Message." Reuters, 11 December 2019. www.reuters.com/article/us-newzealad-volcano-maori-idUSKBN1YF1CR.

Andrews, Robin George. "The Mount St. Helens Eruption Was the Volcanic Warning We Needed." *New York Times*, 18 May 2020. www.nytimes.com/2020/05/18/science/mt-st-helens-eruption.html.

"Mount St. Helens' 1980 Eruption Changed the Future of Volcanology." United States Geological Survey, 14 May 2020. www.usgs.gov/news/mount-st-helens-1980-eruption-changed-future-volcanology.

"Mount St. Helens Visitor Center." Washington State Parks and Recreation Commission. https://parks.state.wa.us/245/Mount-St-Helens.

"Mount St. Helens Fast Facts." CNN.com, 2 June 2020. www.cnn.com/2013/07/26/us/mount-st-helens-fast-facts/index.html.

2018 Update to the U.S. Geological Survey National Volcanic Threat Assessment. United States Geological Survey. https://pubs.usgs.govsir/2018/5140/sir20185140.pdf.

Bonnie, Hannah. "Survivors of the Mount St. Helens Eruption Tell Their Story." *Portland Monthly*, 12 October 2017. www.pdxmonthly.com/arts-and-culture/2017/10/survivors-of-the-mount-st-helens-eruption-tell-their-story.

Bernstein, Robert S., Peter J. Baxter, Henry Falk, Roy Ing, Laurence Foster, and Floyd Frost. "Immediate Public Health Concerns and Actions in Volcanic Eruptions: Lessons from the Mount St. Helens Eruptions, May 18–October 18, 1980." *American Journal of Public Health* 76 (Suppl), 1986. https://ajph.aphapublications.org/doi/pdf/10.2105/AJPH.76.Suppl.25.

Mount St. Helens—Disturbance Zones Map, U.S. Department of Agriculture, Forest Service, Pacific Northwest Research Station. https://www.fs.usda.gov/pnw/galleries/mount-st-helens-disturbance-zones-map.

"Safety on Volcanoes: Volcanic Risk Zones Around Volcano." VolcanoDiscovery. www.volcanodiscovery.com/volcanic_risk_zones.html.

Chapter 22: The Space Shuttle *Challenger* Explosion

Berkes, Howard. "Remembering Robert Boisjoly: He Tried to Stop Shuttle *Challenger* Launch." The Two-Way, 6 February 2012. www.npr.org/sections/thetwo-way/2012/02/06/146490064/remembering-roger-boisjoly-he-tried-to-stop-shuttle-challenger-launch.

Ware, Doug G. "Engineer Who Warned of 1986 *Challenger* Disaster Still Racked with Guilt, Three Decades On." UPI, 28 January 2016. www.upi.com/Top_News/US/2016/01/28/Engineer-who-warned-of-1986-Challenger-disaster-still-racked-with-guilt-three-decades-on/4891454032643.

"*Challenger* Timeline." Spaceflight Now. https://spaceflightnow.com/challenger/timeline.

"Transcript of the *Challenger* Crew Comments from the Operational Recorder." NASA. https://history.nasa.gov/transcript.html.

Reagan, Ronald. Address to the Nation on the Explosion of the Space Shuttle *Challenger*. 28 January 1986. https://web.archive.org/web/20110604013445/http://www.reagan.utexas.edu/archives/speeches/1986/12886b.htm.

"Medallion, Congressional Space Medal of Honor, Armstrong." Smithsonian National Air and Space Museum. https://airandspace.si.edu/collection-objects/medallion-congressional-space-medal-honor-armstrong/nasm_A20200012001.

"Quotes of the Day." *TIME*, 22 August 2007. http://content.time.com/time/
    quotes/0,26174,1655136,00.html.

"Your Letters Helped *Challenger* Shuttle Engineer Shed 30 Years of Guilt."
    The Two-Way, 25 February 2016. www.npr.org/transcripts/
    466555217?storyId=466555217.

"Finally Free from Guilt Over *Challenger* Disaster, an Engineer Dies in Peace."
    Washington Post, 22 March 2016. www.washingtonpost.com/news/
    morning-mix/wp/2016/03/22/finally-free-from-guilt-over-challenger-
    disaster-an-engineer-dies-in-peace.

Report of the Presidential Commission on the Space Shuttle Challenger Accident,
    6 June 1986. https://history.nasa.gov/rogersrep/genindex.htm.

Tonight Show McAuliffe transcript. "Christa McAuliffe: Reach for the Stars."
    CNN.com, 22 January 2006. http://transcripts.cnn.com/
    TRANSCRIPTS/0601/22/cp.01.html.

Banford, Margaret. "Cassandra Complex in Mythology, Psychology and the
    Modern World." Learning Mind, 27 December 2018. www.
    learning-mind.com/cassandra-complex.

"The Cassandra Curse: Why We Heed Some Warnings and Ignore Others."
    Hidden Brain. NPR, 17 September 2018. www.npr.org/transcripts/
    648781756.

"Reagan's Eulogy for the *Challenger* Astronauts." Eulogyspeech.net. www.
    eulogyspeech.net/famous-eulogies/Ronald-Reagan-Eulogy-for-
    the-Challenger-Astronauts.shtml#.XyCW7i2z1hE.

Chapter 23: The Grenfell Tower Fire

Grenfell Tower Inquiry. www.grenfelltowerinquiry.org.uk.

Kebede 999 call transcript. https://assets.grenfelltowerinquiry.org.uk/documents/
    transcript/Transcript-of-outbreak-of-fire-21-June-2018.pdf.

All 999 call transcripts. www.grenfelltowerinquiry.org.uk/
    evidence/999-call-transcripts-7.

Grenfell Tower Inquiry. October 2019. https://assets.grenfelltowerinquiry.
    org.uk/GTI%20-%20Phase%201%20full%20report%20-%20
    volume%202.pdf.

GTI Phase 1 report executive summary. https://assets.grenfelltowerinquiry.org.uk/GTI%20-%20Phase%201%20report%20Executive%20Summary.pdf.

Fagge, Nick. "The Man 'Whose Faulty Fridge Started Tower Inferno.'" Daily Mail Online, 15 June 2017. www.dailymail.co.uk/news/article-4606078/Man-faulty-fridge-started-Grenfell-Tower-inferno.html.

Mills, James, Dan Sales, and Andy Jehring. "Hero of Grenfell Tower." *The Sun*, 15 June 2017. www.thesun.co.uk/news/3810798/hero-pat-catches-four-year-old-girl-thrown-by-mum-from-the-5th-floor-seconds-before-flat-was-engulfed-in-flames.

GTI Phase 1 full report, volume 3. https://assets.grenfelltowerinquiry.org.uk/GTI%20-%20Phase%201%20full%20report%20-%20volume%203.pdf.

Grenfell Tower Fire Fund, 14 June 2017. www.gofundme.com/grenfell-tower-fire-fund.

Grenfell Tower Fire. Grenfell Action Group, 14 June 2017. https://grenfellactiongroup.wordpress.com/2017/06/14/grenfell-tower-fire.

"Grenfell Tower Fire." Wikipedia. https://en.wikipedia.org/wiki/Grenfell_Tower_fire.

Chapter 24: The Boxing Day Tsunami

Walton, Marsha. "Scientists: Sumatra Quake Longest Ever Recorded." CNN.com, 20 May 2005. http://edition.cnn.com/2005/TECH/science/05/19/sumatra.quake/index.html.

Lamb, Kate. "Indian Ocean Tsunami: Survivors' Stories from Aceh." *The Guardian*, 25 December 2014. www.theguardian.com/global-development/2014/dec/25/indian-ocean-tsunami-survivors-stories-aceh.

Anckarman, Lisa. "My Tsunami Story Actual Footage." YouTube. https://youtube.com/watch?v=BP_3zNMk1Y8. [Video subsequently removed.]

Campbell, Bradley. "Survivors Will Never Forget the Day the Tsunami Hit." *The World*, 26 December 2014. www.pri.org/stories/2014-12-26/survivors-will-never-forget-day-tsunami-hit.

"South Asia: Earthquake and Tsunami—Dec 2004." ReliefWeb.
    https://reliefweb.int/disaster/ts-2004-000147-idn.

"Asian Tsunami Anniversary—Thailand Tsunami Then and Now Comparison
    Series." *Zoriah Photojournalist*, 26 December 2008. www.zoriah.net/
    blog/2008/12/asian-tsunami-anniversary-thailand-tsunami-then-
    and-now-comparison-series.html.

The Sumatra-Andaman Islands Earthquake. IRIS Special Report. www.iris.iris.
    edu/sumatra.

"Humanitarian Response to the 2004 Indian Ocean Earthquake." Wikipedia.
    https://en.wikipedia.org/wiki/Humanitarian_response_to_the_
    2004_Indian_Ocean_earthquake.

"List of Natural Disasters by Death Toll." Wikipedia. https://en.wikipedia.
    org/wiki/List_of_natural_disasters_by_death_toll.

"Tsunami Generation from the 2004 M=9.1 Sumatra-Andaman Earthquake."
    United States Geological Survey. www.usgs.gov/centers/pcmsc/science/
    tsunami-generation-2004-m91-sumatra-andaman-earthquake?qt-
    science_center_objects=0#qt-science_center_objects.

"The Devastating 2004 Tsunami: Timeline." *Agence France-Presse*, 26 December
    2014. www.ndtv.com/world-news/the-devastating-2004-tsunami-
    timeline-718329.

"11 Facts About the 2004 Indian Ocean Tsunami." DoSomething.org. www.
    dosomething.org/us/facts/11-facts-about-2004-indian-ocean-tsunami.

"Tsunami Tragedy: Your E-mails." CNN.com, 11 January 2005. www.cnn.
    com/2004/WORLD/asiapcf/12/27/more.emails/index.html.

"Tsunami: Readers' Eyewitness Accounts." Have Your Say. BBC News,
    6 January 2005. http://news.bbc.co.uk/2/hi/talking_point/
    4146031.stm.

"Tsunami Stories: Your Experiences." BBC News, 25 December 2014.
    www.bbc.com/news/30462238.

"Survivors, Victims and Eyewitness Accounts of and [*sic*] the 2004 Tsunami in
    Thailand." Facts and Details. http://factsanddetails.com/asian/cat63/
    sub411/item2543.html.

Intergovernmental Oceanographic Commission. *Tsunami Preparedness: Infor-
    mation Guide for Disaster Planners.* UNESCO, January 2008.
    https://unesdoc.unesco.org/ark:/48223/pf0000160002.

Chapter 25: The Chilean Mining Accident

Compania Minera San Esteban Primera (San Esteban Primera Mining Company). Internet Archive. http://web.archive.org/web/20101125102235/ http://chile.infomine.com/companies/listings/11003/COMPANIA_ MINERA_SAN_ESTEBAN_PRIMERA.html.

"San José Mine Rescue Operation." Internet Archive. https://web.archive.org/ web/20110707010617/http://www.minmineria.gov.cl/574/articles-7093_recurso_2.pdf.

"'Estamos bien en el refugio los 33', a 10 años del mensaje que los mineros chilenos enviaban desde las entrañas de la montaña" [Spanish]. La Voz, 22 August 2020. www.lavoz.com.ar/sucesos/estamos-bien-en-refugio-33-a-10-anos-del-mensaje-que-mineros-chilenos-enviaban-desde-entrana.

Associated Press. "33 Trapped Chilean Miners Found Alive After 17 Days." 22 August 2010. www.ctvnews.ca/33-trapped-chilean-miners-found-alive-after-17-days-1.544872.

Maxwell, Amanda. "Misión Cumplida Chile" [Spanish]. NRDC, 13 October 2010. www.nrdc.org/es/experts/amanda-maxwell/mision-cumplida-chile.

Govan, Fiona, Aislinn Laing, and Nick Allen. "Families of Trapped Chilean Miners to Sue Mining Firm." The Telegraph, 26 August 2010. www. telegraph.co.uk/news/worldnews/southamerica/chile/7966590/ Families-of-trapped-Chilean-miners-to-sue-mining-firm.html.

Bonnefoy, Pascale. "Poor Safety Standards Led to Chilean Mine Disaster." The World, 29 August 2010. www.pri.org/stories/2010-08-28/ poor-safety-standards-led-chilean-mine-disaster.

"Holy Father Gives Thanks for Rescue of Chilean Miners." Catholic News Agency, 13 October 2010. www.catholicnewsagency.com/news/ holy-father-gives-thanks-for-rescue-of-chilean-miners.

Oppmann, Patrick. "Baby Brings Miners Hope and Rebirth." CNN.com, 18 September 2010. www.cnn.com/2010/WORLD/americas/09/ 18/chile.mine.baby/index.html.

"Freed Chile Miner Mario Sepulveda Reveals Darkest Days." The Telegraph, 17 October 2010. www.telegraph.co.uk/news/worldnews/southamerica/ chile/8069092/PIX-AND-PUBLISH-Freed-miner-reveals-darkest-days.html.

2011 incident investigation report by Chilean Commission of Mining and Energy. Internet Archive. https://web.archive.org/web/20150114001810/http://www.camara.cl/pdf.aspx?prmID=381&prmTIPO=MANDATOANTECEDENTE.

"Q&A: How Did Chile's Trapped Miners Survive?" Reuters, 13 October 2010. www.reuters.com/article/us-chile-miners-qa/qa-how-did-chiles-trapped-miners-survive-idUSTRE69B5BP20101013.

Bonnefoy, Pascale. "Inquiry on Mine Collapse in Chile Ends with No Charges." *New York Times*, 1 August 2013. www.nytimes.com/2013/08/02/world/americas/inquiry-on-mine-collapse-in-chile-ends-with-no-charges.html.

Getlen, Larry. "The Untold Story of How the Buried Chilean Miners Survived." *New York Post*, 11 October 2014. https://nypost.com/2014/10/11/how-the-chilean-miners-men-survived-for-69-days-beneath-the-earths-surface.